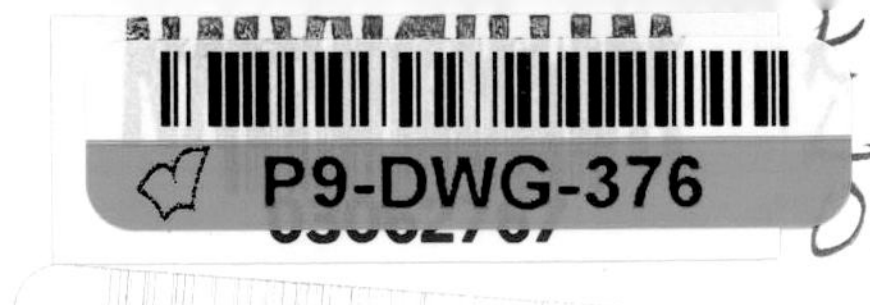

Gravy Training

Gravy Training

Inside the Business of Business Schools

Stuart Crainer
Des Dearlove

This edition published by arrangement with Capstone Publishing Limited.

Jossey-Bass books and products are available through most bookstores. To contact Jossey-Bass directly, call (888) 378-2537, fax to (800) 605-2665, or visit our website at www.josseybass.com.

Substantial discounts on bulk quantities of Jossey-Bass books are available to corporations, professional associations, and other organizations. For details and discount information, contact the special sales department at Jossey-Bass.

Manufactured in the United States of America on Lyons Falls Turin Book. This paper is acid-free and 100 percent totally chlorine-free.

Library of Congress Cataloging-in-Publication Data

Crainer, Stuart.
Gravy training : inside the business of business schools / Stuart Crainer, Des Dearlove.—1st ed.
p. cm. — (The Jossey-Bass business & management series)
Includes bibliographical references and index.
ISBN 0-7879-4931-0
1. Business schools. 2. Master of business administration degree. I. Dearlove, Des. II. Title. III. Series.
HF1111.C7 1999
650'.071'173—dc21 99-6683
CIP

FIRST EDITION
HB Printing 10 9 8 7 6 5 4 3 2 1

The Jossey-Bass
Business & Management Series

Contents

Preface: Welcome to Gravy Training

> *A man can seldom—very, very, seldom—*
> *fight a winning fight against his training:*
> *the odds are too heavy.*
>
> —*Mark Twain*

Gravy Training is the real story behind the rise and rise of the world's business schools. It doesn't try to set up everyone at business schools as fall guys. Nor does it paint an idealistic view of ambitious young MBAs huddled at the feet of an all-knowing management guru.

The book's starting point was to assess the impact, importance, and influence of business schools. Though business schools have now been around for more than a century, they seemed—to our eyes at least—to have skillfully (or inadvertently) avoided some hard questions.

Our questions were simple. We asked:

- Have business schools delivered on their original promises?
- Do they support wealth creation in their national economies?
- Have they helped establish management as a profession?

- Does the research carried out in business schools help the business community become more effective?
- Should business schools be leaders in best practice or reporters of best practice?
- And, perhaps most important of all, do business schools produce better managers?

We did not expect and did not find easy answers. But, hopefully, the responses and our conclusions will succeed in fueling debate.

Inevitably, some business school insiders do not welcome inquisitive journalists with their simplistic questions. They would have us believe that questions are better posed by those who truly understand—namely those who work within the business schools themselves. During our research we were regularly told that business schools can't be judged by the same standards as other organizations. "We're a special case; we're different," people said with varying degrees of conviction.

Even if this were true, it would not be healthy. It is the job of journalists to ask questions. We ask questions of companies all the time. Is it fair, then, to ask the same questions of business schools? Is it reasonable to ask whether they have delivered on their promises, for example? Is it reasonable to expect them to practice what they preach? Is it fair to examine how they are managed? Of course it is. It is also fair to ask whether they are competitive, whether they provide value for money—indeed that is a central issue. (Whether what is studied in business schools stands up to academic scrutiny is a separate issue and one best left to academics.)

Business schools often seem strangely ill at ease with such questions. Some are defensive, others prickly. Perhaps it is human nature. Organizations tend not to be very good at introspection. Their reasons for existing and their ways of doing things tend to go on unquestioned from year to year. Business schools are no exception.

Some, for example, seem to think they are immune to market forces. They see no end to burgeoning demand and limited competition. Yet the one thing business history teaches us is that things will change. Today's supremacy is tomorrow's failing. Arrogance precedes a fall.

The more we looked at the executive education market, the more we became convinced that the world of business schools is about to experience dramatic change. Yet many in the business school world prefer to bury their heads in the sand. They are in denial, denial that they are part of the commercial world—the very world they educate people about.

The reality is that business schools have had it their own way for a long time. Some have become well-endowed managerial comfort zones. While many companies have been through painful downsizing exercises, most business schools are still carrying some fat.

The emerging problem for business schools is that the rapidly growing executive training market is just too tempting for others to resist. Business schools are vulnerable because they are an expensive solution. Competition comes from a number of fronts. In the United States, there are already more than 1,500 corporate universities. The number in Europe is also rising. Then there are the consulting firms. Once the big business ideas came out of business schools. No longer. Thought leadership has become a battleground, as has the market for customized learning. Training and consulting have become intertwined. This creates a problem for American university business schools as their tax-exempt status bars them from consulting activities. Yet increasingly companies want programs that include an element of consultancy. They want help in implementing the neat theory.

Elsewhere, there are upstarts and start-ups in abundance. They deliver executive training at a fraction of the cost of business schools. Some specialize in distance learning delivered by the latest technology. But technology is something university business schools have so far failed to exploit. (Admittedly, there are signs that this may now be changing: witness the programs run by Wharton Direct, for example.)

Those nonuniversity business schools that pride themselves on distance learning should not be complacent either. In the age of infotainment a link between a media or high-tech giant and a top-tier business school could be a dream ticket. What if Microsoft bought a business school? Or Rupert Murdoch?

The education bandwagon is becoming crowded. The media company Pearson won the auction for publisher Simon & Schuster—with its lucrative educational publishing interests. To do so, Pearson had to beat off another contender in Knowledge Universe—the company started by junk bond king Michael Milken and Oracle founder Larry Ellison to target the educational market.

Big brand players are already sniffing out opportunities. The newcomers will take no prisoners. In the battle ahead, brands will be critical. And it's not just executive education that is up for grabs. Chris Lederer of Chicago-based Helios Consulting presents the intriguing scenario of Harvard Business School teaming up with consulting firm McKinsey for a combined program of study and work: "It would be a powerful coupling of brands."

Indeed it would. Of course, the idea of business schools' behaving like brands arouses academic indignation. The trouble is that business schools have never quite established whether they wish to be considered academic institutions or businesses. This, we believe, is a dilemma that causes many of their problems. The time is coming when they will have to make their minds up.

If *Gravy Training* has one message for business schools it is simply: wake up and take a good look around. The real battle is only just beginning. After twenty years of booming business, business schools face intensifying competition and fundamental questions about their role. Those that don't face up to the issues now risk an ambush down the road. The crossroads is here.

Acknowledgments

The idea for this book emerged from our work as management writers. We have written about training and development, and business schools in particular, for a number of years. Along the way we have interviewed hundreds of people involved in the global, multibillion-dollar business of educating managers. We are grateful to them all for their time and interest. In particular, we would like to thank those we have talked to at business schools: Robert S. Hamada, dean of the Graduate School of Business at the University of Chicago; Gale Bitter of the Graduate School of Business at Stanford University; Rory Knight and Peter Snow of Templeton College at the University of Oxford; Warren Bennis of the University of Southern California; Jean Hauser, Allison Adams, and Robert Sullivan of Kenan-Flagler; Ray Wild and Michael Pitfield of Henley Management College; John Quelch, Don Sull, Jeff Sampler, William Connor, Nigel Nicholson, and Dena Micheali of London Business School; Philip Kotler of Northwestern University; George Bain, former principal of London Business School; John Kay and Anthony Hopwood of the Said Business School, University of Oxford; Leo Murray, Andrew Kakabadse, Martin Christopher, and Stephen Carver at Cranfield School of Management; Carlos Cavallé, dean of IESE at the University of Navarra, in Barcelona; Antonio Borges, dean of INSEAD; Sandra Dawson, director of the Judge Institute at Cambridge University; Doug Lamont, author of *Salmon Day* and visiting lecturer at the Kellogg School of Business at Northwestern University; Jean-Pierre Salzmann, former head of public affairs at IMD; Steve Robinson, MBA director, Ashridge Management College; Ian Tanner, director of the executive center at Manchester Business School; Martyn Jones, director of the School of Management and Business at the University of Wales, Aberystwyth; Wanda Wallace, managing director of executive education, the Fuqua Business School at Duke University; Santiago Iniguez of Instituto de Empresa; David Asch, former dean of the Open University Business School; Stephen R. Watson, Jonathan Gosling, John Mackness, and Rick Crawley of the Management School, Lancaster University; Kjell Nordström and Jonas Ridderstrâlle of the Stockholm School of Economics. (Many of these people graciously agreed to allow us to use their words in this book. All quotes not credited to a published source are from our personal interviews with these individuals.)

Among people who would lay claim to residence in the real world, we are indebted to Gerry Griffin of Burson Marsteller; Bruce Tulgan of Rainmaker; Eddie Obeng of Pentacle—The Virtual Business School; Eileen Shapiro, consultant and author; Tom Brown of Management General; Bernadette Conraths, director general of the European Foundation for Management Development (EFMD); business journalist Joshua Jampol; Tom Peters; Peter Brown of The Times (London); Randall P. White of RPW Executive Development; Sam I. Hill of Helios Consulting for his initial idea; John E. Wehrli; Nigel Hall; Nunzio Quacquarelli; Peter Cohan, consultant and author; Stephen Coomber for his research on our behalf; and Art Kleiner. Thanks are also due to Cedric Crocker at Jossey-Bass and Richard Burton and Mark Allin at Capstone.

We hope what emerged from our researches is a fair and accurate portrayal of reality. Any inaccuracies or omissions are our responsibility.

June 1999

Stuart Crainer
Des Dearlove

The Authors

STUART CRAINER and DES DEARLOVE are business writers and founders of the media content, concepts, and consulting business Suntop Media. Their work appears in newspapers and magazines throughout the world.

STUART CRAINER is the editor of *The Financial Times Handbook of Management*. He is also the author of *The Tom Peters Phenomenon* (the biography of the management guru), *The Ultimate Business Library*, *Key Management Ideas*, and a number of other books. His work appears in *The Financial Times* and leading business magazines including *Business Life*, *Human Resources*, *Across the Board*, and *Strategy & Business*.

DES DEARLOVE is a former commissioning editor and a regular contributor to *The (London) Times*. His articles appear in international publications, including *The American Management Review* and *Across the Board*. He is the author of several books on management best practice, including *Key Management Decisions* and *The Interim Manager*.

Introduction: Gravy Tales

The Life of Business

At Wharton Business School, MBA students talk fondly of the "Wharton Walk," a well-known drinking ritual—or bar crawl—that involves ten bars in one night. "A great bonding experience," says one student. This is what happens at business schools. Most students simply get drunk; MBA students bond and network. If you read the books that promise inside stories on business schools you read a lot about caffeine intake as students work through the night and about how boring courses on international finance can be. Most people know that already.

Similarly, if you read brochures about business schools and articles on them, there are a lot of sugary sentiments. "Do something to make the program better for those who follow you," advises one MBA student to his successors. Another adds: "You are in the prime of your life—look for a school that you can enjoy, not just endure, for two years." Noble thoughts, but there is more to business schools than clean-cut, ambitious young men and women absorbing the merits of strategic planning and networking deep into the night. There has to be.

Welcome to the real world of business schools. Welcome to *Gravy Training*.

The Truth

London Business School organized a day-long seminar for the media. It showcased the school's latest ideas and paraded its intellectual heavyweights in front of cynical journalists. It also inadvertently showcased some of the paradoxes that are common in the business school world.

The atmosphere was convivial. In the morning the group witnessed a bravura display from Indian academic Sumantra Ghoshal. Without a note in sight, Ghoshal stalked the platform providing a witty and incisive journey through corporate life. To close the day, the assembled intellectuals were gathered together to answer questions. Visiting professor Gary Hamel was live by satellite from Idaho or somewhere. Questions were fielded routinely. Then a planted icebreaking question struck a nerve. "Were business schools reporters of best practice or leaders in best practice?" It seemed simple enough. A room full of intellectuals could deal with that one. It was slam-dunk time.

Hamel, a mustachioed, tie-less figure on vacation, came to life. Ghoshal looked at his shoes in polite contemplation. "A business school is the closest thing to anarchy where you still get a paycheck," said Hamel in his characteristically breathless delivery. The audience laughed good-naturedly. Ghoshal looked at his shoes with ever greater concentration. Hamel warmed to his themes. "A couple of things have been lost in business schools. They have lost their basic purpose. I ask my colleagues and they tend to be vague. We are trying to improve the competitiveness of the economies we live and work in, but many business schools have a narrow definition of who they are and who they serve. The MBA student is a distribution channel. The product is competitiveness."

Ghoshal smiled. It was difficult to determine whether this was relief, as Hamel drew breath, or annoyance. The American continued. "I worry that those of us in business schools spend too much time writing for each other rather than improving business practice." At the back of the auditorium, the organizer, an astute and chisel-chinned Irishman, was madly signaling to the front that the link should be cut. Hamel continued, oblivious. "If you ask what are the best ideas in organizations over the last ten years, most didn't start with business schools. Most of the top ten business best-sellers didn't start with business school faculty." Exit Idaho.

Free speech is alive and well. In what other business could a highly paid part-time employee lambast his employer with such commendable gusto and honesty? The rules are different in business schools.

Government on the Gravy Train

It is late October again in London, 1995. It will be another eighteen months before Tony Blair's New Labour sweeps to power with a massive majority. A report on the front page of the *Times* reveals that key members of Blair's Shadow Cabinet team have been attending a secret training course at a top British business school. Blair's press handlers have uncharacteristically allowed news of the classes to leak.

"Tony Blair is so concerned at the lack of ministerial experience among his frontbenchers that he is sending them back to school to learn how to run the country," the *Times* declares mischievously.[1] Evidently, key members of the government in waiting have been sent to Templeton College, Oxford, to learn about managing change.

It is, the newspaper notes, a far cry from the old days. "Where once it would have been obligatory for Labour frontbenchers to go down coalmines, the Blair team have been told to attend a weekend course entitled The management of change in government at an elite Oxford business school."

It makes sense. Labour has been out of power for sixteen years, and its people are light on experience. On hand to offer practical tips on running the government of the United Kingdom are former senior civil servants, ex-cabinet ministers, captains of industry, and strategists from the ubiquitous Andersen Consulting.

That same day at Prime Minister's Question Time, John Major, who will remain haplessly in the post for a few months more, jokes about New Labour's sudden interest in business schools, deriding its education policy and its blue-collar credentials. "Labour's Shadow Cabinet went to good schools, yet they want to abolish them," Major quips in the House of Commons. "They send their children to good schools, yet they want to abolish those. I now read that the Shadow Cabinet is going off to Templeton College for the weekend—Templeton College had better watch out for its future."

On the Tory backbenches they roar their approval. John Major grins an impish grin. He's enjoying himself. He doesn't know that in less than two years' time he will be swept aside by a Blair administration and replaced as Tory leader by a thirty-five-year-old business school graduate named William Hague. If he did, he might not have enjoyed the joke nearly so much.

The top business schools are creating a new elite—they exert a growing influence in public as well as business life. They exert a growing influence over the world of politics. Hotshot MBAs are stepping out of the top management consultancies like McKinsey & Co. and into government. Welcome to the new corridors of power. Welcome to the world of *Gravy Training*.

Personal Incentives

One business school had a well-known professor. Meanwhile, an aspiring school had a conspicuous gap in its faculty's expertise. This meant that it wasn't taken very seriously—especially by bodies that gave out money for research. So it made overtures to the esteemed professor. It cemented negotiations with a generous offer. The professor would receive substantially more than his current salary. This sounded good. In addition, he would not have to teach anything. Even better. In fact, so long as he came in once a week to show he still existed, the school would consider it a wonderful deal. The professor speedily accepted.

To this bizarre arrangement was added one extra element: absurdity. The professor continues to work for his original employer as a visiting professor. In fact, he teaches much the same hours, but the school buys back his time. This works out quite expensive. The professor also still has a permanent office, just like any other member of staff. Could this happen in any other business? We doubt it.

Welcome to the world of business schools. There is more to business schools than you ever knew. Welcome to *Gravy Training*.

Gravy Training

1

The Business School Phenomenon

Business schools have managed to create an aura of respectability to cover up what is otherwise a bloody brawl. They have given intellectual attire to what otherwise would pass as folk wisdom. And they have created countless jobs not only for professors but for publishers. Business schools will exist as long as there is business—which is forever.

—Philip Kotler, Northwestern University[1]

Today, after more than a century of unchecked growth, business schools are part of a multibillion-dollar global industry selling business education and executive development.

Their modus operandi is based on the belief that management can be distilled into theory and taught in classrooms away from the workplace. Central to this book is our belief that what goes on within business and management schools is of vital importance to society because of the impact it has on the way business is conducted in the real world. For this reason business schools merit critical examination. (It is for others to consider whether the claims of those who believe that management should be regarded as an academic discipline are justified.) In subsequent chapters we will consider the consequences of the way management is taught.

Here we examine the business school phenomenon, the circumstances that gave rise to these twentieth-century institutions, and the growing influence they wield in the modern world—in particular:

- The meteoric rise of business schools
- Their main activities: qualification programs, research, and executive education
- The 1980s MBA gold rush

THE IRRESISTIBLE RISE OF BUSINESS SCHOOLS

Business schools are among the great institutions of our age. That is a bold statement, but think of where the power lies. If a multinational hits trouble it calls in a management consulting firm. Before long, teams of fresh-faced, business school–trained consultants are assembling a report to save the business. Stock prices can actually go up when companies call in consultants. At last, investors say, they're calling in the professionals—twenty-eight-year-old MBA (Masters of Business Administration) graduates who have virtually no line management experience and who last came across a similar problem in a case study two years ago at business school.

Today, the steps that matter belong to well-heeled business graduates. Politicians once courted clerics, soldiers, and the aristocracy; now they go cap in hand to business school–trained CEOs. Once they listened to learned lawyers and professionals; now Bill Clinton plays golf with Michael Porter of Harvard Business School and is advised by a legion with business school connections. Former Clinton Under Secretary of Commerce Jeffrey Garten is now dean of Yale's School of Management. Laura D'Andrea Tyson moved from academia to become the president's chief economic adviser and returned to become dean of the Haas School of Business at the University of California, Berkeley. The list is long and lengthening.

There is no escape from the ubiquitous power of business schools. Largo Winch is the main character in a French comic-book series. He is astonishingly young, good looking, runs a huge international conglomerate, and boasts an MBA from the top French school, INSEAD. (Author Jean Van Hamme was given an honorary INSEAD diploma for his creative promotional activities.)[2]

Whether it be in a textbook or a comic book, business is the universal language—albeit one characterized by jargon and obfuscation—and the creators of the language are business schools. Recent years, for example, have seen *core competencies*, *strategic intent*, *industry foresight*, and *strategic architecture* become the vocabulary of top executives in organizations the world over—largely as a result of the research carried out by two American academics, Gary Hamel and C. K. Prahalad.

Business schools are the new corridors of power. They change people's lives. And we are not talking about someone undergoing a personal transformation in a leadership seminar. We are talking about people in factories in Illinois and Gdansk, Poland, changing the way they work and live because of business schools. President Clinton is not playing golf with Michael Porter simply for the fun of it. Porter has changed the way individuals, firms, and countries run themselves. His ideas on competitive strategies have been picked up and acted on throughout the world.

From a corporate point of view, business schools are no longer decorative adornments to which poorly performing managers can be dispatched for a spot of executive R&R. There was a time when most senior managers had never been to business school. They looked to executive education to fill in the gaps between knowledge and practice. Attending a course on strategic management was their payoff for long service to their firms. But today, business schools have turned hundreds of thousands of trained managers loose on the world. Exec ed is no longer a gap filler, a pleasantly undemanding diversion from reality. Exec ed's new role is helping executives get things done. Business schools proclaim their ability to help managers change things, solve problems, make a real difference. They make managers better at their jobs—or so they claim.

Curing all known corporate ills—or at least being able to make a diagnosis—is lucrative work. As the proclamations have become louder and more strident, business schools have become big business. They have carved out a share in one of the great growth markets of our time. They have attracted huge donations from corporations and individual entrepreneurs. Along the way, a number of top academics have also used their research to launch successful careers as management gurus and become millionaires. Business school faculty members have become academic rock stars, parading their ideas around the world at conferences and seminars.

Dry figures have given way to dry ice. While their faculty spread their talents widely, business schools themselves have been the largest beneficiaries of the huge growth in demand for business education. The numbers are impressive. This is big business. In the United Kingdom, a report published by the Association of Business Schools suggests that U.K. business schools are among the United Kingdom's top fifty exporters, attracting over £400 million ($640 million) a year from other countries.[3]

Albert Vicere and Robert Fulmer, two business professors from Penn State, calculate that businesses worldwide spend more than $100 billion on training their employees every year. Dauntingly, Vicere and Fulmer also estimate that over half of this is wasted as much is carried out with no objective. The global executive education market has been calculated to be worth in excess of $12 billion. Business schools are believed to account for approximately one-quarter of the total—about $3 billion. If you add on all the many millions spent on management and business education at degree level, the figures become even more impressive—in 1995–1996, 227,102 bachelor degrees in business were awarded in the United States. One survey, by management consulting firm Linkage, concluded that $250 billion is spent annually on executive development. Leadership guru Warren Bennis referred to this as "The Great Training Robbery."[4]

THE BUSINESS OF BUSINESS SCHOOLS

There are three main areas of business school activity:

- Qualification courses
- Research
- Executive education (mainly nonqualification programs)

This doesn't include the lucrative consultancy work that professors and other faculty members do in their own time. Most schools allow their professors one day a week to pursue this alternative income source.

Taking up the first of the three activities, business schools offer a range of qualification courses. These include degrees at undergraduate and postgraduate level. A number of the university business schools have large undergraduate programs as well as postgraduate programs. Others, however, offer only postgraduate qualifications.

The best-known business school qualification is the Master of Business Administration (MBA). But the list of business school degrees is expanding rapidly. At postgraduate level, the choice is wide, including master's degrees in finance and similar programs. Recent years have seen the creation of more specialized offerings. Among them are master's programs in consulting and leadership.

To these have been added a plethora of so-called specialized MBAs (discussed in Chapter Four). Whether these new variations are truly MBAs at all is a matter of debate in academic circles. Traditionalists argue that the MBA is essentially wide in scope and does not lend itself to customization. However, the creation of hybrid degree programs is likely to increase in the future.

The second area of business school activity is research. This area is of particular importance to U.S. business schools, which regard knowledge creation as one of their primary roles. Research is the cornerstone of traditional academic life. Faculty are measured by the quality of their research—as reflected in the quality and quantity of their published articles in refereed journals. Academic tenure is research-oriented.

Finally, the third main activity—and by far the most lucrative—is the provision of shorter executive development courses to corporate clients. These are often nonqualification courses, which cover a wide range of business disciplines—everything from finance for nonfinancial managers to programs on stress management.

As already noted, this market has exploded in recent years. A McKinsey-Harvard report in 1995 found that the nondegree executive education market alone generated around $3.3 billion and was growing at a rate of 10 percent to 12 percent annually. Given the fragmented nature of the market, this may well err on the conservative side.

But the aggregated numbers tell only a small part of the story. Behind them are a plethora of executive education programs—some of them open to the public and others customized to the needs of individual companies with entry restricted to their employees. What they all have in common is a price tag that reflects the buying power of business. Executive education programs range in price from $1,395 for a three-day course at Vanderbilt University on effective management techniques to $40,500 for the nine-week Advanced Management Program at Harvard.

Dramatic growth has been particularly evident in the area of customized—or tailored—programs. These are designed for individual corporate clients or consortia. The degree of customization varies from tweaking existing open programs to make them more relevant to the client's business to developing programs from scratch to meet the client's specific requirements.

At Duke University's Fuqua Business School, custom programs now account for 70 percent of total revenue, compared to 65 percent two years ago. It is expected that this proportion will rise to around 75 percent in the next few years. The continuing rise of custom programs is a common story throughout the world's business schools. A growing number of schools now generate the majority of their executive program revenue from custom work—at Indiana custom programs account for 70 percent of exec ed revenues; at Pittsburgh it's 69 percent; at Carnegie-Mellon 65 percent; at Emory's Goizueta School 65 percent.[5]

Custom programs have mushroomed because companies want programs that directly support their business goals. They do not want their executives laboring through peripheral subject areas. They want them working at subjects and learning skills that will make a difference when they come back to work.

Custom programs offer some economies of scale. Large numbers of managers can be put through a program simultaneously, with cost benefits and the opportunity to create momentum for change initiatives. They are also flexible and ensure that training reflects corporate priorities. But they don't come cheap—a one-week program may cost around $3,500 per participant, and the price can easily be $5,000 or above.

The range and ambition of custom programs is growing rapidly. The World Bank, for example, has an innovative program, led by Harvard but also drawing on leading faculty members from a number of other top schools including Stanford in America and the top Spanish business school, IESE, in Europe. Such partnerships are increasingly common, as are consortium programs customized to the needs of a group of companies. Creativity—and marketing awareness—is also evident in programs targeted at particular industries. Wharton, for example, offers industry-specific programs that include an Executive Management Program for ophthalmic administrators and one on leadership skills for professors of gynecology and obstetrics. Increasing numbers of such niches are being developed by business schools in an effort to fuse the best of public programs with the advantages of custom programs.

"It is very effective to get fifty people in a room and to then debate the issues. Custom programs give companies an opportunity to huddle," says Jean Hauser, head of the Center for Custom Programs at North Carolina's Kenan-Flagler School. "It's a debate among smart people. As outsiders we can raise tough questions. We provoke debate."

The question today, however, is who to huddle with. Business schools are not the only players in what is an increasingly diverse and fragmented marketplace. The lion's share of this highly lucrative market, however, still goes to the business schools. To date, their grip on this market has gone largely unchallenged. That is about to change.

Over the last decade the number of programs and providers has grown rapidly. Providers now include a growing number of corporate universities as well as consulting and training firms. This is already redefining the market for executive education. We believe that the arrival of other muscular newcomers, either alone or in joint ventures with existing suppliers, will redraw the map in the coming years. For example, the combination of a big name business school brand with a major software company or publishing and media group would offer a powerful alternative delivery system.

Some in the business school world shrug off such developments. They believe that their position as professional educators and researchers makes them unassailable. But business schools can no longer afford to be arrogant. They may well wake up in the near future and find that they're in bed with Bill Gates. They have had almost a century to demonstrate their value to their real-world business constituency. Yet their case is still far from cut and dried.

Indeed, business schools continue to attract more than their fair share of critics. The sniping comes from many quarters. Take these asides on the merits of the top French school, INSEAD, and its reputation for working students until they are ready to drop. "INSEAD is the most high powered finishing school in the world. Most MBAs find the time to ride in the forest of Fontainebleau, perfect their skiing and negotiate their way around a wine list," noted one article in, of all places, the society magazine, *Harpers & Queen*.[6] One European telecommunications company CEO quipped: "They are all graduated like identical bunny rabbits. They are very charming, very personable, very intelligent, and incapable of actually doing anything. INSEAD graduates are like robots. Their brains seem to be disconnected from their bodies." Another critic at a London investment bank said: "They are totally obsessed by process. We try not to hire them but they infiltrate the place as consultants."[7]

The comments are harsh, perhaps, but it would be foolish to ignore the sentiment: there is genuine concern that business schools have become MBA factories, churning out clones—and often unhelpful clones at that. There is also a sense that they do not serve the interests of the wider business community, but have been responsible for producing a cadre of career managers—people whose primary concern is their own career advancement and not the welfare or success of the companies they work for.

One source of this criticism is, predictably enough, people who have been successful without attending a business school. Their homespun wisdom usually regurgitates the university-of-life argument in one form or another. With surprising understatement, former Chrysler CEO Lee Iacocca noted: "Formal learning can teach you a great deal, but many of the essential skills in life are the ones you have to develop on your own."[8]

More opinionated was the late Avis chief and author of *Up the Organization*, Robert Townsend. "Don't hire Harvard Business School graduates," he warned. "This elite, in my opinion, is missing some pretty fundamental requirements for success: humility; respect for people in the firing line; deep understanding of the nature of the business and the kind of people who can enjoy themselves making it prosper; respect from way down the line; a demonstrated record of guts, industry, loyalty down, judgment, fairness, and honesty under pressure."[9]

Business schools are also criticized for failing to develop entrepreneurs. In recent years, Microsoft's Bill Gates, Virgin's Richard Branson, and Body Shop's Anita Roddick have all been much-quoted examples of those who didn't attend business school but went on to reach the summits of business success. "A great advantage I had when I started the Body Shop was that I had never been to business school," says Roddick. (Interestingly, she helped create a quasi-business school, the New Academy of Business.) Some entrepreneurs even go so far as to suggest that a business school education could dull the entrepreneurial instincts. Take 1-800-Flowers founder Jim McCann, for example, who believes his company would have not got off the ground if he'd been to business school—"I would have thought too much about why the deal couldn't be done," says McCann.[10]

What is more surprising is that some of the most vituperative criticism comes from business school insiders. The strategy guru Henry Mintzberg is a long-term critic of MBA programs (despite teaching at McGill in Canada and France's INSEAD). "The idea that you can take smart but inexperienced 25-year-olds who have never managed anything or anybody and turn them into effective managers via two years of classroom training is ludicrous," he says.[11]

The venerable Peter Drucker is another persistent critic of business schools. "The business schools in the US, set up less than a century ago, have been preparing well-trained clerks," he wrote as long ago as 1969.[12] More recently, he has predicted the decline of business schools, noting that "Business schools are suffering from premature success. Now, they are improving yesterday a little bit. The worst thing is to improve what shouldn't be done at all."

Drucker has roundly dismissed Harvard Business School—"Harvard, to me, combines the worst of German academic arrogance with bad American theological seminary habits." Drucker, who sees himself as an outsider, has eschewed the well-worn route to business school faculty life. Instead he prefers the relative obscurity of California's Claremont College.[13]

The critics persist, and their voices are likely to get louder unless their concerns are addressed. To date, however, business schools have found it easier to ignore them. They have been able to do so because of the enormous interest in business as a subject, which has largely overshadowed their shortcomings. Business schools are victims of their own success.

BORN IN THE U.S.A.

Two threads dominate the business school success story: the meteoric rise of business as an academic subject and the rise of management as a respectable professional discipline.

The twentieth century will be remembered for many great achievements—putting a man on the Moon, splitting the atom, and inventing the computer—but it is also the century that spawned the new academic discipline of management, which in turn created a multibillion-dollar global industry in management education.

While management has been a fundamental activity throughout history, the recognition and study of it as a discipline and profession is a thoroughly modern phenomenon. Only in the twentieth century did management come of age, gaining respectability and credence. Even now, management as an academic discipline is still in a fledgling state. In fact, the desire to establish academic credentials is largely to blame for many of the failings of business schools.

Business schools like to give the impression of age-old permanence and wisdom. They have a penchant for old buildings. They like ivy and lawns. There are statues of founders and teams of gardeners. They yearn for gravitas as well as air conditioning, but if you look through the ivy their lineage is relatively short. Indeed, by the standards of universities—especially in Europe—business schools scarcely register on the chronometer. (Oxford University is hundreds of years old; its business school is only now getting off the ground—as we write foundations are being laid in an old parking lot near Oxford rail station.)

Invented in the United States, the business school as we know it can be traced to the University of Pennsylvania's Wharton School, which was founded in 1881. The Wharton approach to business was numerical. Its bedrock was finance, and it was the management of money that was drummed into students from the earliest days. Other schools soon followed. These institutions grew out of a desire to train and educate future generations in management techniques and practices, an aspiration often supported by generous donations from industrialists.

Toward the end of the nineteenth century this desire led to the creation of a number of specialized departments and schools attached to leading U.S. universities. For the first time commercial practices, and the philosophies that underpinned them, were elevated to the same sort of level as other academic disciplines. They have been unlikely and often uncomfortable bedfellows ever since.

The origins of the MBA, the best-known business school qualification, date back to this period. The Tuck School at Dartmouth claims to have had the first graduate program in management. Although not technically an MBA, the first postgraduate degree in business was awarded by Tuck in 1902. Originally it was a "three, two" program, with three years' study at undergraduate level at Dartmouth followed by two years at Tuck.

Postgraduate entry courses followed. Harvard Business School claims to have been the first business school to require a university degree for entry to its management program. Founded in 1908, the school awarded its first master's degree in the discipline in 1910.

The idea of business education quickly took off. In some cases it was integrated into other professional disciplines. As early as 1914, for example, the Massachusetts Institute of Technology offered business training for engineers, and its master's degree in management dates back to 1925. Elsewhere it was given a helping hand by a section of the local business community. The Edwin L. Cox School of Business, at Southern Methodist University in Dallas, for example, was founded in 1921 with the help of Dallas businessmen and women. The need to establish some sort of quality control resulted in the creation of the American Association of Collegiate Schools of Business (AACSB) in 1916.

Throughout the 1940s, interest in business schools grew rapidly in the United States. After World War II, a number of private business schools were started, including the American Graduate School of International Management, known as Thunderbird.[14] But by the end of the 1950s, business schools were under attack. In 1959, two reports on the state of American management education were published. One, by Robert A. Gordon and James E. Howell, was sponsored by the Ford Foundation; the other, by Frank C. Pierson, had the financial backing of the Carnegie Corporation. Both complained that business schools were little more than vocational colleges, with mediocre students and second-rate teachers. Business schools were criticized for failing to produce original research and for being out of touch with business.

Business schools took the criticism to heart. Academic credibility was a raw nerve. In the coming years, it was to become an issue that dictated their priorities. The business schools hit back by raising admission and teaching standards. They also initiated the research programs for which the U.S. schools are now well known.

It was also at this time that the classic two-year American MBA model was born, with the first year devoted to the core disciplines and the second year offering more specialization through electives. The business schools were determined to be taken seriously. They would put management on the academic map. If large sums of cash were generated from these programs to pay for more research, then so much the better.

The MBA bandwagon was under way. Over the next forty years it would call at countless new business schools, providing job mobility for several million business school graduates it picked up along the way.

CONQUERING THE WORLD

While American institutions boarded the bandwagon with enthusiasm, in Europe there was a tepid response. In Europe, structured study of management is a much more recent phenomenon. With a few exceptions, Europeans took little interest in business schools in the first half of the twentieth century. (One of the notable exceptions was the Paris Chamber of Commerce and Industry, which introduced a management course in 1931. In many ways it was a precursor of the executive MBA—a part-time program aimed at managers between the ages of thirty and forty, though it did not involve a degree.)

After World War II the Marshall Plan and other U.S.-led initiatives to rebuild Europe's industrial base brought American ideas to Europe. These included recognition that the business leaders of the future required special training.

By the late 1940s and 1950s business schools were springing up on the European mainland. The origins of the Institute for Management Development (IMD) at Lausanne, Switzerland, for example, can be traced back to 1946. In 1958 the European Institute of Business Administration, better known as INSEAD, was established in Paris. INSEAD offered an MBA for the first time in 1959. (The dearth of European business education was such that in 1970 only one member of INSEAD's faculty had a business doctorate—all now do.)

In the United Kingdom, too, seeds were being sown for the business schools that followed. In 1965, both Manchester Business School and London Business School opened. They joined others, including Henley Management College and Cranfield, that were already running courses in management education.[15] But the two new British schools had the backing of the British government and were deliberately created to be centers of excellence that would rival their American counterparts. This represented an important development. The British government of the time believed that the creation of such centers was a necessary precondition to maintain the competitiveness of the national economy.

The American model was the one to follow. Elsewhere in Europe many of the newer schools were heavily influenced by U.S. business schools. IESE at the University of Navarra in Barcelona, for example, was inspired by Harvard, and still makes extensive use of the Harvard case study method. Harvard supported the founding of Paris's Centre de Perfectionnement aux Affaires in 1931. In the Netherlands, Erasmus University's close links with the University of Michigan helped it create Rotterdam School of Management in the early 1970s.

Harvard's influence stretched around the world. The Indian Institute of Management, for example, was established with Harvard's support and remains a devout follower to this day. In Asia, the Manila-based Asian Institute of Management was launched in 1968 and initially used material from Harvard for all its programs. Harvard even offers a one-year program in applied economics with the Ho Chi Minh City Economics University in Vietnam—thus achieving by stealth what the United States failed to achieve through warfare.

But although some European schools copied the Americans, elsewhere a distinctively practical European approach was apparent at schools such as IMD and INSEAD.

Today, business schools operate from within the walls of some of the most respected universities in the world—though those august academic institutions, Cambridge and Oxford, have only embraced management in the last decade. Business schools have influenced and changed the business world. Of that there is no question. But what sort of world have they helped create?

2

Building an Engineer's Paradise

Management is more art than science. No one can say with certainty which decisions will bring the most profit, any more than they can create instructions over how to sculpt a masterpiece. You just have to feel it as it goes.

—*Richard D'Aveni of Dartmouth's Amos Tuck School*[1]

Business schools have succeeded in popularizing management. They have created systems, models, and frameworks by which business can be analyzed. These are notable achievements and should not be underestimated. But business is about much more than manipulating numbers or finding rational solutions to problems. Business is a human activity—it is about people.

However, historically, business school theory has often been sterile, making few allowances for the way real people behave—other than to note they can be obstacles to change. Too often, what is taught in the classroom has had no relation to what is reasonable and practical in situ, preferring to create an engineer's paradise rather than a world based on the reality of the factory floor. Through their use of case studies, in particular, business schools have encouraged blind faith in business solutions—answers rather than questions.

As a result, the world of business management promulgated by business schools has been one of numbers, ratios, and lever pulling. Students are encouraged to regard companies as machines rather than communities of people. You make adjustments to the machine, change the ratios or change the inputs, and it automatically alters the output. (The very name Master of Business Administration reinforces this.)

In this chapter, we examine the *raison d'être* of business schools and ask these pointed questions:

- Do business schools make individuals and the corporations they work for more competitive?
- Do they play a useful role in wealth creation?
- Do business schools develop well-rounded managers with both hard-side and soft-side skills?
- Have business schools succeeded in establishing management as a profession?
- Have business schools created a credible body of knowledge that legitimizes management as an academic discipline?

We also make a number of specific criticisms. In particular, we assert that

- Business schools have contributed to the dehumanizing of management, which has had a damaging effect on the lives of large numbers of people around the globe.
- MBA graduates—a major output of business schools—are admitted on the basis of academic performance, including GMAT scores, and graduate unprepared for the real world of business.

- The teaching in many business schools—especially the Harvard case study method—is fundamentally flawed.
- At a time when most corporations are trying to create a more integrated approach to management, business schools remain wedded to the functional silos approach to business—something that places academic convenience above reality.
- Business schools have failed to provide either thought leadership or continuity. This failure has given credence to passing fads and fashions that have damaged the standing of management as a profession.

THE PURPOSE OF BUSINESS SCHOOLS

What are business schools for? It's a simple question, but one to which the answer is elusive. The truth is that business schools define their missions differently depending on their history and circumstances. What common ground exists lies in three key areas in which the success of business schools can be reasonably judged. Business schools as a species exist to

- Improve the effectiveness of individuals, the organizations they work for, and their national economies through promoting best practice.
- Legitimize management as an academic discipline and to support it as a profession.
- Carry out research (knowledge creation).

Taking up the first of these, it seems reasonable to suggest that a fundamental role of business schools is to improve the effectiveness of practicing managers. This operates at two levels: at the micro level, the aim is to provide knowledge and experience that makes the individuals who attend b-school programs better managers than those who have not done so. In theory, their improved personal competitiveness translates into enhanced performance for their companies. This is supposed to make their companies more competitive.

The competitiveness issue is also relevant at the macro economic level. Many business schools in Europe, and to a lesser extent in the United States, were originally created with government support with the express purpose of bolstering their national economies. This was meant to be achieved by making a contribution to the quality of the management population. In other words, business schools were supposed to enhance wealth creation.

The second role of business schools—and the one where they have succeeded beyond all expectations—is putting management on the map. Today, there is wide acceptance of the importance of management in almost every sphere of life. This extends well beyond the business world to include public sector and nonprofit organizations. Business schools must take much of the credit for this.

The professionalization of management was an explicit objective of some business schools. Management, they set out to prove, was made up of a common set of standards and techniques. Spreading this gospel has, at one level, been an unequivocal success. Today, whether in London, New York, or Tokyo, managers speak the same language—that of management jargon—and understand the same concepts, tools, and techniques. A manager in Manila, for example, will be as familiar with the vocabulary of Total Quality Management or business process reengineering as one in Paris or Chicago. Degree courses such as the MBA have undoubtedly helped create a common vocabulary and curriculum of management theory.

The third purpose is to carry out research. This is supposed to further the understanding of management and business—by creating a body of knowledge akin to other academic disciplines. This is a role the American university business schools have taken more to heart than their counterparts in Europe or Asia. In many cases, however, this has been driven by pressure to establish the credentials of business schools as bona fide academic institutions, rather than by any serious attempt to push out the frontiers of knowledge. In answering the academic calling, rigor has tended to take precedence over relevance to the business community.

BUILDING COMPETITIVENESS

Do Business Schools Make Individuals and the Corporations They Work for More Competitive?

More effective managers, corporate clients believe, lead to better-managed corporations. Corporations are careful with their money. Executives are paid to be careful with corporate money. Perhaps the greatest leap of faith is their investment in training and development. With basic skills, companies can see dividends. Employees acquire skills they put into practice. Training manifestly and immediately improves performance. The benefits of executive education are more elusive, notwithstanding the billions of dollars spent every year at business schools.

This raises a pointed question: what do business schools bring to the party? What do business schools offer corporations that other providers of executive development do not? It is hard to say. What even the business schools are prepared to admit is that managerial effectiveness does not lend itself easily to measurement.

"Being an effective manager is not a black and white issue. Managers are neither good nor bad. In reality, being a good manager is a matter of being marginally better than and different from your competitors," explains Arnoud de Meyer, former dean of INSEAD. "It is a question of being a little bit faster; able to spot an opportunity somewhat earlier; or reacting quicker to a new threat. These are the elements which make the difference between a successful and a less successful manager. This marginal advantage may be based on talent, flair or natural leadership. But, knowledge of management can provide this decisive advantage. A sophisticated manager must, as a result, constantly update his or her knowledge of the latest concepts, insights and experiences in management thinking."[2]

Managerial effectiveness may be open to debate, but the logic is not: better managers create better and more efficient organizations, thus boosting national competitiveness and prosperity. As Gary Hamel says: "The product is competitiveness." QED.

The trouble is that it is difficult, if not impossible, to calculate the performance of business schools in such broad terms. This creates problems with assessing their impact at the macro level.

Do Business Schools Play a Useful Role in Wealth Creation?

Have business schools helped increase managerial standards over the last fifty years and, as a result, helped boost economic performance? Again, hard to say. Arguably, Germany and Japan, which have largely ignored the business school approach, have been the most consistently successful economies of the last fifty years. The success of the Germans and Japanese has been based on corporate cultures vastly different from those of the American multinationals that provided the customers and the case studies for business schools. Germany thrives thanks to a network of innovative *Mittelstands*, middle-sized companies; while Japanese companies created cultures based on mutual support, long-term perspectives and teamwork. The link between the two is perhaps that both preserve a sense of individuality built around small units and teams, albeit often in large organizations.

Elsewhere in the East, business schools are only now getting off the ground or establishing themselves. You may wonder why—after all, Singapore has a higher GDP per person than the United States. Charles Hampden-Turner, coauthor of *Mastering the Infinite Game: How Asian Values Are Transforming Business Practice*, argues that the fundamental difference between Eastern and Western business thinking is that Western corporations play to *win* a finite game while the Tiger economies of the East play to *learn* in an infinite game. Business schools have been playing to win rather than playing to learn. The message of the world's business schools has been resolutely, perhaps religiously, corporate. The world of the Fortune 500 has largely been the world of business schools—if only for the simple commercial reason that only big companies can afford the premium prices charged by business schools.

Business schools have trained managers in the skills needed to survive and prosper in big organizations. Working to the credo that what's good for big companies is good for national prosperity, business schools have traditionally eschewed the arts of running a small business and largely ignored the skills of entrepreneurialism.

It might, therefore, be more practicable and meaningful to use the performance of corporate giants as a measure of business school success. Unfortunately, those large organizations have not actually proved that adept at survival. "The natural average lifespan of a corporation should be as long as two or three centuries," writes Arie de Geus in *The Living Company*, noting a few prospering relics such as the Sumitomo Group and the Scandinavian company, Stora.[3] But the reality is that companies do not head off into the Florida sunset to play Bingo. They usually die young.

De Geus (formerly of Royal Dutch Shell and now a business school academic) quotes a Dutch survey of corporate life expectancy in Japan and Europe that came up with 12.5 years as the average life expectancy of all firms. "The average life expectancy of a multinational corporation—*Fortune* 500 or its equivalent—is between 40 and 50 years," says de Geus, noting that one-third of 1970's Fortune 500 had disappeared by 1983. Such endemic failure is attributed by de Geus to the focus of managers on profits and the bottom line rather than the human community that makes up their organization. Of course, business schools have spent the last fifty years preaching the virtues of the bottom line and largely ignoring any concept of the human community (with a few glorious exceptions—most notably, Rosabeth Moss Kanter).

It is true that we are belatedly starting to recognize some of these issues, but this is largely no thanks to the b-schools, which by and large have found it easier to reduce the art of management to the cold science of numbers.

THE GOLDEN AGE OF STRATEGIC PLANNERS

The cold science reached its peak at the same time as the Cold War. The 1960s and 1970s were the golden age for rational problem solvers. While the rest of the world enjoyed the Summer of Love and Woodstock, business schools discovered Igor Ansoff and strategic management. In retrospect, all had a hallucinogenic quality. Armed with these analytical weapons, regiments of bright young business school graduates advanced into the real world of business and were paid large salaries to sit in strategic planning departments—the corporate equivalent of the command bunker—removed from the cut and thrust of day-to-day operations, gazing into the future. Meanwhile, other business school graduates joined management consultancies such as McKinsey and the Boston Consulting Group (BCG), which built multimillion-dollar businesses from doing clients' strategic thinking for them. Programmed for analysis, the b-school graduates were ideally suited to this work. A string of strategic analysis tools was developed. So influential was the Boston Matrix—one of the tools developed by BCG—that a whole generation of senior managers grew up with cows, dogs, stars, and question marks as a way to classify their businesses. "I was taught at [Stanford] Business School that the manager's job revolved around P.A.T., cash flow, R.O.I., and quick ratios. After too many years, I learned that all of those measures are nothing more than a by-product of a customer," former Levi's chief Pete Thigpen has lamented.[4]

Strategic planning was rational management *in extremis*. Such was the confidence—soon to be recognized as arrogance—of the in-house analysts at that time that some companies had planning departments at work on detailed strategic plans for up to ten years ahead. As strategic planning departments mushroomed in the 1970s, so they became more and more disconnected from the reality of what was happening at the sharp end of the business.

Strategy became a purely cerebral activity, a triumph of rationality over reality. It was the ultimate case study, creating the future out of the past. Figures fed in from the operating companies at one end were crunched by the planners back at corporate headquarters and spewed out as strategic plans at the other end. The strategic planning department was the brain of the body corporate, but it took little or no interest in what messages it received from its eyes and ears in the marketplace.

All that came to an end in the early 1980s. The impact was felt not in the cloistered spaces of Harvard or Wharton, however, but in corporate America where household name after household name lost market share to foreign competitors (who, incidentally, had no MBAs). Not only were the business school graduates of the time ill-equipped for managing real people, their analytical skills also proved ineffective as companies were outflanked by more nimble competitors. The new arrivals—many of them upstarts from Silicon Valley and Japan—broke the mold. They seemed to be making up strategy as they went along. They had not been to business school. When Kenichi Ohmae revealed the inner workings of Japanese strategists, the talk was of intuition and reality. They analyzed, but not obsessively.

For many commentators, the turning point came in 1983 when General Electric CEO Jack Welch (a non-MBA) dismantled the company's two-hundred-strong planning department. In the face of fierce competition, Welch found the GE planners so preoccupied with financial and operating details that they failed to realize that the company's strategic position was being eroded. Freed from the dictates of planners, GE has prospered.

Other strategic planning departments followed. The best-laid plans of giants—IBM, Sears, Digital, Kodak, and General Motors among them—crumbled under a barrage of competition. From what had seemed unassailable strategic positions, many found themselves staring into the abyss. Throughout the 1980s and early 1990s, once-mighty companies were forced to come down from the strategy mountain and engage in a humbling new pursuit called downsizing.

In his 1994 book *The Rise and Fall of Strategic Planning*, Henry Mintzberg seemed to sound the death knell of business strategists. (It is no surprise that this book came from the ultimate outsider in the business school world—one of the few strategists who hadn't been taken in by the importance of their work.) Strategy, said Mintzberg, cannot be planned but must emerge by "synthesis" from changes taking place inside and outside the company. Under this interpretation, strategy is less concerned with handing down "big ideas" from on high and much more concerned with identifying and communicating the best of what's already happening within the organization. The role of senior management becomes the identification, interpretation, and articulation of ideas bubbling up from below.

Others have continued to cast doubt on the rational approach to strategy. Listen to Gary Hamel, for example: "I am a professor of strategy and oftentimes I am ashamed to admit to it because there is a dirty secret: we only know a great strategy when we see one. In business schools we teach them and pin them to the wall. They are specimens. Most of our smart students raise their hands and say, 'Wait a minute, was that luck or foresight?' They're partly right. We don't have a theory of strategy creation. There is no foundation beneath the multibillion-dollar strategy industry. Strategy is lucky foresight. It comes from a serendipitous cocktail," he says.[5]

The trouble, according to Hamel, is that we have sought to explain strategy by a series of simplistic frameworks: "We have an enormous appetite for simplicity. We like to believe we can break strategy down to Five Forces or Seven Ss. But you can't. Strategy is extraordinarily emotional and demanding. It is not a ritual or a once-a-year exercise, though that is what it has become. We have set the bar too low."

Strategy, the cornerstone of business school theorizing, was a carefully wrought castle assembled in the clouds. Over decades, business schools taught techniques that tied managers in a theoretical straitjacket before eventually realizing that there is more to business life than logically thought-out strategies that bear little relation to reality.

Where does this leave business schools? A generous interpretation would be that the impact of fifty years of business school education is just now making its presence felt, as witnessed by the strength of the U.S. economy. Perhaps it has taken this long to make up the gap in competitiveness between American and Japanese companies that began to appear in the 1970s. A less generous interpretation would be that business schools have not provided the competitive advantage and corporate strength they were supposed to.

In terms of new wealth creation, too, business school performance is questionable. If business schools were supposed to turn out entrepreneurs who would go forth and multiply—creating jobs and adding to GDP—then they have not succeeded. When it comes to successful business start-ups, with a few notable exceptions such as Dell Computers, business school graduates are conspicuous by their absence.[6] Wharton MBA, consultant, and author Peter Cohan is among those who argue that the role of business schools should be "to prepare leaders of established companies *and* entrepreneurial ventures."[7]

In reality, business schools are much more geared toward developing *intrapreneurs*—managers who are good at working within the structures and career frameworks of large corporations—than entrepreneurs. The one area where they excel at starting their own firms is in the field of management consultancy—and the value such firms add to the economy is debatable.

Of course, there are exceptions. Business schools are increasingly adding entrepreneurial programs to their more standard fodder. Some schools put entrepreneurial skills at center stage. Babson College, for example, makes much of its entrepreneurial pedigree. A college ad features well-known executives with the line, "Their entrepreneurial leadership began at Babson." The Instituto de Empresa (IE), one of Spain's leading business schools, makes it an explicit part of its mission to "encourage enterprise." This includes helping graduates launch their own companies. Some 15 percent of those in IE's International MBA program go on to start their own business, and there is an annual award of two million pesetas to help MBAs get their companies off the ground. In the last ten years, more than 350 firms have been set up by IE graduates, amounting to about £2.25 million ($3.6 million) of investment. However, such enterprise remains the exception.

While business schools have proved somewhat blinkered adherents to corporate gigantism, they have achieved a great deal in promoting the idea of management as a profession. In recent years, too, they have communicated the message of continuous professional development to a wide audience. There is, of course, a self-serving element to this, but the achievement should not be underestimated.

Today, the desire for self-improvement is remarkably and unusually strong among managers. It is commonplace to find executives paying their way through an MBA or working at night to achieve another business qualification. Fifty-year-old executives are likely to be investing time in developing their knowledge and skills—reading magazines, journals, and books, attending conferences and exec ed programs. Fifty-year-old lawyers are unlikely to be so committed—you don't find many of them reading *The One Minute Attorney* or going back to law school for a refresher course. Business schools have helped inculcate executives with a restless urge for learning. Whether they are actually learning the right thing in the right way at the best time is another matter entirely—and one that is increasingly being called into question. (The issues of teaching methods and program contents are discussed further in Chapter Eleven.)

To a large extent, the argument about whether managers are more effective has become buried beneath one undoubtedly exceptional aspect of business school performance: few other academic qualifications have done so much for the earning power and career prospects of their graduates. Business schools have done all right by their graduates. Their effect on corporate and national performance is difficult, if not impossible, to gauge, but they have boosted the salaries of countless thousands of executives. For this executives are eternally grateful—witness their willingness to give money to business schools.

INVENTING MANAGEMENT

The third grand mission of business schools is knowledge creation. Business schools aim to create and promulgate a theory of management—indeed, *the* theory of management. (Ford Foundation grants in the early 1950s were given to Carnegie-Mellon to define the science of management in order to make it a legitimate profession.)

These original intentions were given added impetus at the end of World War II. In the United States, the need to optimize economic growth was a political imperative as the Cold War standoff with the Soviet Union intensified. At the same time, there was a growing sense that, as with the established professions such as law, architecture, and medicine, the business leaders of the future would require special training if they were to deliver managerial effectiveness. In the struggle ahead, capitalism would have to demonstrate its superiority and that would require a well-trained army of managers. The battle is won, but in the intervening years, the business academies have fallen behind.

In their role of creating and disseminating management theory, business schools have failed to keep pace with the constituencies they serve. The vast majority continue to take a functional view of what managers do. Teaching remains organized around functional disciplines, or silos, that mirror the traditional departments of corporations.

In recent years, however, corporation after corporation has attempted to restructure itself to get away from these functional fiefdoms. But while much of the business world now accepts that this silo approach is outdated, most university business schools have stoutly resisted this trend, continuing to teach management as though it were made of compartmentalized areas of knowledge and expertise. The vast majority of MBA programs, for example, teach the so-called core subjects: accountancy, economics, finance, human resources management, information management, marketing, organizational behavior, quantitative analysis, and strategy. What is in question here is not whether these are important basic subject areas but whether teaching them in silos is the best preparation for the managers of the future.

Most business schools still make little serious attempt at integrating these areas of knowledge into a coherent view of what it means to run a business. (One notable exception to this is Wharton—when he took over as dean at the beginning of the 1990s, Tom Gerrity immediately reviewed the Wharton MBA and shifted it radically toward integration and away from its traditional functional emphasis.)

Most schools remain structured into departments that are themselves mirrors of the traditional silos. So, for example, marketing professors are to be found in the Marketing Department and finance professors in the Finance Department, with little interaction between the two. What practical hands-on experience the schools offer is provided through project work, as if everything will magically fall into place when students step outside the classroom. Yet the dissonance between the different disciplines is rarely discussed.

How do you balance human resources issues against financial considerations, for example? Sadly, the answer is implicit in the culture of many business schools, which reinforces the belief that numbers are more important than people.

It is interesting that much of the experimentation with issue-based learning has actually occurred outside the United States. Henry Mintzberg has said that a great deal of the innovation in executive education is occurring in Europe. He himself has championed one of the most innovative projects—the International Masters Program in Management (IMPM). This involves five business schools from around the world—McGill, INSEAD, the Indian Institute of Management, Hitosubashi University in Japan, and the UK's Lancaster University. The IMPM is run as a consortium with a limited number of companies sending several participants. The ten members of the consortium are also a truly international selection and include Fujitsu, Lufthansa, Matsushita, Royal Bank of Canada, and Alcan.

The program, over three years in the making, is miles apart from the MBA approach. The classroom activity takes place in five modules of two or three weeks each, spread over almost a year and a half. The content is structured around *managerial mind-sets:* the reflective mind-set, the analytic mind-set, the worldly mind-set, the collaborative mind-set, and the catalytic mind-set. "Organizing the program in this way gives a different perspective," says Lancaster University's program director, Jonathan Gosling. "Managers need to understand the world around them. The question is not just how people act economically or politically or creatively, not just how economies function or social ethics develop, but how these different perspectives interact to create the behaviors we see around us. Any manager is only as good as his or her understanding of these phenomena." Clearly, such notions are a world away from the functional emphasis still pursued by most MBA programs.

The IMPM does not mark the death of the MBA. "It aims to bridge weaknesses on both sides of the management development curtain—MBA programs removed from the actual practice of management and in-house or public programs lacking a certain depth," says Gosling. "The conventional MBA is still a good product if it is aimed at the right people and if it is clear what it is there to do. But it doesn't develop people fit to lead companies." The unconventional MBA program is clearly the future.

Have Business Schools Succeeded in Establishing Management as a Profession?

Business schools may not have created a legion of leaders but management has become a profession—even a respected one. Celebrations may be premature. In their book *Management Redeemed*, Frederick Hilmer and Lex Donaldson argue that "a respected profession is distinguished by a number of core values." These are

- Professions tend to be based on lofty ideals that transcend self-interest.
- Professionals give form to their ideals by mastering a craft or body of knowledge.
- A professional body of knowledge is based on sound reasoning, not dogma or unproven rules.
- Reasoning, especially in fields such as management, rests on the ability to use language clearly and precisely.
- Professions operate according to high ethical and technical standards.[8]

Placed against such criteria the creation of a profession of management begins to look tenuous. In one area in particular, business schools have proved disappointing. Not only have they failed to instill lofty ideals, in some cases they have actually encouraged ignoble values. The image of the grasping MBA graduate whose primary concern is career advancement and personal gain may be a legacy of the "greed is good" ethos of the 1980s, but certainly was not discouraged by most business school professors. Indeed, it could be argued that they played an active part in the deification of market forces. Of course other professions are far from pure, but they do aspire to a higher calling. Why isn't business ethics a core part of every MBA program?

Do Business Schools Develop Well-Rounded Managers with a Balance of Both Hard and Soft Skills?

Of course, the very nature of management—a practical art as well as an awkward science—means that the parameters of managerial theories are continually being tested. This is something that business schools have struggled to come to terms with. They have been seeking to lay down, in tablets of formidable stone, the theory of management. Just as they are about to do so, management slips from their grasp, developing another idiosyncratic quirk.

When it comes to teaching management theory, business schools attempt to make the complex practice of business comprehensible to novices by setting out hard-and-fast rules and principles. In this way, they attempt to provide clarity. Yet in recent years there has been a growing sense that business schools should be helping practicing managers cope with an increasingly complex business environment. The true art of management, by this understanding, isn't clarity of classroom analysis at all, but coping with ambiguity. "Uncertainty is the new reality," says Randall White of Greensboro, North Carolina–based RPW Executive Development, who teaches in programs at Duke and Cornell. "Managers and organizations remain addicted to the quick fix. There is an air of desperation in the way managers cling to new ideas. Fads and fashions are grabbed with gusto and then discarded. They emerge in a fanfare of superlatives only to disappear almost as quickly. Organizations and managers obey the 'law of the refrigerator' without apparently realizing it. The law of the refrigerator is that the things that come to hand are not the things you want to hand. The things you most need are not the things you can easily get. And the things most easily observed and measured are the most often studied."

The trouble is that business schools have built their reputations and modus operandi around the citadels of certainty, the things most easily observed and measured.

THE CASE IN POINT

The desire to offer clarity and certainty is exemplified by the use of the case study method of teaching. Exported around the globe, the case study has been one of the educational building blocks of MBA programs throughout the world. The case study method was established as the primary method of teaching at Harvard Business School as long ago as 1924.

It presents students with a corporate example. From the narrative, they are expected to reach conclusions about what was the right or wrong thing to do, identify best and worst practice, and learn something about managerial behavior. Whatever its current and historical limitations, the emphasis on the case study method greatly aided the development of management theory. It froze management in time. It espoused rational contemplation, analysis, and decision making. In doing so, it made management theory more understandable and accessible. It regarded management as a science.

However, case studies generally eschewed the intricate and complex human side of management. It is this fundamental shortcoming that is increasingly being exposed. Business schools have placed too much emphasis on teaching students analytical techniques and not enough on managing people. The end result is that many top managers are notably dysfunctional when it comes to interpersonal skills. (Indeed, like the rest of us, many are notably dysfunctional. Period. Don't be taken in by their positions of power.)

There are a myriad cases to choose from, covering every business eventuality. With over fourteen thousand titles, the European

Case Clearing House, based at the United Kingdom's Cranfield University, is the largest single source of management case studies. During 1996–1997, it supplied nearly three hundred thousand cases in response to requests from throughout the world. Harvard alone has generated 5,310 cases—the most prolific case generator in Europe is Lausanne's IMD with 1,058.

It is an indictment of business schools that the case study has become such a sacred cow. To question its relevance is seen by some as an attack on the very temples of learning—which is precisely our point. Rather than welcome debate about their teaching methodologies, too many of those within business schools regard this as treasonous. While it is true that some business schools eschew the Harvard model, the case study method remains a widely accepted and practiced approach, in the United States and in many other parts of the world. Harvard alone continues to churn out six hundred cases a year (as well as around forty books). Its example is followed in places far distant from Cambridge, Massachusetts. Take the China Europe International Business School in Shanghai. "Case writing on the development of selected enterprises in China is CEIBS's most important research activity," its publicity material announces. "These cases are not only used in the school's own programs, but also published to serve as teaching material at other institutions."

Despite the profusion of cases and the wide usage of the case study method, doubt and invective have been aimed in its general direction. Peter Drucker surely had the case study in mind when he said, "Classrooms construct wonderful models of a non-world."[9] Once again one of the most consistent critics has been Henry Mintzberg. "Superficial and disconnected," he says. "It's somebody else's world. You read twenty pages the night before and pronounce the next morning. Business schools using cases, like Harvard, train managers to be glib, that's all."[10]

Elsewhere, he has noted: "Business schools train people to sit in their offices and look for case studies. The more Harvard succeeds, the more business fails." Unlike many other critics, Mintzberg has the courage of his convictions—the IMPM, with which he is closely involved, is case-free.

"The case study was introduced to bring a level of reality to a student in a remote environment so that theoretical concepts could be brought to life," says London Business School's Jeff Sampler. "The case study is not dead. The issue is finding different ways of bringing the business world into the classroom in a dynamic, realistic, and lively way. Today's case studies take that still further with video clips of chief executives talking with real feeling and passion, as well as simulations which show what happens if you do a or b." In practice, Sampler argues that the case study's chief role should be to introduce and explain fundamental principles. He warns against overdependence on the case study: "Doing everything by case study leads to paralysis by analysis, an unwillingness to do anything or decide on anything unless there is a supportive case."

The chief gripe against the traditional case study is that it represents an idyllic, one-dimensional portrait of reality. "Business schools have been case study–based and have followed an intellectual model. The heritage has been about managing structures we wanted to control. If you build industries on change, people rely on processes which they can't control so business schools have to emphasize the people side much more," says Kurt Vickersjo, director of strategic human resource development at Electrolux.[11]

There is an inbuilt tendency also for case studies to err on the positive side. A company is unlikely to agree to a case study that shows its executives to be consistently inept. And companies usually do exercise some control over the end result of academic endeavors. Similarly, academics are likely to favor case studies that confirm their prejudices or offer easy teaching lessons. They then master a basic repertoire of cases and regurgitate them year after year. Once the key learning points are established, they are unlikely to change.

The case study helps breed a culture based on dangerous assumptions. "Laying events down in a neat narrative can lead students to overlook the complex, confused, and messy reality," says Phil Hodgson, joint director of Ashridge Management College's Action Learning for Chief Executives program. "The traditional case study is classroom-oriented and marred by 20-20 hindsight. This is the Achilles' heel of the case study: history cannot be used as a blueprint for a future which is liable to be significantly different."

The reality is that the case study method is alive and well, though the typical Harvard case study now bears little resemblance to its predecessors—in terms of delivery at least. Under Dean Kim Clark, Harvard has sought to revitalize the case study method. The grand old school was on the point of outsourcing its information systems network to IBM when Clark took over as dean in 1995. He balked at the idea and turned Harvard's attentions and its considerable spending power to modernizing the case. Clark has dragged Harvard into the late twentieth century just in time. Along the way he has shocked academics with his brazen use of new technology. His first message to the faculty was delivered through e-mail—Clark's predecessor, John H. McArthur, never used e-mail. (McArthur refused to have an e-mail address as he believed, quite rightly, that students would flood him with messages. McArthur closed the only computer lab open to students in 1993.)

Harvard put its first electronic case to work in 1996 and now boasts that its MBA curriculum is "virtually paperless," with an expanding number of electronic cases incorporating on-site video sequences and links to real-time information on the Internet. "Cases have always had that kind of flavor, when you think about what you would do and why. We can now take it further because the technology allows us to do things like create a case structure in which the students actually have to search for data," says Kim Clark. "It's not a linear narrative, it's more like what the world's like—it's messy and the problem isn't framed for you."[12]

Inevitably, though it may save trees and be more colorful and interactive, the modern case study is not without its problems and critics. "In reality, multimedia cases are very expensive to construct, and they confound the student with a huge array of raw data," says Brandt Allen of the University of Virginia's Darden School. "The random access capability adds no value because students want to see all the relevant data and it's frustrating because you never know whether you've found it all. Finally, what could be more debilitating than an executive class that begins with one smart aleck saying 'I stayed up all night and in the back of those old documents, buried away in the company's old spreadsheets, was an error which probably explains everything.'"[13]

Here, as in many other situations, technology is not the simple savior. Producing generic lessons from unique situations is a risky business and one that some find has no relation to their business—"We have stopped sending our executives to business school. It is frustrating to learn about the marketing of Listerine mouthwash and have what is of primary interest to us treated as an aside," one executive recently told *Strategy & Business* magazine.

KNOWLEDGE CREATION

In their third grand mission—knowledge creation—business schools face more problems. In terms of pure quantity, business schools have performed amazingly in promoting management as a distinctive activity. No other discipline has produced as much research and debate in such a short period. It is unclear yet how much of it will stand the test of time, but for sheer industry, the business schools deserve credit. Not a day goes by without another tranche of research papers, books, articles, and journals.

In these terms, schools have produced a generally accepted theoretical basis for management. When it comes to knowledge creation, however, they find themselves in difficulties. They are caught between the need for academic rigor and for real-world business relevance, which tend to pull in opposite directions. The desire to establish management as a credible discipline leads to research that panders to traditional academic criteria. The problem for business school researchers is that they seek the approval of their academic peers rather than the business community. In the United States this has led to the sort of grand paper clip counting exercises that stand up to demands for academic rigor but fail to add one iota to the real sum of human knowledge.

Once again, business schools have too often allowed the constraints of the academic world to cloud their view of the real world. B-school researchers seek provable theories—rather than helpful theories. They have championed a prescriptive approach to management based once more on analysis and, more recently, on fashionable ideas that soon disappear into the ether. The one best way approach encourages researchers to mold the idiosyncracies of managerial reality into their tightly defined models of behavior. Figures and statistics are fitted into linear equations and tidy models. Economists and other social scientists label this *curve smoothing*. Meanwhile, reality throws out yet another curve ball.

Central to this is the tension between relevance and rigor. In a perfect world, there would be no need to choose between the two. But in the business school world, the need to satisfy academic criteria and be published in refereed journals often tilts the balance away from relevance. In other words, it is often easier to pursue quantifiable objectives than it is to add anything useful to the debate about management.

To a large extent, the entire tenure system works against useful, knowledge-creating research. Academics have five years in which to prove themselves if they are to make the academic grade. It seems long enough. But it can take two or even three years to get into a suitable journal. The novice, therefore, has around three years, probably less, to come up with an area of interest and carry out meaningful and original research. This is a demanding timescale. The temptation must be to slice up old data in new ways rather than pursue genuinely groundbreaking, innovative research. Too many business school faculty choose the easy option. Research, to them, is concerned with analytics rather than insights.

It is a criticism also made by some b-school insiders. "Academic journals tend to find more and more techniques for testing more and more obscure theories. They are asking trivial questions and answering them exactly. There has to be a backlash," says Julian Birkinshaw of London Business School.

In large part, the problem goes back to a time when business schools were trying to establish themselves. Up until the 1960s, American business schools were dismissed as pseudo academic institutions. Other academic institutions, including their own universities, regarded them as little more than vocational colleges.

Over the next two decades, the business schools managed a remarkable transformation. In the 1960s and 1970s, they did everything they could to gain academic respectability. A key tactic in this, and one that many felt they were misguided to adopt, involved taking on the traditions and ways of mainstream academia. They took on the airs and graces of other academic institutions, requiring the same high standards of their faculty members as those applied to other parts of the universities they belonged to.

As part of their attempts at elevating their work to academic respectability, schools also began recruiting junior teaching staff from the top doctoral programs in American universities, a tradition that continues. But perhaps most important of all, they adopted the tenure system. This meant that members of faculty had job security, but were required to carry out research that was recognized by other university faculty. The tenure system meant that the new business academics were obliged to publish their research findings in academic journals. But many of those required to referee this work had a limited knowledge of the business world. The methodology had to meet academic criteria, and the research had to be original. The results are predictable. If you reward one sort of behavior—academically rigorous but largely irrelevant research (paper clip counting)—and penalize another—academically tenuous but potentially useful fieldwork—you will end up with a lot of the former and much less of the latter.

The effects of this can be seen today. From a purely academic perspective, it has been a success. A number of U.S. business schools have prize-winning faculty members. In 1982, Chicago became the first business school in the world to have a Nobel Laureate on its faculty, when George Stigler won a Nobel Prize for his work in Economic Sciences. He was followed by his Chicago colleagues Merton Miller in 1990, Ronald Coase in 1991, and Robert Fogel in 1993.

"During the fifties and sixties, academics in business schools always felt inferior," says Robert Sullivan, who has worked at the University of Texas, Carnegie-Mellon, and now at the University of North Carolina at Chapel Hill. "They were not at the same level as physicists and the like. Consequently, in the sixties everything became a mathematical model. This served the peer community but not the professional community. Now there is no inferiority complex, but we haven't returned to the sense of creating value. We don't ask, Is the profession that we serve better or more efficient or more knowledgeable?"

By the late 1980s, the business community had had enough. The U.S. business schools in particular faced growing criticism from companies that what they were teaching was too theoretical and lacked real-world relevance. When a highly critical report was published by the Graduate Management Admissions Council (GMAC) in 1990, the schools realized they had to respond. Wharton and Columbia, two of the most prestigious schools, took an immediate decision to overhaul their approach and their curricula. Since then, most of the other leading schools have undergone major reassessments and introduced sweeping changes. It is questionable whether those changes have gone far enough.

In effect, the business schools have swung some way back toward the practical aspects of management. However, they have also tried to retain their academic rigor. In recent years, they have tried to ensure what they teach is relevant to what managers do in the real world of business. At the same time, they have also tried to inject more relevance into research. Today, despite much talk about relevance, the problem persists.

ICY HEARTS AND SHRUNKEN SOULS

In some ways, business schools have failed their subject. Sterile theory breeds simplistic responses. At a reengineering seminar we listened to a consultant talk for over an hour on the background of reengineering. It was accurate, predictable, and reasonable, talking of the nature of continuous change and the deficiencies of traditional management structures and management tools and techniques. However, the assembled executives were plainly ill at ease. The consultant asked, "Am I covering the areas you want to look at?" One plucked up the courage to express dissatisfaction. "What I want are one-liners so I can sell the idea to my people," he said. He believed in solutions. He knew what he wanted to achieve—a lean, flat, process-based organization. If only he had the means of persuading the people he could do it. If only he had the one-liners, the pithy, persuasive phrases that encapsulated it all.

"In the U.S. business education has been construed more and more narrowly as applied science. Business school professors are engineers and managers are mechanics. Management education is about knowing the right thing to do and getting people to do it," says Harvard-trained Don Sull, now at London Business School. "The fundamental assumption is that there are universal laws which can be extracted. I don't believe there are global business laws other than in finance. There are useful generalizations, but in management, context, timing, personality, and history are everything. The challenge lies in developing judgment, knowing which tool to use rather than reaching for the hammer every time." The trouble is that taking hammers out of the hands of those who are in the habit of using them is easier said than done.

As Peter Robinson, author of *Snapshots from Hell,* observes: "Sometime during the two-year curriculum, every MBA student ought to hear it clearly stated that numbers, techniques and analysis are all side matters. What is central to business is the joy of creating."[14]

For all their success, then, business schools have failed in this crucial area above all others. They have been party to a process that can be traced back to Frederick Taylor's Scientific Management. Business schools have been part of a dehumanizing of management that has been a characteristic of the last hundred years.

"While we teach many of the right things in our MBA programs, we don't teach some critical things we ought to teach . . . like leadership, vision, imagination and values . . . the major reasons we don't is because if we teach those untaught things it will become more difficult to teach and to justify what we design for MBA-level education. We then lay it upon well-proportioned young men and women, distorting them (when we are lucky enough to succeed) into critters with lopsided brains, icy hearts, and shrunken souls," says Stanford Business School's venerable Harold Leavitt.[15]

In time, scholars may come to regard the twentieth century as a period when mechanistic solutions were misapplied to what are essentially human issues. This is now beginning to change. But business schools have been slow to acknowledge the human dimension. For fifty years they have been happy to churn out MBAs who went out into the real world to play their number-crunching games with real people's lives.

As we have noted, it is an indictment of business schools that business ethics is still not mandatory on the vast majority of MBA programs. It is no defense to argue that b-schools are not there to teach morality; the fact is that they are quite happy to provide frameworks and tools for other business decisions, so why not provide young managers with some help with the really important issues that affect people's lives?

Some schools are beginning to do this: Cranfield School of Management in the United Kingdom, for example, provides training in termination interviews. Much more still needs to be done, however, in helping managers understand the real impact of their decisions, and their responsibilities to stakeholders such as employees and customers as well as stockholders.

"Business schools have raised certain kinds of managerial standards, principally numerical. I think there is a more easy cross-talk now between all kinds of managers on assessing lots of numerical benchmarks. I think some of it is globalized business, but a lot of it is business school mantra," says Tom Brown, mastermind of the influential Management General Web site. "On the other hand, if you were to check on whether performance appraisals or any other softer skills are being done better than thirty years ago, it just isn't there."[16]

The softer human side of management is in the ascendancy. A vast new market in executive coaching and mentoring is emerging as training companies and consulting firms help executives develop what many would regard as basic managerial skills. Stella Sinden is senior executive coach with the U.K. firm GHN Executive Coaching, which specializes in providing senior managers with the human skills they require. "The people we deal with are very talented and successful. The areas where they struggle are positioning, people, and politics. They tend to have analytical skills. Often they are engineers, IT or finance specialists who have won through because they are so analytical and rational," she says. "Making the transition to becoming a first-rate director requires skills in managing people. If you look at boards, they are peopled by individuals who tend to be aggressive and successful. They have risen through organizations because they negate the competition. Suddenly they find themselves in the boardroom and have to understand and take on completely different roles. They have to adapt their behavior in new contexts. They have to be responsive, take lateral perspectives, understand opposing positions."

New roles mean that managers—and business schools—have to move beyond regarding their role as problem solving. There are no clinically correct solutions to business problems. Solutions are the easiest way out, but not the answer. (From a teaching point of view, the advantage of solutions is, of course, that they can easily be marked and ranked. In economics and engineering this works, but not in management.)

Harvard's Chris Argyris has spent his entire career revealing just how poor managers—and others—are at learning. "Most people define learning too narrowly as mere *problem solving*, so they focus on identifying and correcting errors in the external environment. Solving problems is important. But if learning is to persist managers and employees must also look inward. They need to reflect critically on their own behavior," he says.[17] Despite Argyris's work and insights, business schools have nurtured a faith in problem solving; a faith that has conspicuously failed to produce the desired results.

3

Business or Ivory Tower?

The MBA programs of the very best U.S. schools—Harvard, Chicago, Stanford, Wharton, and Kellogg—tend to have many people teaching who have never worked in industry. The divide between the academic and real world is growing at these schools, not shrinking. There comes a point where academic theory is totally meaningless.

—Doug Lamont, visiting scholar at Kellogg Graduate School of Management, Northwestern University, and author of Salmon Day

Business schools face a dilemma. It is a dilemma they have occasionally wrestled with, but one that remains essentially unresolved. It is the cause of many of their current difficulties. The dilemma is this: On one hand, business schools present themselves as bona fide academic institutions. On the other, they try to demonstrate their ability to manage themselves as businesses. Indeed, many have to manage themselves as businesses because that, effectively, is what they are. This leads to the business school equivalent of schizophrenia. Full-fledged academic research rests uneasily with full-fledged commercialism. There is constant tension between rigor and relevance.

At present, many of the fault lines are simply papered over. The cracks are disguised by a combination of fudge and self-denial. But the cracks are there to see for anyone who takes the time and interest to look. They cannot be ignored forever. Sooner or later business schools will have to face up to their dual identity—and either come to terms with its challenges in a way that affords transparency or choose between the two roles. We believe it would be better for all concerned to have that debate sooner rather than later.

A number of developments make this debate increasingly necessary, including the following:

- The corporate desire for solutions rather than theory brings business schools into competition with consultancies. This is fueling a war of ideas, but there is a serious question mark over whether business schools should be competing in this market.
- Intensifying competition for corporate clients makes it increasingly difficult to maintain the independence of thought and action required of academic institutions.
- Much business school activity is currently driven by commercial pressures that can conflict with academic standards.

THE CREDIBILITY GAP

Business schools are caught between a rock and a hard place. They try to please the business community and the academic community at the same time. It is a thankless task. Their academic pedigree is far from established. Many of the schools are not readily accepted by their universities—even now. Harvard Business School is situated on the other side of the Charles River from other parts of the university—and some see that line as significant.

It is not uncommon for new academic disciplines to experience resistance when they are first introduced to university curricula. Several of the social sciences, including economics, took some time to establish themselves as "proper academic subjects." Arguably, others, such as sociology, have still to be accepted as rigorous disciplines in their own right. It is hardly surprising then that management and the core subjects taught at business schools have yet to be fully accepted at many leading universities.

There is often a good deal of suspicion—jealousy even—from other disciplines when a new subject area is in the ascendant. To make matters worse—much, much worse—the newcomers have been remarkably effective in attracting funding, both in the form of donations for new buildings and equipment and in the form of private sector funding for research.

This issue surfaced at Oxford recently when the siting of the new Said Business School was being debated in Congregation—the dons' parliament. A number of speakers from other academic disciplines questioned the legitimacy of management at the university, and one described it as a cuckoo, an imposter. No doubt we haven't heard the last of such sniping.

Beneath the surface, there is another issue. What has ruffled feathers in traditional seats of learning is the fact that the professors at the upstart business schools earn large fees for private consultancy work. Those who cross the line, like Michael Porter, are liable to raise academic hackles. Crossing the river is not a way to make friends—though you may come to influence people. In recent years, a number of business school professors have also become millionaires on the proceeds of books that have come out of what some in academia regard as fatuous research.

On the other side, when academically rigorous research is produced by business school faculty it can be greeted with blank expressions among the business community. The corporations that buy the expertise of business schools want knowledge, but they want usable knowledge.

The question that business schools struggle with is whether their work should be theory-to-practice or practice-to-theory (and back to practice). Again, the difficulties they face in this area originate from trying to be at one and the same time both credible academic institutions and beacons of best practice. At present, lack of clarity is bringing business schools into competition with consultancies that traditionally concentrate on enabling companies to put the latest theory into practice.

"Business schools have a real dilemma here," notes Bernadette Conraths, director general of the European Foundation for Management Development. "On the one hand, they have to follow the market call; on the other, they have to provide the thought leadership role and think beyond the present to the future. These two demands can contradict each other. Hopefully it is a fertile dilemma, which can create creative conflict."

GETTING REAL

How then are the twin imperatives to be reconciled? The answer, we believe, is by facing up to the issue rather than fudging it. Different schools come from different traditions and, as a result, have different imperatives.

In much of the discussion in this book we have lumped together business schools and institutions that call themselves schools of management. There are differences between these two traditions. When it comes to research, the latter are often much more concerned with relevance to the business world—or at least are more inclined to say they are. This may be due to differences in their origins. In the United Kingdom, for example, Henley Management College, Ashridge Management College, and Cranfield School of Management were created specifically to serve the needs of industry—rather than as academic institutions. As a result, they consider relevance to be at the heart of everything they do.

Even here, however, research is problematic. Some self-styled schools of management, like many of their business school brethren, belong to universities and compete for research funding, both from government and from other sources. Their ability to attract funding depends crucially on their academic standing. Cranfield, for example, is part of Cranfield University. As such it is subject to periodic assessments of its research by the Higher Education Funding Council (HEFC). The HEFC research assessment exercise covers the spectrum of university departments. A score of between one and five is awarded based on meeting rigorous academic standards. On one hand, then, a school such as Cranfield is philosophically dedicated to producing research that is relevant to the business community it serves, while the other hand is tied behind its back by the need to be academically rigorous.

Observes Andrew Kakabadse, professor of international management development and deputy director at Cranfield: "As business schools become more involved with organizations on a strategic level the boundaries between them and consultants will blur. Development of intellectual property and dissemination of knowledge will become a key way in which business schools differentiate themselves.

"Central to this issue of intellectual property and knowledge production is the question of research. However, here there is a tension arising from the current relationship between management research and management practice. In the American model of management research, knowledge production is driven by an academic agenda which assumes fundamental theories arise ahead of practice. This approach has dominated the field of management research in the U.K., too, not least because of the pressures of the Research Assessment Exercise."[1]

However, this prevailing approach does not sit comfortably with the trend toward increasing consulting activities. In this context, research with a broad business relevance is needed, which involves setting and solving problems in the context of applications and thereby informing business practice.

Cranfield recognizes the fundamental tension between these two different but equally valid types of research. "What is required is a portfolio of research activities which are both theory sensitive and practice led, providing the intellectual property base for our role," Kakabadse says. "The problems addressed by management research should grow out of the interactions between the world of practice and the world of theory rather than out of either one alone."

Many U.S. schools take a different view. "At Stanford, we pride ourselves on offering a research-based framework that managers can apply to any situation," says Gale Bitter, director of executive programs at Stanford Graduate School of Business. "Our programs don't just try to teach the latest flavor-of-the-month ideas and techniques, they are based on research over many years. What we teach is substantial. It will stand the test of time."

Notes Martin Christopher, director of executive programs at Cranfield School of Management: "Business schools would like to think they are setting the agenda. But the reality is that it's being set on a global stage now, with ideas and issues coming from many sources."

From a business point of view, research is the route to competitive advantage. From an academic point of view, research is the route to credibility. Research is central to one of the main objectives of business schools: the creation of management theory. The creation of management theory is based on the foundation of research, even though, at times, its creation appears to owe more to marketing and the fevered workings of overambitious imaginations. Research is, business schools would have you believe, central to their purpose and being. They claim that carrying out new and original research is one of their most important roles.

"Research at business schools is often denigrated. Practitioners are quick to talk of ivory towers, academic playgrounds, and categorize research as esoteric and overly theoretical. Yet, good management research is absolutely essential to the competitive performance of companies," says INSEAD's Arnoud de Meyer. "In order to serve its partners, the business community, a business school must carry out research, and further the understanding of management practice. Management research is essential to the business community. Collaborating with a business school is for many companies a privileged method of gaining access to the latest management thinking, before it gets published in trade journals or popular books. And working with the scholars who developed these concepts may be one of the fastest ways to discover not only the *what* of the concept, but also how to implement it effectively."[2]

Such protestations place business schools firmly in the long tradition of academic institutions whose primary purpose is to advance the frontiers of human knowledge. But here again is confusion about whether business schools should take their lead from the real world of business, or whether enlightened members of the business community should take their lead from the business school theorists. The polarity of such learning should be reversible, and b-schools should strive for partnership relationships with industry and commerce. At present, however, the need to satisfy the academic community too often takes precedence. If b-schools exist to serve their business communities, then it follows that the needs of those communities must come first. If, however, their academic credentials are more important, then it is time to say so and be done with it. There are arguments to support such a position. Freedom from purely commercial concerns, argue such schools, makes them better able to break new ground. But the comments from those inside leading business schools indicate a desire to have it both ways.

"The class is the raw material. You can't be in an ivory tower. We have to be at the cutting edge of our disciplines. There is a virtuous circle: the best ideas attract the best people," says Nigel Nicholson, research dean at London Business School. "The best consulting is research for the client's benefit. The line between consulting and research is sometimes quite fine. Research is cheaper than consulting."

As Carlos Cavallé, dean of IESE in Spain, puts it: "It's not just about best practice, it's about next practice." If only it was so simple. Once again, business schools are regularly criticized on two fronts. Although the schools spend millions of dollars on research every year, many business practitioners question the usefulness of the resulting findings. Much of what is researched, they claim, is highly esoteric and of limited practical use.

Practitioners demand research that can be fed directly into best practice. They want to do it and they want to do it now. This says more about the unrealistic expectations of managerial practitioners than it does about business schools. However, it is a point that is made and made repeatedly.

"There are two sins in research," says Harvard dean Kim Clark. "One is getting too far away from practice. A lot of academic research is essentially a conversation among a very small group of people about stuff that only they care about. The other sin is work that doesn't have depth—a poorly conceived idea that gets out there in the public domain with a lot of flash and glitz and doesn't have much substance behind it. Academics can commit both kinds of sins."[3]

No wonder they are criticized. Academics from other disciplines suggest that business school research is superficial and lacking academic merit and rigor. They remain scornful of management as a discipline. Management is the adopted child of social sciences and economics. In their eyes, business school research isn't theoretical enough; it is driven by publicity and corporate fashion rather than intellectual coherence.

We accept that b-schools are in a difficult position here. Our main criticism, however, is that rather than nail their colors to the mast, many try to be all things to all men. Given the twin pressures of accessibility and rigor, it is perhaps little wonder that they have an instinctive and unfortunate urge to trumpet the phrase *leading edge*. Every piece of research is heralded as being at the forefront of corporate thinking. One intellectual fanfare follows another and the sound becomes hollower with each retort.

This is ultimately self-defeating. It leads b-schools into direct competition with the management consultancy industry, a war of ideas that most b-schools are ill-equipped to win. In fact, looking back over the past two decades, the b-schools appear to be losing ground. This is because they have been lured into competing in the wrong arena. Rather than attempting to map uncharted seas they are often simply surfing the next big wave (whatever it is, wherever it is going).

IN SEARCH OF THE HOLY GRAIL

How do you extract lessons from intuitive decisions? How do you replicate inspiration? These are the uncomfortable issues that business schools prefer to ignore. After all, how do you write five thousand words about the inexplicable?

The problem (or delight if you are not a business school) with the real world of business is that it is complex, based on abstract notions such as intuition. It is all too human, and all too difficult to measure and rationalize. But business schools like measuring things.

Arrogant, out of touch, or commendably persistent, business schools haven't been dissuaded from their faith in a rational approach driven by a need for solutions. Indeed, their blind faith in solutions continues. It is just that the solutions are different. They are no longer the grand analytical panoramas and neat models created by strategists. Instead, they are the solutions of management gurus.

The entire management guru industry is based around the belief that there is a Holy Grail of management, a solution, a cure, a potion, a quick fix that will work. Rather than remain above this simplistic line, many business school academics have leapt on the guru bandwagon and become rich in the process. Managerial effectiveness may or may not have improved but the managerial capacity for wishful thinking has certainly been enhanced in the business school era. Business schools have allowed themselves to become diverted by this superficial sideshow.

While they have not been to blame for creating many of them, business schools, as much as the people who attend their courses, have been victims of management fashions. Business schools have joined in the hullabaloo accompanying a series of cure-all business wonder drugs. In recent years, for example, these have included TQM, downsizing, empowerment, business process reengineering, and the learning organization. They are managerial Viagra.

These ideas were all supposed to make businesses more competitive, and were adopted wholesale by companies. Yet many of the initiatives they inspired failed to deliver the goods. Some middle managers have reported the onset of "initiative fatigue," caused by an unrelenting barrage of management wonder drugs. This has led to a backlash against the preaching of the management evangelists.

Business academics have been tarred with the same brush. This has done little for their credibility with employees, who are increasingly disillusioned and cynical about management theory. Some business school professors have criticized the "big ideas," usually after the event. Very few were prepared to stand up and be counted when the ideas were the height of fashion.

By offering a lead in debunking management snake oil, business schools could do much to legitimize management as a profession. Rather than seeing themselves as competing with the big consultancies as they presently do, by questioning the management cure-alls and providing a sense of continuity they could regain some of the thought leadership high ground they have lost. At present, however, too many business school academics are themselves caught up in the guru industry, selling their services as consultants and riding the latest bandwagon—or gravy train. Those in glass houses prefer not to throw stones.

Once again, an exception is Henry Mintzberg, who was among the most critical of the reengineering fad: "There is no reengineering in the idea of reengineering," he said. "Just reification, just the same old notion that the new system will do the job. But because of the hype that goes with any new management fad, everyone has to run around reengineering everything. We are supposed to get superinnovation on demand just because it is deemed necessary by a manager in some distant office who has read a book. Why don't we just stop reengineering and delayering and restructuring and decentralizing and instead start thinking?"[4]

The answer is simple: thinking is hard; action, even if it is foolish, is easy. Managers retain an unquenchable desire for instant solutions that tackle all their problems in one fell swoop. Managers and business schools believe in the big idea. This is akin to the way adolescents believe that a fashionable set of clothes will change their personality and lead them into a new world of happiness and romantic fulfillment. The result can be that executives are in touch with the gurus, but woefully out of touch with reality. Just as strategists forgot about what was really happening, fashion-conscious organizations end up attempting to implement every bright idea their senior executives come across—research by George Binney and Colin Williams of the United Kingdom's Ashridge Management College found one company with nineteen initiatives simultaneously under way. Inflicting ill-advised ideas on their organization occupies the time of many thousands of managers. For some it is a full-time job.

There appears little chance of this cycle of dependency being broken. Business schools—and executives—remain wedded to the idea of solutions to management problems. (And, from a commercial point of view, the bigger and more dramatic the solutions, the longer the programs they can run.) So recent years have seen a profusion of exec ed programs based on the latest management fashions. Schools launched their own courses on reengineering when it was popular, then—as its fame grew tarnished—either ditched the programs or subtly renamed them. Indeed, the renaming of programs is part and parcel of business school marketing. This year's Reengineering Program is next year's Strategic Process Management Program.

Little thought is usually given to the impact of these fashions on managerial effectiveness and individual managers. In both the public and private sectors management mantras have exacted a high human cost, raising stress levels in the workplace and leaving demotivated employees in their wake. More cynical observers say that "big ideas" are often little more than window dressing and doublespeak for layoffs. The toll in terms of derailed careers is especially high.

In Stockholm, we spoke with the then head of the Swedish engineering group Atlas Copco, Michael Treschow. He explained that the company had been successful over a long period without recourse to management gurus. "It takes a year for any initiative to be absorbed by each level of management," he said. Since the company has about five layers of management, it would be counterproductive to introduce more than one "big idea" every five years. Business schools should take heart from this. You can do an awful lot of research in five years.

WHO IS WINNING THE WAR OF IDEAS?

Inevitably, many of the ideas presented as great leaps forward are simply repackaged versions of hardy theoretical perennials. Little that is written, published, or unearthed by diligent business school researchers is truly original. Similarly, little that consultants encounter is truly unique or universally applicable.

And yet, few would disagree with the notion that ideas are the fuel that drives the businesses of consultants and business schools forward. For management consultants, a fresh insight is highly marketable. It can speedily be integrated into a package sold to companies en masse. It is an obvious commercial fact that consultants who appear to be a step ahead of the game will attract more clients.

The same commonsensical rule applies to business schools. A school with a reputation for being genuinely innovative and fresh in its thinking and its insights has a head start on one that simply follows in the wake of others. This explains why business schools fall over themselves to attract the intellectual thought leaders.

Amid the brain drains and brain gains, business schools can point to a lengthy pedigree of innovative research that has unquestionably changed management and shaped management theory. Early management theorists such as Chester Barnard and Mary Parker Follett had strong academic connections. The human relations school of the late 1950s was inspired by MIT-based Douglas McGregor, who attracted the likes of Warren Bennis, Ed Schein, and Chris Argyris to his team. Harvard Business School has its own lengthy lineage of original thinkers. These include Alfred Chandler in the 1960s, marketing guru Ted Levitt, Chris Argyris, Rosabeth Moss Kanter, Michael Porter, Christopher Bartlett, and John Kotter.

Undoubtedly, too, there remains a nucleus of highly original thinkers at the world's leading business schools. The present Harvard group—Argyris, Kanter, Porter, and the rest—have repeatedly broken new ground and are genuinely influential. Harvard's near neighbor MIT can point to Peter Senge, Ed Schein, and Lester Thurow. Elsewhere, London Business School can boast the formidable Sumantra Ghoshal, as well as having Gary Hamel as a visiting professor. Other notables, such as Henry Mintzberg and Philip Kotler, are business school–based. Charles Handy came to theorizing at MIT and then went to London Business School. In fact, of the great management theorists, Peter Drucker is the only—but the greatest—exception.

And yet, despite the names and brains, recent history has seen business schools gradually lagging behind in the war of ideas. Indeed, it is increasingly reasonable to ask whether business schools have run out of big ideas. A review of the significant management ideas of the 1980s and 1990s quickly reveals that most had their origins in management consultancies rather than in business schools.

First came what could loosely be termed "excellence," spawned by Tom Peters and Robert Waterman's best-selling *In Search of Excellence*. The book was the result of a substantial investment in research by consultants McKinsey & Co. At the time it marked a significant development. After decades of largely untroubled success, McKinsey had encountered difficulties in the 1970s with the growth of the Boston Consulting Group. Crucially, McKinsey identified ideas as the key battle area. With its profit-share matrix, BCG had positioned itself as a thought leader. McKinsey sought to reestablish itself as a competitor in the world of ideas by launching various research projects—of which the excellence research was but one. Peters and Waterman both had business school contacts and enlisted the assistance of Anthony Athos from Harvard and Stanford's Richard Pascale along the way. The result was a book that sold massively and launched a torrent of books by consultants. (This has continued. After being largely ambivalent about publishing, McKinsey has embraced it with gusto, producing a continuing stream of books.)

Excellence led to the quality movement of the 1980s. Once again its inspirations came from outside business schools. The likes of W. Edwards Deming, Joseph Juran, and Philip Crosby were more likely to be sneered at by business schools than welcomed into the fold. Despite the fact that many business schools now run programs and courses on quality, TQM, Just-in-Time, and other techniques, there are comparatively few influential books on the subjects written by business school academics.

Then came the concept of the learning organization. Here, at least, the business schools can claim to have played the leading role. The best-selling *The Fifth Discipline*, which effectively launched the subject into public consciousness, was written by MIT's Peter Senge. The entire concept could also be seen as building on the work of Chris Argyris at Harvard.

The 1990s, however, have seen a steady procession of big ideas generated by consultants rather than business schools. Reengineering was a classic consulting big idea, one that could be easily converted into a package and given the hard sell. (It helped propel the consulting firm CSC Index into the major league.) The current fascination with knowledge management and intellectual capital is also manna for consultants. It is notable that of the three books currently boasting the title *Intellectual Capital,* none came from business schools. (The authors are Annie Brooking, director of a company called the Technology Broker; Leif Edvinsson, director of intellectual capital at Skandia, and author Michael Malone; and finally Thomas A. Stewart, who is on the board of editors at *Fortune* magazine and whose articles on the rise of intellectual capital did much to bring it to the forefront of the executive agenda.) The business best-seller lists are bereft of big business school names. In the last five years only Hamel and Prahalad's *Competing for the Future* was pioneering, successful, and business school generated.

The business schools' defense to accusations that their ideas have dried up is that consultants are highly adept at taking academic work and popularizing it. This is undoubtedly true. The reverse is also equally true: business schools are very good at coming up with ideas and then burying them in the same way dogs bury particularly tasty bones. Business school research—often written in tortuous prose—is published via academic journals and expensive research reports with limited circulations. (Tom Peters has pointed out that a lot of the material in *In Search of Excellence* was actually dug up from research that lay buried in business schools.)

"We spend too much time creating theories and not enough on practice," laments Gary Hamel. "Most other science researchers are more experiential than we have been in management. In business we tend to be glorified journalists. There is a need for a more active partnership between business school professors and managers. If you say that we transfer best practice from company A to B then consultants do it better."[5]

While the ability—or willingness—of business schools to reach out to broader business audiences with their latest thinking appears to remain limited, a number of other trends have had an impact on their ability to generate new ideas. The business school world has undergone a series of significant changes over the past two decades. Simply glancing at the courses offered by an individual school gives you some idea of how the product range has expanded. Most now offer a variety of options on their MBA programs, a growing array of open executive programs, and a range of custom programs.

But it is not only that the basic product offering has expanded significantly. Successful schools have sought to grow their businesses—something academic institutions have never previously contemplated. As we have seen, the University of Chicago offers an International Executive MBA at Barcelona with all courses taught by Chicago faculty. This has the advantage of widening the international perspectives and experience of the faculty. It also means that teaching demands on the faculty have multiplied.

The reason for such initiatives is simply that competition has increased. There is continuous pressure to deliver. And, in the short term, this encourages a focus on delivering courses and programs rather than world-class research to be written up in an academic journal.

BLURRING THE GREAT DIVIDE

While increased competition has created obvious pressure on resources, the blurring of the divide between consultants and educators is perhaps even more significant. Large, well-known consulting firms have moved into the ideas business with great enthusiasm. And business schools and their academics have moved into consulting, often more tentatively, but equally significantly.

"Consulting companies tend not to do the pure education as well as business schools," says Blair Sheppard of Duke University's Fuqua School. "We are not in the advice business and consulting firms aren't in the education business. There is too seductive a predisposition for consulting companies to start selling the consulting side of their business."

In the past consultants and educators tended to view each other with skepticism and not a little snobbery. Consultants sought to distance themselves from the ivory towers of academia. While academics dealt in theories, consultants proclaimed themselves to be masters of implementation.

This conveniently overlooked the fact that management consultants from top firms like McKinsey, Booz•Allen & Hamilton, and Bain are recruited from business schools. Consulting firms took one-third of the class of 1994 from Stanford and Wharton—ten years before it was 15 percent; of 610 MBA graduates from Kellogg in 1996, 42 percent joined consulting firms. Consulting firms go to great lengths and invest a great deal of money in ensuring that they find and recruit the best of the MBA class. No stone is left unturned. McKinsey has held recruiting dinners for gay and lesbian students at Harvard Business School—"We were losing qualified gay and lesbian candidates either because we were unable to connect them with the gay and lesbian network within the Firm, or because they viewed the Firm as a hostile place to work. It is not in our interest to lose qualified candidates," a McKinsey spokesman told *Harbus News*.[6]

With consultants generating new ideas, theory and practice appear more closely intertwined. (This has not made it any easier for bright ideas to become best practice—look at reengineering.) Conversion to the need to combine implementation with theory has not come cheaply. It is estimated that McKinsey now spends between $50 and $100 million a year on "knowledge building." It claims, somewhat dauntingly, to spend more on research than Harvard, Wharton, and Stanford combined. To put this in perspective, London Business School's annual revenue from its research activities is a meager £4.5 million ($7.2 million).

Academics are dubious about consulting claims to the role of thought leaders. "There is a lot of brilliant translation. Consultants learn from experience and then generalize, but it is not systematic and their work is limited. Ideas such as organizational culture or empowerment weren't invented by consultants and can be traced back to Kurt Lewin in the fifties," says London Business School's research dean, Nigel Nicholson. "When you trace ideas back you usually find yourself with academic research. Though academics may write for academic journals, ideas do get picked up. It is just that it is a longer conduit through to consciousness. Helping people to think or to think differently is something we do all the time in the classroom. Best-selling books by consultants get attention and appear to be unearthing new ideas, but usually the consultants are midwives. You shouldn't confuse midwifery with conception." The sentiment is echoed by Kenan-Flagler dean Robert Sullivan: "The roots of what consultants put forward can often be traced back to business schools. Big ideas have been popularized by consultants."

The borders between consulting firms and business schools are likely to become even more blurred in the near future. "It is very natural that there be a close relationship between a top management consulting firm and a top business school," says Brian Dickie, president of Booz•Allen & Hamilton's worldwide commercial business. "We share a mission to help shape the ideas and practice of business on a global basis, and we share a mission to educate and place future generations of business leaders."[7] Booz•Allen has a research alliance with the French business school, INSEAD. As part of this alliance, Booz•Allen will sponsor a major research program through the Center for Integrated Manufacturing and Service Operations at INSEAD.

The end result of such relationships remains a matter of conjecture and debate. What, for example, if the research included a critical appraisal of a Booz•Allen & Hamilton client? Would INSEAD enter into alliances with other consulting firms? Would INSEAD be more prone to provide research critical of Booz•Allen's competitors?

Most b-schools would claim that such circumstances would not affect their professionalism. They would simply uncover the facts

Thinkers and Ideas

	Affiliation	
Thinker	*Business School*	*Consulting*
Russ Ackoff	Wharton	—
Igor Ansoff	U.S. International University (ex Carnegie-Mellon)	—
Chris Argyris	Harvard	—
Chester Barnard	Harvard	—
Christopher Bartlett	Harvard	—
Warren Bennis	University of Southern California	—
Robert Blake	University of Texas	Scientific Methods
James Champy	—	CSC; Perot Systems
Alfred Chandler	Harvard	—
W. Edwards Deming	—	—
Peter Drucker	Claremont College	—
Henri Fayol		—
Mary Parker Follett	Harvard University	—
Sumantra Ghoshal	INSEAD; London Business School	—
Gary Hamel	London Business School	Strategos
Michael Hammer	MIT	Hammer & Co.
Charles Handy	London Business School	—
Bruce Henderson	—	Boston Consulting Group
Frederick Herzberg	University of Utah	—
Geert Hofstede	University of Maastricht	—
Joseph Juran	—	—
Rosabeth Moss Kanter	Harvard	Goodmeasure
Allan Kennedy	—	McKinsey
Philip Kotler	Kellogg, Northwestern	—
Ted Levitt	Harvard	—
Douglas McGregor	MIT	—
Abraham Maslow	Brandeis	—
Elton Mayo	Harvard	—
Henry Mintzberg	INSEAD; McGill	—
Kenichi Ohmae	—	McKinsey
Richard Pascale	Stanford	—
Tom Peters	—	McKinsey
Michael Porter	Harvard	Monitor
C. K. Prahalad	Michigan	—
Edgar Schein	MIT	—
Peter Senge	MIT	Innovation Associates
Alfred P. Sloan	—	—
Frederick Taylor	—	Own firm

and report and interpret them. Claiming the high ground is all well and good. However, while such issues remain undiscussed there is potential for misunderstanding. Making relationships—and the expectations that flow from those relationships—explicit is the best way forward. At present there is an unhealthy environment where implicit understandings and commercial pressures could, and we emphasize the word *could,* lead to awkward situations.

There are a number of different business school traditions adding to the confusion. Depending on which tradition they are from, business schools occupy different positions on this issue, but all have elements of this conflict within them.

Schools that are part of traditional universities tend to operate in a way much more similar to the institution they are part of. (Although more than one business school dean complains that most of his time is spent finding ways to get around or short-circuit the bureaucratic university administration.)

The other great business school tradition is independent institutions, typically with tax-exempt status but not part of a university. Although some products and services they provide generate surpluses, business schools that enjoy tax-exempt status don't make a profit in the traditional sense of the word. Their numbers include many of the leading European schools such as INSEAD and IMD. Both these schools make much of the fact that they receive no government funding and have to operate and survive in the real world. Those that must sing for their supper, as it were, are more inclined to behave like commercial organizations. But no university-based business school of serious standing can survive on government funding alone. (At London Business School, for example, the government grant amounted to just 11 percent of the school's $47.6 million income in 1996. Some 55 percent—$26.18 million—came from master's courses and executive programs.)

When it comes to degree qualifications such as MBAs, schools from the two traditions compete with one another. University schools have the academic clout of their university behind them, but many of the independents, whether they have degree-awarding powers themselves or are validated by partner universities, have established strong reputations as quality educational providers in their own right. But in their other activities business schools come into competition with a variety of commercial organizations.

In particular, both the independent schools and their leading university-based counterparts provide executive education—short, nondegree courses for corporate customers. Naturally, this brings them into direct competition with each other, but it also means they are in competition with other executive education providers including training companies, and, increasingly, consultancies and corporate universities. This is where lines can become blurred.

GLORIOUS DETACHMENT

Schizophrenic business schools flit desperately from one persona to another. They can, for example, be seen glorying in their academic splendor. Their selling line, when the occasion demands, is that they provide the academic and physical detachment that enables an objective perspective. Executives need to get away from it all to take a broader view. Business schools argue that their academics are not stuck in the mire of everyday corporate life, and are thereby able to provide a balanced and informed overview.

At the same time, business schools are equally adept at presenting themselves as businesses so as to gain credibility with their corporate customers. This adds to the confusion.

Few have the courage of Scotland's Herriot-Watt University, which floated off its business school as Edinburgh Business School. A university department was transformed into a business with a turnover of £7.5 million ($12 million). It is now linked with the media company Pearson in delivering its distance learning products throughout the world. In the eyes of some, such deals are akin to selling your soul to the devil. Undoubtedly, such deals put commercial imperatives first and academic independence second. Unless we are totally mistaken, Edinburgh Business School is unlikely to produce a critical case study of Pearson's performance.

The more general confusion within business schools is largely of their own making. And everything they do appears to make it worse. Schools have tried, for example, to keep their "academic" programs (MBAs, DBAs, and so on) entirely separate from their "commercial" programs (public and custom programs). At many schools it was (and still is at some) acceptable for academics to refuse to countenance teaching on executive programs. The marketing professor could turn his nose sniffily in the air at the prospect of distilling his six-week MBA elective down to three hours for a group of middle managers. On one level, this is academic snobbery. On another, it is a deliberate attempt to distance academic from commercial activity. Trying to have the best of both worlds is fine in theory but, in practice, things get messy.

When Success Fails

A highly successful entrepreneur thought she would add academic varnish to her accomplishments by studying for an MBA. The business school she approached was only too pleased to see her. But life as a student proved harder than she anticipated. Indeed, she struggled on every single assignment. Her marks were poor, but thanks to some imaginative marking, she got through. Eventually, her MBA came down to a particularly thorny project. She talked to the course administrator, who suggested she talk to a particular tutor. The tutor was well briefed on the situation and came up with her own solution: she would write the project for the student. This proved successful. The entrepreneur departed with her MBA, and the school's alumni list was enhanced. The story serves to underline the sorts of conflicts that can exist when academic standards get in the way.

The reality is that when money talks, academic standards can all too easily become negotiable. In the example above, a true story, the school faced a dilemma. Its MBA program came with a premium price because of its high-quality faculty. But if its faculty were so good, how could someone fail? In addition, the economics of allowing a single candidate to retake examinations are unattractive. Other academic disciplines face their share of problems, too, of course. But it is rare in other academic walks of life for someone with a proven track record in the real world to fail the academic subject they have clearly demonstrated competence in. In other words, it is awkward for business schools when businesspeople fail the theory but have already passed the practice. There is a suggestion that perhaps the theory isn't what it's cracked up to be. The waters become all the more murky when the individual concerned is sponsored by a corporate client. Corporations are not paying the school to fail their best managers.

If a corporate client is paying for a customized executive program, for example, this provides some leverage. If the company wants the red carpet treatment, with the very best the school can offer—including the attention of its top professors—then it is likely to get it. There will always be a temptation to say yes in such situations, especially with so many other business schools and other providers hungry for the work.

At the same time, the growing demand for part-time master's programs taught in the evenings or on weekends at whichever sites are most convenient, and pressure to provide academically accredited in-company programs, makes it much harder to know where to draw the line between the pure academic and less academic. The lines are, inevitably, largely imaginary.

Dressing for Success

"Executive programs cover much the same issues," confided one anonymous academic we talked to. "You can, for example, find yourself delivering the same program to a completely different audience. Marketing may be dressed up as strategic marketing if you are talking to more senior executives. You can keep the material the same. The secret is to wear a darker suit the higher level the program is. Women tutors have found that a shorter skirt for more senior executives has a similar effect. It is also advisable to talk more slowly when addressing more senior executives."

All this is done in the name of competitiveness. There are good reasons why business schools need to be competitive. A healthy income stream, for example, enables them to pay the higher salaries required to attract top academics. In reality, most schools are only too aware of the bottom line. What few are prepared to admit is that the desire to maximize returns can sometimes take precedence over the educational role and traditional values of an academic institution.

Feedback

In 1996, the *Business Week* rankings of American business schools relegated the Graduate School of Business at the University of Chicago from third to eighth place. This fall from grace was mainly thanks to criticism from Chicago's own MBA students. As a result, it found itself in the interesting position of offering a Master of Business Administration program that had been roundly condemned by its own graduates for deficiencies in administration.

More Feedback

Chicago students rated their school so poorly on administration and career services that it would have fallen to twenty-third place had it not been saved by its popularity with company recruiters—who placed it fifth among the U.S. business schools. But even the recruiters bemoaned its career service as one of the worst.

The Price of Victory

A school had a particularly successful program. It was a bastardized version of the MBA. Media coverage was excellent. The program was lauded as a giant leap forward in exec ed. The school, anxious to calculate the full extent of its good fortune, examined its highly computerized financial systems. It found that such was its investment in the marketing and delivery of the program that it was losing $750 every time another candidate signed up.

SCHOOLS BEHAVING BADLY

Chicago is not the only business school to attract criticism for the way it manages itself. The Judge Institute of Management Studies at Cambridge University opened its doors to MBA students in 1991. Since then, it has learned about the MBA market the hard way.

Its original MBA offering—an ambitious three-year sandwich course based on the ideas of management writer Charles Handy—was short-lived. Billed as the most practical MBA in the world when it was launched in 1991, the idea was that students would spend one term a year at Cambridge, then return to their employers to apply what they had learned in the classroom to their jobs. At the time, it boasted the ideal blend of classroom theory and work experience.

The trouble was that Cambridge's much-publicized entry into the MBA market coincided with the downturn in the economy, when employers were more concerned with slashing headcount than sponsoring MBAs. A three-year commitment was certainly not what they had in mind, as Cambridge soon discovered.

Privately, too, one of those involved with launching the original course admits that its design was influenced as much by the internal politics and rules of Cambridge University as the needs or demands of the market. The university simply would not accept a one-year master's program, even though that was clearly the direction in which the European market was moving.

The Judge Institute bit the bullet. It reduced its MBA to twenty-one months, but stuck to its guns on the idea of a sandwich course. The revamped program involved six months of study followed by a twelve-month work period, finishing in a series of electives and a dissertation.

That's how it remained until the end of 1996 when Cambridge bowed to market pressure once more, announcing that from 1997 it would be offering a twelve-month MBA in line with most other U.K. business schools. (The shorter course, which will run alongside the sandwich course, is the same basic program without the work break, and uses project work with local companies to provide practical focus.)

According to Professor Sandra Dawson, director of the Judge Institute, the decision was prompted by two things: the confidence that the school could condense the Cambridge MBA into a shorter course without losing its distinctive character, and a recognition of external changes in the MBA market. Ultimately, the longer course may be phased out altogether.

"The original MBA," she explained, "was designed around some explicit pieces of ideology. In particular, it aimed to marry management practice with management theory, something which we remain committed to. At that time, it was felt that the sandwich course was the best way to achieve that. Now, we are confident we can achieve the same aim in twelve months.

"Because it meant that employees wouldn't be away from work for so long, the sandwich course was also designed specifically for sponsored students. But the nature of employment has changed enormously in the past four or five years. In Europe, there is less sponsorship now, and employees don't stay with the same company for as long. In the light of those changes, we also felt that limiting ourselves to sponsored MBA students was too restrictive."

The decision may also have been influenced by Oxford's entry into the MBA market with a one-year course. Oxford later ran into problems of its own—over the siting of the new building for the school of management. That is one problem Cambridge avoided. The Judge Institute—named after its main benefactors Paul and Anne Judge—moved to its new building in the center of Cambridge in 1995.

Elsewhere, business schools remain perpetual hostages to charges of not running themselves according to the precepts they champion in the lecture theater. Business schools may protest the unfairness of being judged by their practical application of the theories they so eloquently espouse. But how many business schools can truly claim to be learning organizations? How many have identified their core competencies and, as a result, changed their organizational structure? How many really know what business they are in?

Until such issues are clarified, a steady stream of stories of managerial incompetence will continue to surface. There's more than one business school that doesn't actually know which programs do and do not make money. As they don't monitor the resources that go into each program, calculating program profitability is impossible.

Unfair? Undoubtedly. There is an inherent unfairness attached to such stories. No organization is perfect. Management is an imprecise art. The trouble is that business schools have led managers to believe that running a business can be a precise, measurable, and therefore manageable science. Being measured by their own yardsticks is inevitable. The challenge for them is to reevaluate the yardsticks.

4

The Industrialization of the MBA

From the seventies until the late eighties, we were riding high. There was so much demand and so few faculties that we didn't have to be responsive. Money flowed in. We became complacent from our own success.

—*Kenan-Flagler dean Robert Sullivan*

The split personality of business schools is demonstrated by the way they have developed the MBA. With the MBA, business schools, almost inadvertently, stumbled upon a mass market product. They then began to behave like mass producers, MBA factories, churning out managers like so many products on a conveyor belt.

In recent years, many business schools have embraced the idea of brand extensions by creating hybrid variations on the MBA theme and in-company MBA programs designed for specific corporate clients or consortia of clients. Business schools have been extremely busy reinventing and adapting their flagship product to extract the maximum commercial benefit. Aware of the restraints imposed by their academic affiliations, the serious-minded university business schools have been much slower to embrace these new products. They have preferred to expand their activities in other ways, promoting their tried and tested programs to overseas markets.

What does this frenzy of international expansion and brand extension demonstrate? It is hard to see what it has to do with maintaining academic standards. Rather, we believe it shows business schools behaving like businesses rather than academic institutions. Having developed a successful mass market product, the challenge was to provide some form of differentiation from the competition—hence the development of decidedly untraditional MBA programs. Those constrained by their university status took another route—to carpet the world with a successful product. The Graduate School of Business at the University of Chicago even went so far as to open a second campus in Barcelona, to pick up European business, and plans to set up shop in Singapore. INSEAD, too, has confirmed it is to open a second campus in Singapore.

Here, we advance the following arguments:

- In the MBA, business schools discovered a degree with mass market appeal and helped hype the qualification in a way that created a mythology around it.
- Variations on the traditional MBA are driven by commercial imperatives rather than academic standards.
- With a few exceptions, business schools have adopted a bigger is better attitude to their MBA programs, which is a step toward cloning.

THE JEWEL IN THE B-SCHOOL CROWN

The story of the MBA is unique among academic qualifications. The best-known degree offered by business schools, no other qualification has ever been so glamorous, so hyped, or, for those who possess it, so lucrative.

Elevated from modest beginnings in the United States in the early part of the century, today the MBA is the fastest-growing postgraduate qualification in the world. Its appeal transcends national borders. In the past decade, the number of students graduating with

MBAs in Britain, for example, has quadrupled—from about two thousand per year in 1985–1986 to its current level of more than eight thousand.[1] That's more than the rest of Europe put together. But it is little more than a drop in the ocean compared to the number of MBAs graduating from U.S. schools each year, which is close to eighty thousand. This means that, in total, there are now some eight hundred or so business schools in the United States and Europe producing a hundred thousand MBA graduates a year.[2]

The history of the MBA mirrors that of business schools. It began life in the United States, where the institutions teaching it were keen to prove their academic credentials. Originally, it was a two-year academic course and most students enrolled immediately after taking a first degree. This model won rapid acceptance in the United States and was widely copied. In Europe, some of the up-and-coming business schools—started not by governments or universities but by groups of companies—opted for shorter MBAs. Switzerland's IMD, France's INSEAD, and the United Kingdom's Ashridge Management College, for example, all offered one-year MBAs.

These European schools placed much greater emphasis on work experience prior to entering their MBA programs. As a result, students at these schools tended to be slightly older, with a minimum of two or three years of management experience. The European schools also included a more practical focus, with many including in-company projects as an integral part of the MBA qualification. American schools, by contrast, were more concerned about participants' academic ability, placing greater emphasis on high GMAT scores and often accepting applicants with limited experience.

During the late 1960s and 1970s the MBA established itself on both sides of the Atlantic. For many it was a respectable means of extending student life, a solution to indecisiveness. It is surprising how many admit to taking an MBA because they simply couldn't think of what else to do. "Why did I decide to get one? I was in a pickle and it was the best way out that I could think of," says Peter

Robinson, author of *Snapshots from Hell*—which recounted his experiences in the Stanford MBA program. "I had spent six years in the White House, most of the 1980s. Good friends had gone on to law school, gone on to business school, gotten established in journalism, and I had gotten established as this Presidential speechwriter, and there's just not much of a market for them. I thought about going to law school; read, in fact, Scott Turow's book, *One L*, which helped to persuade me that law school was not for me."[3]

Robinson wasn't the first—and certainly won't be the last—to fall into business school simply for the want of any better ideas. Management guru Tom Peters did much the same twenty-odd years before when he was at a loose end after serving in Vietnam. "I didn't know what to do after the Navy. I didn't have any better ideas than doing an MBA," he says. It was a move not exactly fired by a burning interest in the subject he would be studying. "I went to business school because that's what people were doing. My half-dozen best friends had decided the MBA was hot. The MBA became a popular phenomenon at the time and two-thirds of my buddies went to Harvard," says Peters.

While the MBA cemented its place during the 1960s and 1970s, its apotheosis came in the 1980s. Suddenly it seemed that recruiters couldn't get enough of the newly minted business school graduates. The investment banks and management consultancies that had always valued the analytical skills provided by the MBA were joined by blue-chip companies from other sectors.

With a flourish, the MBA seemed to epitomize the free market philosophy that dominated Western democracies during that decade. In America, Reaganomics championed the values of self-sufficiency and personal achievement, while in Britain, a generation of young people grew up on the political philosophy of Margaret Thatcher. Thatcher's and Reagan's children were bottle-fed on the enterprise culture. Suddenly, commerce in all its guises was not just a respectable activity but a moral imperative. Market forces were elevated to the status of elemental forces. Business was suddenly the one true social force, cutting through weak socialist notions of economic equality. "Let the market decide" became the mantra of a new generation. For that generation, Thatcher's own phrase "you can't buck market forces" was a truism. Where better to learn the rules of the new game than at business school?

The MBA *was* the 1980s as much as Gordon Gecko or *The Bonfire of the Vanities*. Masters of the Universe, in Tom Wolfe's phrase, came armed with an MBA. It was part of the zeitgeist. The spirit of the decade was embodied in the well-heeled young managers who stepped straight out of business school into high-powered executive jobs. Simply having the three letters after your name was believed to be enough to add a zero to your salary. Never before or since has a qualification been so lucrative—or so hyped. Stories about the "golden hellos"—joining bonuses—on offer to MBA graduates at the time abounded. Especially popular among business graduates joining investment banks on Wall Street and in the City of London and those going into the leading management consultancies, they became part of the mythology of the MBA.

The mood was captured by Peter Robinson in *Snapshots from Hell*. Robinson was one of Ronald Reagan's speechwriters before enrolling in an MBA course at Stanford Business School. Robinson saw the MBA as part of something bigger: "I had spent six years writing speeches about how the private sector was creating jobs at the rate of more than 100,000 a month, far more than any government program could attempt, and about how blacks and other minorities were benefiting from among the most dramatic gains in income they had ever experienced in American history. I had become convinced that free markets represented an enormous force for good. I had also witnessed—all too plainly, and increasingly over time—the good that free markets were doing my friends."[4]

As applicants stampeded to get the qualification, business schools benefited from the gold rush. It became apparent just how lucrative the market for MBAs was. Others jumped on the bandwagon. The result was an explosion of institutions offering MBA programs.

As Thatcher and Reagan disappeared into the sunset, reality kicked in. With a degree of inevitability, the boom of the 1980s was followed by recession and a downturn in the MBA market. The hype that had fueled the gold rush lost some of its momentum. With no guarantee of a better job at the end of it, many MBA wannabes were more inclined to stay put in their jobs. Business schools, many of which had jumped on the MBA bandwagon just a few years earlier, hit the ground with a bump.

But rumors of the death of the MBA in the early 1990s were greatly exaggerated. What followed was a period of reevaluation. After what turned out to be little more than a dip during the recession, the MBA revived. Business schools report that demand for the qualification is now strong once more. At the beginning of the new millennium, the qualification of the 1980s is alive and kicking.

Today, those who sign up for MBA programs are less inclined to be capitalist ideologues. If current MBA students remember Gordon Gecko at all, they are more likely to criticize than idolize him. Indeed, business ethics is now offered in some MBA programs—a change the schools say has been driven by student demand. Outside classrooms, too, the talk is more likely to be about "stakeholders" and "corporate citizenship" than "asset stripping."

Perhaps, the repackaging of the Yuppie degree is simply a sign of the times. In the caring 1990s, greed has become unfashionable. But that does not mean that profit maximization is not admired. A 1997 survey of new Cornell MBA students found that 60 percent admired Chainsaw Al Dunlap and "results-oriented leaders" of the brutal downsizing kind.[5]

THE GOLDEN GRADUATES

Insiders suggest that the 1980s created a mythology that now bears little relation to reality. "The idea of the grasping MBA is a caricature," says George Bain, former principal of London Business School. "There are a few exceptions, of course. On the whole, though, most people who take an MBA are career-changers. They want to have an experience that will change their lives." Ambitious, youthful managers are now building business school qualifications into their career game plan. For them, the question is no longer whether to do an MBA, but where and when.

"In the U.S., and increasingly now in other parts of the world, the MBA is seen as a credential almost like a union card," observes Robert S. Hamada, dean of the Graduate School of Business at the University of Chicago. "It is a signal to the potential employer that the applicant is serious about business. In a way, it tells them who is serious and who is not serious. Some people are in business just to make the salary and go home. Those people would not make the investment—as much as $100,000, and two years out of their life.

"Business school is now seen as a very important career pit-stop for ambitious people. This is definitely true in the U.S., and increasingly in other parts of the world including Europe and I would say even more so in Asia."

An MBA from one of the world's top business schools has the sort of cachet normally reserved for lifestyle accessories—making it the BMW, Cartier, or Versace of postgraduate education. One commentator recently described the qualification as the "luxury brand of the management education world." That's quite an achievement for a degree that's been around for less than a hundred years.

So what is it about the MBA that gives it such enormous pulling power? A few years ago, when MBAs were in short supply and employers were prepared to pay big bucks for what were seen as the golden graduates, the answer was simple: the chance to make more money. Today, the supply side is more developed but the qualification is still highly lucrative for those coming off the assembly line at Harvard, Wharton, Kellogg, or INSEAD. The latest edition of *Which MBA?*—the guide to the top MBA courses—reports six-figure paychecks for graduates from the top U.S. programs. MBAs from the Stanford Graduate School of Business, for example, start at an average of $105,000, while graduates from Harvard Business

School and MIT Sloan School of Management can expect to earn $102,000 when they reenter the job market.[6]

American graduates aren't the only lucky ones. The figures also suggest the leading European schools are closing the gap with their U.S. counterparts. MBAs from IMD (the Institute of Management Development) at Lausanne in Switzerland top the pay table on both continents with an average starting salary of $106,904, followed by Cambridge University's Judge Institute, which claims its graduates start at $93,104.

The Pacific Rim still lags behind in the salary stakes, but is coming up fast with the Australians leading the charge. MBAs from Melbourne Business School, part of Melbourne University, average $73,586 in their first job after graduating, and those from the Australian Graduate School of Management average $68,164.

Even allowing for some creative accounting by the schools to make themselves look good, these are big bucks. Possessing an MBA gives you a great chance of substantially increasing your salary. Beyond the smell of money, however, there are other factors that explain the popularity of the MBA.

A master's degree is now becoming an entry requirement for the top jobs. Many young managers see business school as a rite of passage to the ranks of the corporate elite. Functional specialists, in particular, use the qualification to make the vital step into general management. For many, it's also the last chance to play at being a student, before getting down to the serious business of making money. Some even gain intellectual stimulation from all that number crunching.

"The idea of being a student for two or more years appeals to anyone stuck in the suit and commute rat race," comments one MBA student. Adds another: "The MBA program has truly changed my way of thinking—like Plato's parable of the caves." Well, yes. The MBA is a passport to better things. Plato wrote of an elite band of rulers who, through careful training, would emerge from the shadows of the cave to perceive the truth. And there are those who believe that, like Plato's Philosopher Kings, MBAs will inherit the corporate world.

"Fifteen to twenty years ago accountancy was the qualification to have," observes Professor Paul Geroski, director of London Business School's full-time MBA program. "Many of the people who fill the top jobs today have accountancy qualifications. But that is no longer the dominant model. There's a shift now to MBAs. My guess would be that given the choice recruiters wouldn't include accountants on short lists for general management jobs now, they'd opt for MBAs. If that's true, then that represents an important shift from the 1980s."

The accountants seem to sense it, too. In 1997, the Arthur Andersen accountancy firm announced a new program with Manchester and Warwick business schools aimed at broadening the management expertise of staff. Under the new initiative, the firm is to send up to a hundred partners and managers on MBA programs each year.

There is an element of self-fulfilling prophecy to this. The influx of MBA students in the past decade means there are a lot more graduates out there than there used to be—a hundred thousand is a lot of competitive brainpower. This has upped the ante for those who want to reach senior management.

The growing pool of MBAs is also creating a discrete market segment: a group of high-fliers hungry for the latest management thinking—as well as big houses and fast cars. New magazines have been launched aimed specifically at MBA graduates. Publishers take one look at the numbers of MBA graduates—and the credit rating of these people—and see easy money. But it's largely a mirage. MBAs may be a soft touch when it comes to giving money to their schools, but they are an incredibly demanding audience. These days, they're more likely to read *Fast Company* than *Forbes*, but they barely have time to read the essentials—*Harvard Business Review* and the *Wall Street Journal*. They don't read or surf the Net for fun, they do it to protect their career investment.

From being a statement, a fashion accessory, the MBA is increasingly seen as a passport to success. Some would have us believe that a business school education is now crucial if you want to climb the greasy pole to senior management. "If you really want to do something, you have to have a master's degree," says George Bain. A first degree, Bain argues, is essentially only an entry requirement.

Expectations remain high. A 1998 survey of MBA students found that 24.25 percent wanted to work for consulting firm McKinsey. Second most popular was Goldman Sachs, and other Wall Street luminaries such as Morgan Stanley Dean Witter (fifth), J. P. Morgan (sixth), and Merrill Lynch (eighth) featured prominently. None of these organizations is renowned as an underpayer. Just over 10 percent picked Hewlett-Packard; Procter & Gamble managed 6.36 percent. DuPont, Caterpillar, and General Electric failed to make the top fifty. Nor did any car maker. MBA graduates do not expect to get their hands—or their suits—dirty. The students expected a starting income of $80,665 and $385,323 after ten years.[7]

BIGGER IS BETTER

In terms of the numbers of students on their MBA programs, the big U.S. business schools dwarf their European counterparts. Harvard Business School, for example, has an intake of close to 900 full-time MBA students a year; Kellogg, at Northwestern University, takes around 1,200 on its full-time program and another 70 or so on its part-time program; Wharton has 750 on its full-time program.

There are many other U.S. schools with student intakes of more than 400. Thunderbird, the American Graduate School of International Management in Phoenix, admitted almost 500 students into its full-time MBA program in 1997, the Graduate School of Business at the University of Texas close to 450, Michigan Business School around 425, Columbia 470, and the Graduate School of Business at the University of Chicago well over 500.

Whether such large intakes can be justified on purely academic grounds is a moot point. They inevitably lead to larger class sizes and less personal attention from members of faculty. They represent a step toward sheep-dip training. There is nothing wrong with treating managers like sheep, of course, as long as you are happy for them to act like sheep. The mass production of MBAs continues apace.

The economics are simple and attractive. Large student intakes generate increased revenue.

In Europe, INSEAD has the largest MBA program and in recent years has made no secret of its plans to expand the number of places further. In 1996, for example, it opened its doors to 486 MBA students, a figure it expects to rise to around 600 by 1999 (an increase of about 20 percent). "We do not see it as a substantial increase," says INSEAD's dean, Antonio Borges, "but as a step-by-step process."

The prestige of the INSEAD brand means the school will have little difficulty filling the additional places. Given that it is already picking the cream of applicants, however, the question is whether it will be able to boost the numbers without diluting the quality of its intake, and if so where the additional students will come from. Insiders at the school report that it is already stretched to capacity and will not be able to maintain teaching standards without a substantial increase in the number of faculty. Here, the twin pressures of the commercial drive to increase revenue and the academic imperative to maintain standards are clearly in conflict.

Borges insists that there is no question of lowering standards. "I have absolutely no concerns in that regard," he says. "If anything, standards are rising. What is extraordinary is the number of outstanding people we are turning down, and the number of companies who come to INSEAD to recruit and cannot get enough people."

Although large by European standards, however, the INSEAD program is still relatively small by U.S. standards. For the time being at least, Antonio Borges says, the school has set an upper ceiling at six hundred. Beyond that, he says, a considerable expansion of faculty and facilities would be required if quality was not to suffer.

On the other hand, Switzerland's IMD has always favored a "small is beautiful" approach to its MBA program, with fewer than a hundred students admitted on its full-time program each year.

GILDING THE LILY

Commercial pressure is also evident in the recent extensions to the business school flagship products. Today, there is growing demand to use variations of the MBA formula for corporate purposes. In Europe, for example, so-called company MBAs are increasingly common.

Company MBAs involve partnerships between a sponsoring company and an MBA provider. They offer employers a cost-effective way to put part of their management population through an MBA program. Course content can also be tailored to make it more relevant to the company's industry.

Very much a U.K. phenomenon, company MBAs have been around since the mid-1980s. They are offered by a number of British institutions—although typically not the traditional university schools.

In the past, some companies sent their high-fliers on full-time MBA courses only to find that time spent away from work and raised expectations meant they didn't come back. In effect, the companies were paying for the training but weren't getting the benefits. Company MBAs are, in part, a response to that dilemma.

The way they are structured—usually modular, with a combination of distance learning and residential workshops—means that managers get the opportunity to achieve the prestigious qualification while remaining in post. At the same time, they offer economies of scale for companies wishing to send large numbers of managers on MBA programs. Despite their popularity in the United

Kingdom, however, company MBAs have been slower to take off in other parts of Europe and North America.

American schools, in particular, have traditionally preferred to keep their MBA programs centered on the requirements of individual students rather than companies. The needs of corporate clients are catered for through executive programs. In the past, many American schools effectively fenced off their academic programs, making it difficult to combine the two activities even if they wanted to.

In recent years, however, they have shown more interest in the idea. Through its global MBA program, the University of Michigan Business School, for example, has provided customized MBA programs via videoconferencing to managers at Daewoo Corporation in Korea and Cathay Pacific Airways in Hong Kong.

In preparing the core courses, Michigan faculty visit partner companies to develop teaching materials that are directly relevant to the company's requirements. The program is designed in conjunction with senior managers.

But company MBAs have also caused some controversy in academic circles. Critics, some leading U.S. and European business schools among them, have argued that students on company programs miss out on important aspects of the traditional MBA learning experience. One concern is that employers can influence the content of custom programs to fit their own management styles, making them less academically rigorous. Another is that by restricting places to candidates from a single or small number of organizations, peer learning through contact and exchange of ideas among students is reduced.

Other critics of company MBAs point out that they lack the prestige of the traditional MBA. Because they are oriented toward a single company culture, some commentators argue, they may be less attractive to other employers, reducing their portability in the jobs market. On the other side, however, advocates of company MBAs argue that the degree of tailoring involved in most company MBAs is relatively minor—typically between 5 percent and 10 percent of course content. Moreover, by holding the purse strings, they claim, companies are able to insist on high standards of teaching and value for money.

As Richard McBain, manager of Henley's corporate qualifications program, explains: "The last thing a sponsoring company wants is a program that doesn't meet the standards of other Henley programs. And the last thing we want is a program that doesn't meet their business needs. We believe you can combine academic rigor with an ongoing partnership with corporate clients. We don't alter the core contents of the MBA syllabus, but we do add value to the sponsor by focusing the theory on their business."

Such claims are open to challenge. Corporate MBAs run real risks of tiptoeing around controversial subjects or ignoring important areas that are simply not relevant to the company footing the bill. Of course, from a corporate perspective, the company MBA is a welcome alternative to traditional MBA programs. It is because they believe theory can be focused on real issues that many employers believe the company MBA approach provides a better return on their investment.

The reality is that these programs are significantly different from the traditional MBA experience. Company MBAs are part-time programs and typically take between two and three years to complete. Being part-time, they lack the rarefied campus atmosphere of a full-time residential course, but they have other important advantages for students. One is that classroom theory can be immediately put into practice in the workplace. Another obvious attraction is that they are completely sponsored.

The key to the success of a company MBA is *contextualization*. By ensuring that classroom theory is set in the context of real issues facing the company, the idea is that knowledge and ideas are imported directly into the organizations and can be applied immediately. For example, course assignments can be used to look at issues facing the company and provide a steady stream of internal consultancy.

Corporate MBA programs are set to continue to grow. Also growing in importance are consortium programs that involve a group of companies—usually between three and six—from a cross-section of industries. Again, the course content is tailored to the needs of the participating companies, and project work offers a useful form of consultancy.

Consortium programs give students the additional benefit of exposure to other corporate cultures. Participants have the opportunity to see how managers in other companies view key issues, as well as the chance to increase their professional networks.

The Ashridge European Partnership MBA, for example, run by Ashridge Management College and validated by City University, involves a consortium of three international companies, Lufthansa, Deutsche Bank, and the pharmaceutical group Merck. Thomas Sattelberger, Lufthansa's senior vice president of executive development, explains the advantages for his company: "We share risk and cut costs. In-house learning tends to enforce old patterns, whereas consortium learning is an opportunity for mutual benchmarking, seeing how people in other companies solve problems."

CORPORATE TROPHIES

Once upon a time, companies that wanted to reward their senior managers—or simply retain their top guns—would send them to the cream of the executive programs. Highly prestigious courses such as Harvard's famous Advanced Management Program fit the bill perfectly. (Started in 1943, the Harvard AMP has been widely imitated by other business schools. In recent years it has been shortened from twelve weeks to nine, but it retains much of its gold-plated appeal.)

These open courses were highly prized among executives. They were expensive and proud of it. In 1998, a place on Harvard's AM cost a cool $40,500 including tuition, accommodation, most meals, and course materials.

Those who attended these top-of-the-line executive programs gained access to high-powered alumni networks. What they didn't get at the end, though, was a master's degree. Business schools, by and large, kept the executive perks programs separate from their degree programs.

Today's executives want a piece of paper with more than just telephone numbers on it. They want an MBA, or some other master's qualification. In recent years demand for Executive MBAs (EMBAs), in particular, has been growing, especially in the United States, where traditional full-time programs have dominated in the past. Managers benefit because they are sponsored by the company, while employers see them as a way to develop and reward the brightest and best of their up-and-coming managers. Business schools like them because they can justify a premium price.

EMBAs combine many of the most attractive elements of part-time, modular, and consortium programs. Companies pay a bit extra for a course that often combines a number of different delivery mechanisms to optimize the learning experience of busy executives.

Such courses are touted as a deluxe version of the MBA. Schools ensure that the big hitters among their faculty teach on the EMBA program and participants enjoy greater access to the top professors. Participants are typically older than the average full-time MBA student and already occupy more senior posts. Places are generally reserved for people identified as having high potential—managers the company wants to feel wanted. Foreign study tours provide both a touch of added class and an opportunity to get away from it all.

Typical of this new MBA brand is the Global Executive MBA offered by Duke University's Fuqua School of Business. Launched in 1996, the nineteen-month course is aimed at high-flying executives. It includes mandatory two-week sessions in Eastern Europe, Asia, and Latin America, as well as study in the United States and Western Europe. Coursework is done via e-mail and the Internet.

With fees at $86,000, the school admits the course is expensive, but argues that it still works out cheaper than sending managers on full-time two-year programs. (But not as cheap as allowing them to pay for their own education.)

In Europe, where part-time courses have been popular for some time, demand for EMBAs is now increasing, too. The emphasis is on offering a prestigious learning experience that is flexible enough to fit in with the lifestyle of busy executives. That's the selling point, anyway. The opportunity to study in other cultures is a bonus.

IMD launched a new Executive MBA in August 1998, the first nonweekend global executive MBA by a non-U.S. school. With study trips to Shanghai and Silicon Valley, the new course is clearly intended to compete with other globetrotting master's programs. "It's relevant, it's rigorous, and it's global," proclaims Peter Lorange, IMD's president. These are the three key words designed to appeal to both managers and their companies.

With fees of 80,000 Swiss francs ($51,200), the course is clearly aimed at the top end of the market and, at that price, should provide red carpet treatment for participants. The way the program is delivered is also designed to provide a more flexible learning experience. Unlike other European EMBAs, which rely on studying over the weekends, the IMD offering is modular in structure, with classroom learning concentrated into a series of residential sessions at the Lausanne campus. Course participants spend a total of nineteen weeks out of the office, and can take as little as sixteen months or as long as three years to complete the course.

The international element of EMBA programs is a useful enticement for faculty. As noted earlier, the University of Chicago runs an International Executive MBA program in Barcelona, Spain. Spreading one- and two-week modules over an eighteen-month schedule, executives from Europe to Asia can take the same program in Barcelona as students at the Chicago campus. They are taught by the same professors, who are flown in specifically to add gravitas to the EMBA course.

EMBAs are becoming increasingly global in their reach. A number of business schools in Asia now offer part-time programs. The Hong Kong University of Science and Technology (HKUST) and the Chinese University of Hong Kong both boast an EMBA course, as does the Asian Institute of Management in the Philippines. Monash in Australia offers an EMBA lasting between three and four years, and the Australian Graduate School of Management offers a three-tier EMBA program similar to the United Kingdom's certificate, diploma, and MBA structure.

The partnership model is already finding favor with EMBA providers. Three universities in the United States and Europe have combined to offer an International EMBA. Tilburg University in the Netherlands, the Budapest University of Economic Sciences in Hungary, and Purdue University in the United States are offering a two-year course comprising seven two-week residential sessions, alternating between the three countries. Called the International Masters in Management, the program leads to two degrees: a master's degree in Management from Purdue and an Executive MBA from either Tilburg or Budapest.

PUSHING THE BRAND

While Executive MBAs take the MBA brand upmarket, business schools have also proved adept at generating MBA programs with added alluring extras. The ultimate general management qualification can increasingly be found with added specialties. After being stretched, the MBA brand is being pushed and pulled in any manner of directions.

Italy's most famous business school, SDA Bocconi, offers an MBA in fashion and design, for example, while a British school offers an MBA degree in church management (Lincoln). The MBA of the new millennium is as likely to feature a specialty in design as in strategy and may include fashion as well as finance.

Some programs have shifted the boundaries even further.

Among the most innovative—or alarming if you are a traditionalist—is the University of Liverpool's football (soccer) industries MBA. Most business school brochures feature pictures of people in lecture theaters and libraries; this one includes soccer stars. They are not in a library. Most MBA interviews seek to get to the bottom of your knowledge of strategic management; for this program you have to know which team you support.

The MBA (Football Industries) is designed for those intending to work in soccer administration, on the commercial or marketing side of the sport, or in related sporting fields such as advertising, broadcasting, and print media.

"We think there is demand for a business education that explores a fast-growing industry and which allows people to study something they are genuinely interested in," says Sam Johnstone of the Football Research Unit, who teaches in the program. "Soccer is a massive, fast-growing, and truly global business. In China, for example, it is reputed to be the third-largest growth industry. But as well as being interested in the business side of the game, we want people who understand and love soccer." Over 150 applied for the first intake and there have been a thousand inquiries since the program was announced. Such is the game's international appeal that over half a dozen nationalities will be represented in the first two intakes—and that's without any overseas advertising.

The actual content of the program covers the familiar fundamentals—organizational behavior, marketing, strategic management, and the management context are compulsory modules. Students move on to study soccer and society and a module on organizational structures in soccer worldwide. Two options have then to be selected from world perspectives on soccer, soccer and the media, and the international business of soccer. Finally comes a dissertation on a subject related to soccer management. "We are a few years ahead, but other institutions will surely follow with similar programs," predicts Sam Johnstone. An MBA (Basketball) is only a matter of time.

While the world's first football industries MBA is a guaranteed headline grabber (except in North America), other developments from the traditional MBA formula are less dramatic but, en masse, represent a significant change in emphasis. The ultimate general management qualification increasingly has a specialist element. The University of Westminster, for example, offers an MBA (Design Management). This is a two-year part-time program and is the first of its kind in Europe. What is interesting is that transforming the traditional MBA format into a design-oriented program does not take a great leap of the imagination. Design, as the content of the Westminster program makes clear, has direct relationships with core subjects such as project management and information management.

Others are following suit. After decades of attempting to follow the American business school model, European business schools are in the vanguard of more imaginative approaches to the standard MBA. Often these elements are based on local expertise or industries—such as Liverpool's soccer initiative. At SDA Bocconi in Milan, for example, students in its MBA program can study "orientation itineraries." These include fashion and design, small- and medium-sized enterprises, and information systems. The fashion and design element draws on the Milanese fashion industry. Similar local expertise led to the creation of an MBA in luxury brand management by ESSEC Graduate School of Management on the outskirts of Paris. This is a one-year, English-language program covering everything from luxury brand logos and trademarks to legal protection against counterfeiters. The MBA, the luxury brand of the management development world, may never be the same again.

PRACTICING WHAT THEY PREACH

What does this frenzy of new programs demonstrate? It shows business schools behaving like businesses rather than academic institutions. Of course, the corollary of this is that if another school develops a new variation on the MBA, others have to be quick to follow. The emphasis is now on keeping pace with the market—matching the programs on offer elsewhere—and developing programs quickly to take advantage of small windows of opportunity.

This is even more apparent in exec ed, where b-schools are constantly tweaking the names and content of their programs. Increasingly, too, they are creating customized programs for individual clients or groups of clients. "You have to be fast. Developing programs once took eighteen months. Now custom programs are instigated and delivered in four months," says Ray Smith of the University of Virginia's Darden School. "This has an effect on open programs—they are developed faster and are more in-tune with the marketplace."

In these areas, business schools are practicing what they preach. They are increasingly market-led, responsive to the needs of corporate clients. In any other business this would be automatically interpreted as a good thing. But whether it is in the field of academic studies is more problematic.

Kenan-Flagler dean Bob Sullivan recalls an event when he was dean of Carnegie-Mellon's Graduate School of Industrial Administration in the early 1990s. Carnegie-Mellon invited Xerox chief Paul Allaire, a 1966 graduate, to speak. "There were lots of people in the audience who had graduated in the sixties. The associate dean gave a presentation on the curriculum," recalls Sullivan. "Allaire said that what we presented was the same as he had studied in 1966. Later he and Heinz's Tony O'Reilly spoke. They both recalled that business schools once defined the key questions and issues for their businesses. Now, they said that industry was setting the questions and leading the way." Sullivan's conclusion: "As professional schools we've often lost contact with the profession. But how can we then anticipate what we need to be doing tomorrow?"

Intellectual purists might argue that business schools should be leading the market, setting the agenda. The suspicion is that a profusion of similar fashionable products creates opportunities for competitors better suited to speedy product development and more adept at finding and developing original niches. Commercial followers are unlikely to be intellectual leaders—and vice versa. Attempting to be both appears both self-defeating and impossible.

INTERNATIONAL EXPANSION

In another important aspect, business schools have been aping the behavior of large corporations. Their international aspirations have grown year by year over recent decades. Now they regard the world as their marketplace and loudly pronounce their international credentials. There is a perpetual struggle to fill faculty and courses with as many different nationalities as possible. Clearly, some are more international than others in practice and perspective.

In trumpeting their global makeup, business schools are only reflecting the demands from corporate clients and students for a global view of business issues. HR directors of leading multinationals confirm that they see executive programs as an important way of providing a "big picture" of the global economy and as a vital resource for creating a cadre of top managers with the competencies to manage transnational businesses.

The question for business schools is whether to deliver global programs from their base or to deliver the same programs elsewhere in the world. Some choose the former option and globalize their faculty and program content. These tend to be European schools, though Harvard has now joined their ranks. Dean Kim Clark has referred to the "aggressive recruiting effort" the school is using to attract more international faculty.

Following a similar route is IMD, which attempts to keep its faculty in Lausanne as much of the time as possible. It reasons that if it started providing programs in other regions this would inevitably involve faculty spending more time away from IMD. This would prove both highly expensive and counterproductive.

Says IMD's Steve Daverio: "We have an ongoing conflict here about running programs outside Switzerland. We only do two: one in Singapore has been established for about fifteen years, and we have one we do in Shanghai and Beijing. This is always a big question for us. The external reason is that one of our biggest strengths is the claim to an international environment. It's something we are proud of, the high percentage of Asians, Africans, South Americans on our programs. It's very powerful on a program to hear how different nationalities deal with issues, so for example to hear how a Mexican might deal with a people issue compared to a Scandinavian. If you start running programs all over the world, there's a danger we could lose that."

Daverio points to the experience of IMD's great competitor, INSEAD—"INSEAD has found most of its Asian business is done in Asia—so the representation of Asians on the programs is not so high as it used to be. We still try to persuade Asian companies to send their managers here to Switzerland. We have the best international mix—18 percent Asians, 6 percent Latin Americans. The U.S., though, is low."

Others take the second approach: seeking out opportunities to deliver the same programs somewhere else. There is increasing pressure from corporate customers on the leading American and European schools to deliver programs wherever in the world they are required. Those schools that have followed this strategy toward international expansion have, in essence, pursued the colonial approach favored by American companies of the 1950s and 1960s. At that time, big American corporations sought to establish themselves in other countries simply by exporting a management team and waiting as they inculcated the locals with the corporate culture. This approach overlooked cultural nuances. In fact, it overlooked nuances. Period.

Business schools remain wedded to this simplistic strategy. Faculty are now exported en masse, like touring circus troupes. Faculty from MIT's Sloan, for example, fly to Barcelona to teach a five-day program with IESE. Their work done, they fly home.

The more imaginative and pragmatic adopt different approaches. "A number of companies are requesting delivery around the globe," says Wanda Wallace of Duke University's Fuqua Business School. "This is met partly through partnership relationships with other schools and institutions in these regions, and partly by flying members of faculty out to company sites or to convenient hotel locations." The world is their oyster, the future a European hotel room.

The international issue is likely to become even more important as globalization continues. With shortages of top-quality faculty, the pressure will be on to find more innovative solutions than simply exporting faculty en masse to Europe.

5

The Business of Professorship

For the top thirty schools, the biggest problem now is getting the best faculty, that means people who know how to create information and knowledge and also know how to pass it on. That requires a cross between a Nobel Prize winner and a Hollywood actor.

—Steve Daverio, IMD

The stakes are high in the world of business school academia, where professional acclaim often goes hand in hand with huge financial rewards. The talk is all about real-world solutions that can be conveniently turned into lucrative consulting projects. Meanwhile, the traditional backbiting among academics has reached new heights.

Never before have academic sinecures carried so many perks. This is creating a unique environment at leading business schools where the traditional career structure has been transformed into a major business opportunity. The rewards for those who reach the heights of stellar faculty are riches and influence far beyond their academic peers in other disciplines. This distorts the salary structures and career expectations of faculty, and is a step toward the commercialization of academic posts. The financial incentives offered by the leading business schools to attract the top Ph.D. graduates threatens to create a brain drain away from other disciplines.

In particular:

- The competition for top jobs is fierce because the rewards are disproportionately high.
- A combination of the traditional tenure system and too much emphasis on faculty superstars distorts the career path of professors, with little incentive to teach.
- Stellar faculty are part of the guru industry, which is served by a secondary industry in ghostwriting. This makes nonsense of traditional academic standards. Where will it end?
- The pressure on salaries this causes undermines academic pay scales in other disciplines as business schools outbid other departments for top Ph.D.'s.
- The spectacle of professors fighting for money is unbecoming.

Digging a Pit

When Professor Tom Robertson was passed over for the job of principal at London Business School, losing out to Harvard's John Quelch, he took the post of dean at Emory University's Goizueta School in Atlanta. Urbane and immaculately dressed, Robertson was walking into a bizarre storm.

The decision about Robertson's appointment was made in November 1997. He was well qualified for the job and had narrowly missed the top job in London where he had been based. But, if there is a winner, there is always a loser. Among those who had their eyes on the Goizueta job was Jeffrey Sonnenfeld. Sonnenfeld was a forty-four-year-old who had moved to Goizueta from Harvard University in 1989. Executives he had taught described him as "brilliant and charismatic." Sonnenfeld was director of Emory's Center for Career and Leadership Studies. Though he failed to get the dean's job at Goizueta, as some consolation, Sonnenfeld got the job of dean at Georgia Tech's DuPree School of Business.

Then the local newspaper, the *Atlanta Constitution*, created a sensation—while also revealing a fascinating picture of the pressures of academic life at a U.S. business school. On December 12 it reported that Sonnenfeld would no longer be going to Georgia Tech as dean because of "allegations that [he] vandalized Emory University's new business school building." Indeed, the newspaper reported that Sonnenfeld, "a highly visible professor," was to leave a month early. "We can confirm that the withdrawal of Dr. Sonnenfeld's nomination to the Board of Regents was done at our initiative based upon personal and medical reasons pertaining to Dr. Sonnenfeld," Bob Harty, a Georgia Tech spokesman, told the newspaper.

Emory and Georgia Tech officials refused to comment publicly about the unusual turn of events. But the *Atlanta Constitution* report said that interviews with people close to the situation at both universities had produced the following account: "A security camera was installed in the Roberto C. Goizueta School of Business building after deep scratches were noticed on the walls and wood-veneer doors in the fifth floor hall leading to the office of retiring dean, Ronald E. Frank. Similar marks were made on the dean's conference table. Sonnenfeld allegedly was videotaped in an act of vandalism."[1]

In an interview with local reporters, Sonnenfeld repeatedly denied any involvement in vandalism. However, it was reported that his story had changed several times. Originally, in a press release issued to newspapers, he claimed he had resigned from Emory a month early for medical reasons. Later, he said that he had asked officials at Georgia Tech if he could take some time off for a semi-sabbatical before starting his new post. The next day he gave the reason for resigning as "high blood pressure."

Still later, he told reporters that he had decided to "take some time out for living." Then he said he wanted to start a stand-alone college for corporate chief executives that would not be affiliated with a university. He said several leading executives had expressed an interest in helping him start such an institute.

Bradley Currey Jr., chairman of Emory's board and chairman of the packaging company Rock-Tenn, described Sonnenfeld as a friend. "He needs some time off," Currey told reporters.

BACK TO MEDIOCRITY

The stakes weren't always so high. The truth is that a job at a business school was once relatively humdrum. In the 1950s, 1960s, and 1970s it was a secure but unexceptional living. Academics worked at their research and taught. The average business school professor of that time was about as likely to wiggle his butt at a seminar to promote a populist potboiler as he was to get fired. Times change.

Business school faculty can now be superstars. "Professors have brand names. The stronger the brand, the more mobile they are," says Emory dean Tom Robertson.[2] People like Harvard's Michael Porter and Rosabeth Moss Kanter are internationally renowned and—thanks to consulting fees, seminars, book royalties, and academic salaries—rich. Their ideas change the way managers manage. They reap the rewards of their influence. This has turned the entire culture of business school faculty upside down.

Of course, the majority keep their heads down and research and teach. Business school faculty are much better paid than they once were. (Business school faculty at the top U.S. schools can command salaries of several hundred thousand dollars.) And there are a few perks—the astute can clinch attractive jobs as visiting professors in major European cities of their choice.

The hungry ones have their eyes constantly on the mass market, the lucrative circuit of seminars and best-sellers. At the top of the pile are the major leaguers, the stars in the business school firmament. These are a select few, including those described in the following sections.

Rosabeth Moss Kanter

As well as being Class of 1960 Professor of Business Administration at Harvard, Kanter is chairman of the consulting firm Goodmeasure. She and Barry Stein founded the company in 1977. Based in Cambridge, Massachusetts, Goodmeasure offers consulting (around 80 percent of clients are Fortune 500 companies), a Speaker's

Bureau, training, research services, and organizing "state-of-the-art business meetings."

Michael Porter

"If anyone is capable of turning management theory into a respectable scholarly discipline, it is Michael Porter," noted *The Economist*.[3] Porter is the C. Roland Christensen Professor of Business Administration at Harvard. Porter's consulting company, Monitor, numbers countries and regions among its clients. Rather than pursuing a career as a professional golfer, Porter took a Harvard MBA (1971) and followed this with a doctorate in business economics (1973). While completing his Ph.D. Porter came under the influence of Richard Caves, the economist, who became his mentor. He joined the Harvard faculty at the age of twenty-six—one of the youngest tenured professors in the school's august history.

Porter's genius has lain in producing brilliantly researched and cogent models of competitiveness at a corporate, industrywide, and national level. For example, Porter took an industrial economics framework—the structure-conduct performance paradigm (SCP)—and translated it into the context of business strategy. From this emerged his best-known model: the five forces framework, which states that "in any industry, whether it is domestic or international or produces a product or a service, the rules of competition are embodied in five competitive forces." This was a brilliant example of a traditional academic theory making the leap downmarket to business theory.

Peter Senge

Director of the MIT Center for Organizational Learning and author of the best-seller *The Fifth Discipline*, Senge has not taken to the guru seminar trail. He is no rock star. Senge's strategy has been more subtle but hugely successful. Senge is also cofounder of consulting and training firm Innovation Associates, now part of the consulting firm Arthur D. Little. This creates an interesting potential conflict of interest. After all, Senge works for MIT's Sloan School, in effect a local competitor to Arthur D. Little's own School of Management.

Gary Hamel

Hamel is chairman and founder of Strategos and visiting professor at London Business School. Hamel has astutely and energetically built from the success of the book he coauthored with C. K. Prahalad, *Competing for the Future*. He now claims to be Concorde's most frequent flier. The Strategos team includes Mike Cornell, Gary Getz, Pierre Loewe, Jim Scholes, and Steve McGrath. "Strategos is a leader in helping foment industry revolution and strategy innovation within and across companies," trumpets the firm's publicity material. "Strategos seeks to liberate the institution's sense of identity, embolden people to create the future, and increase emotional connection between individuals and their institutions." The company's bold words are only matched by the big bucks it charges.

Lesser Lights

Beneath this group are a host of other business school academics who are prospering without hitting the global heights of the superstars. They have yet to turn themselves into industries—either through choice or lack of opportunity to do so. Among them are the following familiar names:

Philip Kotler. Prolific marketing guru based at Northwestern's Kellogg School.

Arie de Geus. Former Royal Dutch Shell executive, now a best-selling author and academic at London Business School.

John Kotter. Kotter is Konosuke Matsushita Professor of Leadership at Harvard Business School. He joined the Harvard faculty in 1972 and, in 1980, aged thirty-three, and was given tenure and full professorship—one of the youngest full professors in the history of

Harvard. Amazingly productive and wide ranging. His books intriguingly include *Matsushita Leadership* (1996).

Warren Bennis. Based at the University of Southern California, Bennis is a world-renowned leadership expert. Now in his seventies, he continues to tread the boards. Bennis is also one of the few guru academics who has actually tried his hand at academic administration at the State University of New York, Buffalo, and as president of the University of Cincinnati. He found that his practice disappointed his theory—a rare example of an academic putting his reputation where his ideas are. "When I was at the University of Cincinnati I realized that I was seeking power through position, by being president of the university. I wanted to *be* a university president but I didn't want to *do* it. I wanted the influence," says Bennis. "In the end I wasn't very good at being a president. I looked out of the window and thought that the man cutting the lawn actually seemed to have more control over what he was doing."

Sumantra Ghoshal. London Business School's Ghoshal has made his reputation working along with Harvard's Christopher Bartlett. Together they are the authors of *Managing Across Borders* and *The Individualized Corporation*. Ghoshal is one of the few who remain committed to the traditional academic approach. "I spend 15 percent of my time teaching; 15 percent consulting and writing and 60 percent doing academic work that people never see," he says.[4]

Would-Be Luminaries

Beneath this level crowd a host of aspiring academics, anxious to board the gravy train. Among the best are:

- *Oren Harari:* Columnist, formerly with the Tom Peters Group and academic at the University of San Francisco.

- *Barry Nalebuff:* Coauthor of *Co-opetition*, a 1990s take on game theory. Nalebuff is based at the Yale School of Management.
- *Hermann Simon:* Visiting professor at London Business School and author of *Hidden Champions*. Simon is chairman and CEO of Simon, Kucher & Partners, a strategy and marketing consultancy with offices in Bonn, Germany, and Cambridge, Massachusetts.
- *Leonard Berry:* Professor of marketing at Texas A&M University.

Daily rates rather than the number of hours spent in class are the basis of competition between these thinkers. Ask Tom Peters, who earns more than most—$90,000 for a day's work outside the United States. "I am not a bad economist and I understand the market logic, the fee structure," says Peters. "In the U.S. there are ten or eleven thousand trade associations and all have annual meetings with three or four speakers. Looking at the economics it isn't that strange. The U.S. has set the market. It is good, simple economics. Every year produces another hero—Schwarzkopf, Ford, Kissinger, Thatcher, Powell. That sets the top of the market and we glide in between them. Every time there's a war it puts the price up. It's like the spot market for speeches. You can explain it all the way down. The bread and butter are seminars for the general public." Market forces *über alles*.

RECRUITING SUPERSTARS

The leading business schools now use resident gurus—or faculty stars—as a key part of their marketing strategy. The presence of top names carries weight with students and corporate clients alike. This adds to the financial rewards now on offer. Top names get top salaries and freedom to take on private consultancy work.

The presence of a big name professor on the faculty of a school can do wonders for its reputation and international standing. As a result, the leading business schools are engaged in a constant battle to attract—by almost any means available—the most talented teaching and research staff. This leads to jealousy among other members of faculty. Some schools suffer from this more than others.

There is now a merry-go-round of top business school academics, reminiscent of that of the top sports stars, who join a club for a season or two and then move on if they get a better offer. Big names are traded and hawked. The annual meeting of the American Academy of Management is compared by one senior academic to an "intellectual meat market."

Some are poached—Professor Sumantra Ghoshal's move from INSEAD to London Business School was one instance of a big name taking the bait. It also caused a great deal of infighting and backbiting among notoriously fractious faculty. Such high-profile appointments serve to underline the growing gap between the superstars and the rest of the faculty.

"In every business there is the dross and the achievers. There are a lot of workmen at business schools. They are the middle mass," reflects London Business School's Nigel Nicholson. "If you want the leading thinkers in management then you have to allow people to pursue their own interests. If you don't do that, they'll go elsewhere. We help people pursue their interests. We get the best people and give them freedom to do what they want to do and to do it well. People who come here want to be in an international environment close to business centers in an elite institution."

As U.S. schools tend to pay more generous salaries, importing a foreign star often means that European business schools break the salary system. "If you are willing to pay you can get people," says Professor David Norburn, director of London's Imperial College Management School. "But where does that leave the other faculty? Alternatively, you could pay all faculty the same, in which case you would fail to attract people."

To attract superstars, business schools have a number of lures. They sometimes offer a package that involves little in the way of teaching. Clearly, this shifts the burden to other faculty. The second lure is the offer of a free rein when it comes to research. More attractive is the offer of consulting opportunities. The bottom line for schools must be whether having a guru-in-residence actually attracts new students or adds to the experience of existing students.

Imperial's David Norburn acknowledges that attracting high-quality faculty without breaking the bank is fraught with difficulty, but not impossible. "We have succeeded in bringing in some big names because we have a very flat hierarchy, no pompousness, and because we laugh a lot. It sounds romantic but we have a better culture. We compete on the basis that this is an enjoyable and fulfilling place to work." Norburn approaches the matter of recruiting faculty with the persistence of a Major League talent scout. "You court people over a number of years," he says. "You may not be able to get the big stars of today, but who is their brightest Ph.D. student? We have a database of U.K. academics working abroad who may, at some point, be interested in returning to the U.K."

In some ways, of course, this is no different from what happens in any other sector. But as the divide between the superstars and the rest widens—in terms of both recognition and financial rewards—the full impact is unclear. Certainly, it is likely to breed resentment among midranking faculty who are likely to feel that their efforts are not valued. Does that matter? Maybe not. But the question is one that the elite business schools do not seem to have considered. There is a very real danger that the business schools could become caught up in a bidding war akin to that of the Hollywood studios. How long will it be before the top professors get themselves agents to negotiate their salaries? Some of these factors are already making their presence felt.

SHOW ME THE MONEY

One inevitable consequence of the battle to recruit faculty superstars is to push up salaries. The establishment of new business schools is already putting intense pressure on the traditional salary structures in a number of famous universities.

At Oxford and Cambridge, for example, the tenure systems—and pecking order among faculty—have endured for years and are part of the fabric of the institutions. These universities have traditionally been able to enforce a pay ceiling on teaching staff. It is unclear how much longer this will be possible.

Pressures to pay business school faculty salaries more in line with the private sector have so far been largely masked by allowing professors time to pursue their own outside interests. This is a novel concept. Anywhere outside academia it would be speedily described as commercial madness.

Many business schools allow their faculty one day a week to do private work and, as we have seen, a number of professors also run their own consultancy firms. Even Harvard Business School dean Kim Clark has time to work with Integral, an international management consulting firm he founded with Steven Wheelwright of Harvard and Bruce Stangle. Integral, with offices in Cambridge, Massachusetts, and Menlo Park, California, employs around seventy professionals and is an affiliate of Analysis Group Economics.

The consulting system means that averagely motivated academics at averagely ranked business schools should be able to double their salary through consulting and other external opportunities such as seminars and speeches. As working arrangements go, this is highly flexible. In fact, so flexible that there have been several instances at leading schools where star professors have had to be politely reminded that their presence at the school from time to time to teach courses is part of the deal. (One well-known professor we know of worked four days a week as a consultant—his business school employer rather pathetically protested that he did work on weekends. Another claimed not to have visited his business school office for two years.)

Schools don't make life easy for themselves: one major school found that it didn't actually have a system to calculate how many hours faculty taught during the year. Obviously, they all claimed to have exceeded their contractual obligations.

Most schools would say that consultancy work is vital to ensure that professors remain in touch with the real world of business. Some, such as Ashridge Management College, even go so far as to insist that all members of faculty have regular experience of the private sector. Ashridge has its own consulting firm, Ashridge Consulting. This provides another angle. Ashridge's staff can be competing against their employer's consulting firm for clients.

More generally the potential pitfalls of the academic-as-consultant arrangement are many and varied. How do students know that the diagnostics offered by academics aren't driven by consulting interests and vice versa—the consultant's report might conclude that extensive training for managers is required.

Schools that choose to venture into such minefields invite danger. Most do, and there is some truth in the argument that consulting is a useful means of keeping up-to-date with developments in the field. Balance appears elusive. The lure of lucrative outside work can sometimes get the better of academics.

At IMD in the 1980s too many professors were spending too much time consulting and not enough teaching, something that prompted strong words from the school's governing body. As Jean-Pierre Salzmann, IMD's former head of public affairs, admits: "Yes, there was a time a few years ago when there were rather too many Porsches in the staff car park. The school had to lay down the law to some people. They had to remind some professors that they were supposed to be teaching on our programs." IMD is not the only school to have experienced some tension in this area. But it is one of the few prepared to admit it publicly.

Today, there are also additional calls on the time of business school professors. The emergence of new players in the executive education market is creating a lucrative new sideline. A number of the big management consultancies have started offering executive programs in recent years. Several use business school faculty to teach in them—and pay handsomely for the privilege.

At the same time, the establishment of their own corporate universities by a growing number of large companies is also creating a secondary market for enterprising business professors. An increasing number now moonlight for this new sector.

Publicly, business schools say there is no conflict of interest in the current situation. But as these alternative providers move into the market for custom programs in particular they will compete more and more directly with the business schools. This could present some serious conflicts of interest.

With higher fees on offer, professors may prefer to teach in programs offered by a consultancy rather than pull out all the stops to secure the work for the business school that pays them a retainer. To get around this potential problem, business schools may have to include restrictive covenants in their tenure arrangements. They are also likely to have to pay their faculty higher salaries.

Money is a powerful drug. At present, many of these issues and their implications remain hidden from view, but the pressure from them is already evident in some places. In time this pressure is likely to blow traditional academic pay scales to smithereens.

The presence of so much tension just beneath the surface makes the job of dean of a business school far from easy. For the man—there are still very few women deans at business schools, and even fewer black deans—who has to massage the egos of so many prima donnas, the task is often thankless. *Business Week*'s John Byrne has called the Harvard faculty "perhaps the largest single conglomeration of out-sized egos and intellects anywhere in business."[5] As *Fortune* noted: "The relationship between a dean and his or her faculty is that of a fire hydrant to a pack of male dogs."[6]

If the going gets too tough, the deans can always share the grief. The deans of the top schools get to know each other quite well. Like all true gentlemen they are generally charming to one another when they meet. They reserve their attacks on rival schools for private discussions with journalists. In Europe, the "Three Deans" of London Business School, INSEAD, and IMD hold regular meetings several times a year. They have a lot in common. All have to put up with the constant demands of egocentric faculty members, and with the school governors' asking why they don't top this or that ranking, or why their school isn't mentioned in glowing terms in some obscure journal. In between, too, they have to run a large and unwieldy organization. Pity the poor dean, then—his body bloated by too many rich dinners, his mind addled from the constant buzz of management theory, and his soul corrupted by the lure of corporate gold.

Leo Murray, director of Cranfield School of Management, reflects (not entirely seriously): "Each year, business school heads from all over Europe meet in solemn conclave. Actually, it is a mass therapy session where we reassure each other that there are one hundred or so other victims just as ineffectual as we are."

THE GREAT PH.D. GOLD RUSH

The reality is that there is a world shortage of high-caliber faculty to teach in business schools. Business schools have grown so rapidly in the last half century that there are too few excellent business academics to go round. Business schools are also in constant competition to spot and recruit the faculty stars of the future.

Among the top U.S. schools, this has already prompted a scramble to recruit up-and-coming teaching stars from the top Ph.D. programs. "It's almost like the pro-football draft," Robert S. Hamada, dean of the Graduate School of Business at Chicago, said of the annual Ph.D. recruitment drive. "By the time offers are made, everyone knows who is Number 1, 2, and 3."

Among the most sought-after are the finance wizards once destined for the top research universities, like Chicago and Harvard, where tenure was the career goal. Now, ambitious up-and-coming business schools—as well as the usual Wall Street pack—are on constant lookout for finance Ph.D.'s.

In recent years, the need to be seen as "international" in their outlook has also led to the leading U.S. schools' recruiting faculty from different national cultures. It's something that can give a fledgling academic that all-important edge over his or her peers.

The Player Draft

In 1996, *Business Week* described thirty-two-year-old graduate student Ming Huang as "the hottest newly minted PhD in the country." Chinese-born Huang received offers of teaching jobs from a dozen top business schools, including Chicago, Harvard, Wharton, MIT, Michigan, and Northwestern, and the Olin School of Business at Washington University. "Ming was no. 1," Kerry E. Back, associate dean at the Olin School of Business, told the magazine. "But no. 2 wasn't far behind."

Financially, the report said, Huang's job offers were close, somewhere in the neighborhood of $100,000 for the academic year, plus $25,000 as a summer stipend. Huang chose to accept an assistant professorship at Chicago partly because of the caliber of faculty he would be working alongside—the school has four Nobel Prize winners.

At the time, he had virtually no teaching experience. At Stanford, he graded papers, and last worked as a teaching assistant at Cornell in 1987. The fact that America's top business schools should be fighting to recruit someone with hardly any teaching experience reflects the importance they still attach to identifying the stars of the future.

Huang was not the only freshly minted Ph.D. to benefit from the attentions of the top business schools. That year, salaries for the top Ph.D.'s in Huang's discipline, finance, rose almost 15 percent, taking them above $100,000, and causing A. Michael Spence, dean of Stanford's business school, to predict a 10 percent to 15 percent hike in pay for finance faculty at top schools throughout the United States.

Elsewhere, upward pressure on salaries gave rise to some strange goings-on at some of America's best-known business schools. At New York University's Stern School, the dean had to ask for special permission to raise salaries of the current finance faculty members so that they wouldn't be earning less than the new recruits. The bill—believed to be in the region of $400,000—didn't include a big pay rise paid to international business professor David Backus to reward his loyalty after Columbia had tried to lure him away with a 70 percent increase on what Stern was paying.

Elsewhere, other schools took a different approach. In a separate move at Chicago, where Huang ended up, the school managed to persuade the American government to proclaim one of its graduate students an official "genius"—making him eligible for a special work visa that would let him stay in the country and join its staff.

Fishing in Troubled Waters

Meanwhile, Columbia, which in recent years has been aggressively recruiting some of the top business school faculty in America, also demonstrated its determination by putting together a special deal of its own. In 1996, by arrangement with three other schools in the university, the business school successfully recruited finance professors Robert J. Hodrick and his wife, Laurie Simon Hodrick—and her ex-husband, Kyle Bagwell, an industrial organization specialist. All three had to go as a job lot, it seems, because of child custody arrangements.

Columbia was also involved in a farrago with Harvard's Professor Robert Barro, an "economics all-star" according to the *New York Times*. Barro was in negotiations to join the faculty at both Columbia University and Columbia Business School, but eventually decided to remain at Harvard. In April 1998, the *New York Times* outlined the details of Barro's compensation package at Columbia, but reported that "cold feet" had prompted him to stay put.

Those close to Barro were at a loss to explain the professor's decision. "Robert is a very unusual guy," said Professor Elhanan Helpman, an economics instructor at Harvard. "My sense is that it was emotionally a big problem to make this move." Compensation was not the issue, it seems. In addition to the $300,000 salary Barro was promised at Columbia, he was also offered a remodeled, rent-subsidized apartment on Riverside Drive, and there was a $50,000-a-year job for his wife at Columbia. At the same time, reports said, he had been given approval to recruit five permanent tenured professors and one visiting professor to Columbia.

The original announcement in April that Barro was leaving Harvard was greeted with surprise from his colleagues. Some felt that he risked compromising his reputation and career by leaving the country's top economics department for Columbia's, ranked fourteenth in the country. His decision to stay in Cambridge was welcomed in the Harvard camp. "Better a broken engagement than an unhappy marriage," Harvard's dean of faculty, Jeremy Knowles, told reporters. Not surprisingly, the reaction from Columbia was less understanding.

THE GURU INDUSTRY

The creation of business school superstars has also had other curious repercussions. The first is the sudden desire by academics and their business schools to be quoted by members of the media. Part of the career strategy of any ambitious business school professor today is to make sure he or she appears as often as possible in newspapers, magazines, and television and radio programming.

For their part, journalists are often only too pleased to find a quotable business school professor—often useful in their daily work. Someone with *professor* before their name has the instant authority of an expert. For the academics, the name of this particular game is to make themselves and their areas of specialist knowledge known to journalists, and to be ready to step in at a moment's notice to provide comment or instant analysis of any business development. In this regard, business school professors are learning from politicians, who literally line up at TV stations to offer their expert opinions whenever a big story breaks.

From the journalist's point of view, the aim is to have an expert on hand whenever analysis or interpretation is required—or some space needs to be filled. Some business academics are better at getting their name in print than others. (A certain professor appeared

Faculty Stars

Amos Tuck
James Brian Quinn, strategy
Richard D'Aveni, strategy

Anderson School—UCLA
William Ouchi, *Theory Z* author

Ashridge Management College
Steve Seymour, finance
Andrew Campbell, corporate strategy
Philip Hodgson, leadership

Carnegie-Mellon
Richard Cyert, *Behavior of the Firm* author
Herbert Simon, artificial intelligence and decision making
Paul S. Goodman, technology and organization

Columbia University
Kirby Warren, long-range planning
Donald Hambrick, top management

Cornell—Johnson School
J. Edward Russo, decision making
Randall P. White (exec ed), leadership

Cranfield School of Management
Andrew Kakabadse, top teamworking
Gerry Johnson, strategy
Adrian Payne, relationship marketing
Steven Carver, project management

Emory University—Goizueta School
Tom Robertson, dean, marketing

Haas School—Berkeley
Peter Schwartz (visiting), co-founder Global Business network
Paul Schoemaker (visiting), planning
David Vogel, *California Management Review* editor
Ikujiro Nonaka, knowledge management

Harvard Business School
Michael Porter, competitiveness
Rosabeth Moss Kanter, human relations
Chris Argyris, learning
John Kotter, leadership, general management
David Arnold, branding and marketing

Henley Management College
Bernard Taylor, corporate responsibility
David Birchall, future of organizations

INSEAD
Henry Mintzberg (visiting), strategy
Paul Evans, organizational behavior
Daniel Muzkya, innovation
Chan Kim, value creation

IMD
Peter Lorange, joint ventures
Fred Neubauer, corporate governance

London Business School
Gary Hamel (visiting), strategy
Sumantra Ghoshal, organizations
Don Sull, organizations
Jeff Sampler, technology and organizations

McGill University
Henry Mintzberg, strategy

MIT—Sloan School
Edgar Schein, corporate culture, careers
Peter Senge, learning organization
Jay Forrester, systems

Northwestern University—Kellogg School
Philip Kotler, marketing

Penn State University—Smeal College
Al Vicere, executive education

Stanford University
Jerry Porras, coauthor, *Built to Last*
Andy Grove (visiting), Intel chief

University of Michigan
C. K. Prahalad, strategy

University of North Carolina at Chapel Hill—Kenan-Flagler
Benson Rosen, organizational behavior

University of Pennsylvania—Wharton School
George S. Day, marketing

University of Southern California
Warren Bennis, leadership
Morgan McCall, executive careers, leadership
Ian Mitroff, crisis management

University of Texas at Austin
Robert Blake, Managerial Grid originator

so regularly in articles in one publication that the editor in charge banned reporters from quoting him.)

This and the development of business lectures as a performing art—as popularized by the stars of the international conference circuit such as Tom Peters—have had other strange side effects. Both these trends favor polished performers. All too often, business professors are rewarded for their presentational skills rather than the quality of their thinking—or ideas. (Certainly, there is an inbuilt tendency for the media to opt for sound-bite solutions rather than intellectually rigorous points of view. As a result, certain media-friendly academics find themselves much in demand, often asked to comment—and usually pleased to oblige—on areas that they know their colleagues are more qualified to discuss.) None of this reflects well on the institutions they purport to represent. At the same time, business schools are madly chasing the management gurus whom they mistakenly see as the competition. (As we shall see, the competition is more likely to come from elsewhere.)

"Management gurus and business schools are both competing to convince the management audience that they are at the forefront of management innovation. If the ideas developed and disseminated by business schools are perceived to be less valid than those of management gurus then they will increasingly become seen as peripheral institutions," says guru watcher Timothy Clark. (Clark, of King's College, London, has recently received a government research grant to study the presentation tricks of the guru business.)

The management guru industry has much to answer for, too, in other areas. It is not that the top gurus aren't bright—they patently are. Or that they don't come up with original ideas—they have to have at least one to make them famous. The problem is that they are so well rewarded that their example tempts others, less brilliant, less charismatic, to try to emulate them. Some of them are business school academics.

The result is that beneath the stars there exists a nebulous cloud of mini gurus competing for attention (the *guritos*—or baby gurus).

Their light is not so bright. Some of these guritos will one day make it into the premier league. Many more will never achieve the stardom they seek but will build moderately successful secondary careers as national (rather than international) speakers and pundits.

The problem is that the guru business is largely a personality-driven one—as opposed to an ideas-driven one. Sure, you need a good first idea, but after that, staying at the top requires stage presence and a certain cultish appeal. It is these intangible qualities that are rewarded with fame and fortune. Anyone who has actually seen Tom Peters do his stuff will admit the man is a natural stage performer. The business academics who have risen to fame in recent years—people like Gary Hamel and Peter Senge—share this ability to entertain as well as inform. They enthuse audiences with their ideas. (So should all good teachers, you say. True up to a point. But the ability to communicate complicated concepts and ideas is a different skill.)

The guru aims for maximum impact. His (most are men) tools are one-liners and drumroll statistics. (These have traditionally been the tools of the journalist, whose job it is to make information interesting to a wide audience, but whose personal opinion is less regarded.) In the case of the gurus, however, entertainment passes for enlightenment. The corporate catchphrase is a relatively recent development. Forget the detailed academic argument. The idea is to distill the very essence of your business philosophy or message into a simple but highly memorable sentence. In so doing, the owner and originator hopes to achieve two not entirely unrelated objectives. First, to become instantly recognizable to managers around the globe, and second to sell business books and consultancy services.

The intellectual sound-bites are phrases such as *Only the Paranoid Survive*, a best-seller for Andrew Grove, head of Intel. We can only guess at how the book might have fared had his original—and altogether less snappy—title *Navigating Strategic Inflection Points* not been rejected by the publisher. "Managers do things right; leaders do the right things" is an oldie but goldie from leadership guru Warren Bennis. "Don't automate, obliterate" is from Michael Hammer and James Champy of *Reengineering the Corporation* fame. Also from the same team, "Good products don't make winners; winners make good products."

Some have been quicker on the uptake than others. The man who coined the phrase "nanosecond nineties," for example, former McKinsey consultant turned rebel Tom Peters, has had more catchphrases than just about anyone in the guru game. More recently, his catchphrase has been: "Crazy times call for crazy organizations."

Over the years, too, not only Peters's catchphrases but his book titles have become progressively catchier. His 1980s seminal work with Robert Waterman, *In Search of Excellence*, for example, had by the mid-1990s evolved into *The Pursuit of Wow!* His next book? *In Search of a New Catchphrase*, maybe.

It is unfair, of course, to reduce the work of any writer to a single sentence. But the move toward the catchphrase culture seems to confirm the emergence of what can best be described as a new troupe of "management entertainers," whose primary function seems to be to entertain and stimulate rather than to inform their audience—a point underlined by a picture of Peters on the cover of one book dressed in jacket and tie with Bermuda shorts—or is it his boxer shorts?

It was the former head of Scandinavian Air Services, Jan Carlzon, who said: "All business is show business." How right he was. The trouble with this is that it leads to business schools' getting sucked into the fashion business. Lured by the promise of publicity, professors are susceptible to focusing research on sexy topics—ones that can be easily converted into consultancy products. The current interest in so-called soft skills can also lead to soft thinking and soft research.

As Carlos Cavallé, dean of IESE, notes: "There is a growing interest in everything on the human side. The softer skills if you like. But also attitudes. Social responsibility is not a skill like communication or negotiation. Research in these areas can be worthwhile. But some areas are ephemeral. For me intuition is in that category. A lot of noise but nothing left at the end but a bad smell. There is no stream of research to build on. It is a fashion thing. There is a danger that business schools follow whatever is popular at the time. If you think about it as fashions for clothes—if you like a yellow tie, then go buy a yellow tie, but I think blue and green ties will be more useful in the long run."

None of this is a big problem (after all, as Dean Cavallé says, you pays your money and you takes your choice) except that it makes it hard for someone doing serious research to get the message across. (This is not the same thing as the business school professor who has spent ten years calculating the correlation between paper clips and profit and thinks it should be on the front page of the *Wall Street Journal* and every other newspaper in the world—and there are plenty of them around.)

It can, although it needn't, involve a dumbing down of business thinking. Interesting is good. But it is no substitute for quality ideas. Some people think the answer lies in taking the best business school thinking and adding some razzmatazz.

GHOSTS IN THE MACHINE

Media-friendliness is just part of the makeover. They may run programs on niche marketing and customization, but academics find the mass market impossible to resist. Where they might once have written for the approbation of their peers, today, business school academics want to appeal to a wider audience. For many, it is no longer sufficient to be published in academic journals, they want to reach the wider business population through newspapers and business magazines. They want to be in show biz.

This brings them into competition with a wide variety of other writers. Most obviously, there are other academics, but increasingly, too, the business school professors are in competition with management gurus, pundits, columnists, and an array of charlatans.

TO GURU OR NOT TO GURU, THAT IS THE QUESTION

What makes someone stellar faculty? Hard to say. Timing is important, being in the right place at the right time with the right idea has got many a guru started. But based on the ones we've met over the years, we'd say that to stay at the top they need some other characteristics. An original turn of mind helps, but in most cases there is also an indecipherable mix of charisma, academic gravitas, and street credibility. They are typically very bright people and know it, which can manifest itself as arrogance or alternatively as disarming modesty (real or projected). A deep competitive streak is also par for the course, along with a genuine fascination with the activity of business.

Overall, to be a serious contender for the major leagues, it helps to have some of the following:

- The name of a major business school on your résumé. (Harvard is good, so is Stanford. In Europe, INSEAD, LBS, or IMD are popular.)
- Some serious academic research under your belt.
- A best-selling business book (or two) to your name (mass market).
- A particular concept or area that people associate with you. Best of all is to actually coin the concept by giving it a popularizing name. (Actual originality is less important—most new concepts are old ones with a new twist.)
- A regular place on the guru speaking circuit, flitting effortlessly and with very few changes to your speech from one major event to another.
- The nerve to charge a ridiculously large fee (plus excessive expenses) to turn up and give the same talk you've given hundreds of times before.
- Polished performing skills—somewhere between a stand-up comedian and a university lecturer.
- An animated delivery style—shout a lot and bang your fist on the lectern.
- The knack of turning complex ideas into punchy one-liners.

Sales and publicity are the fuel that transforms professors into gurus. This desire for publicity is seen in the involvement of academics in the burgeoning business of ghostwriting. For those who seek fame and fortune, there is a whole industry that has grown up to package them and their ideas for the mass market. What price academic credibility when you didn't even write the book? Business school professors appear quite happy to go along with this Faustian pact.

If you open *Jamming* by Harvard Business School academic John Kao you read plaudits to "Donna Sammons Carpenter and her extraordinary team of creative talents." Ms. Carpenter is a busy woman. In *Reengineering the Corporation* by consultants James Champy and Michael Hammer, the authors pay tribute to "Donna Sammons Carpenter, Tom Richman, and Abby Solomon, whose extraordinary editorial skills helped turn an inchoate mass into a coherent narrative." She is also mentioned by Tom Peters in *The Circle of Innovation* and others of his books. Michael Treacy and Fred Wiersma were grateful to her for her work on *The Discipline of Market Leaders*. Michael Milken and Senator John Kerry are also thankful for her editorial support in their literary endeavors.

Ms. Carpenter is, according to *Business Week*, "the Queen of ghostwriters" and CEO of her own ghostwriting factory, Wordworks, in Boston, Massachusetts. (The location, within striking distance of Harvard and MIT, is no coincidence.) In just over ten years, Wordworks has all but cornered the market in business blockbusters. Its service covers everything. It writes, edits, and researches. It will put you in touch with an agent and even send along one of its staff to hold your hand at a key interview. It cannot guarantee a bestseller, but its track record is exceptional.

Almost single-handedly, Wordworks has rewritten the economics of business book publishing. Traditionally, an author receives an advance on royalties from the publisher. In the United States, where the market for business books is substantial, sizable advances are commonplace. An author who is using a ghostwriter—or a company such as Wordworks—will usually enter into a separate agreement with them. The trouble is that in many cases the publishers' advances fail to cover the ghostwriting charges. The author is effectively using the book as a loss leader, the ultimate calling card to open doors for consulting business, to secure engagements on the lucrative speaking circuit or to further an academic career.

In some ways, such arrangements are a dream ticket. The publisher is happy. From its point of view, ghostwriters are useful because they mean that it is likely that a manuscript will be delivered more or less on time—journalists meet deadlines, academics tend not to, and consultants are usually too busy making money—and that it will be more or less readable. These are highly persuasive factors. For publishers, ghostwriters often represent no additional expense or risk.

The ghostwriter is also usually happy. One calculation of the fees Wordworks charges put them at a massive $60,000 for a mere proposal—suggesting that Wordworks staff are going to produce something pretty persuasive. Alternatively, a complete book project could cost $300,000. (Fees for ghosts range from $20,000 to $200,000 depending on the project.) In addition, Wordworks receives royalties. Clearly, in such deals, only massive book sales would allow the authors to recoup their costs.

The final winner is the so-called author with the calling card. It is a card with a substantial price tag. Winning is expensive. Some consultants go a stage further by employing a ghostwriter and then buying thousands of copies of their own books to distribute to clients. This can also ensure they reach the best-seller lists. Most famously the authors of *The Discipline of Market Leaders* arranged the purchase of over 10,000 copies of their book. James Champy bought 7,500 copies of his *Reengineering Management*. There is, as yet, no evidence that academics indulge in this particular practice.

Of course, ghostwriting is nothing new. Sports stars have been using ghosts for years and the recent flurry of celebrity novels proves that the fictional ghost is alive and well. What is new is that

Wordworks has created an industry and others are entering the fray. Journalists can increasingly be found credited for their input into business books.

Ken Shelton, editor of the newsletter *Executive Excellence*, is the ghost behind one of the biggest business best-sellers of all time, Stephen R. Covey's *Seven Habits of Highly Effective People*. Shelton has also worked on *Smart Talk* by Lou Tice, *Managing People Is Like Herding Cats* by Warren Bennis, *Twenty-First Century Leadership* by Larry Senn and Lynn MacFarland, and is currently working on *Twenty-One Keys of Success*. He argues that ghostwriting is simply part of a media process that is radically different from the traditional one. "Publishing today implies multimedia presentation. Often the book is merely part of a package of product that follows a certain line of thought," says Shelton. "The package may include audiotapes, video-based training, CD-ROM games, presentations, and speeches. Covey's *Seven Habits* book, for example, was the last item in the *Seven Habits* product line—the cherry on top." But what a cherry—*Seven Habits* has sold over six million copies.

Another star name in the ghostwriting pack is the writer and researcher Art Kleiner. In his own right, Kleiner is author of the successful book *The Age of Heretics*. As a ghost, his credits are many and varied—he worked as "a consulting editor" on *The Fifth Discipline* by MIT's Peter Senge, *The Art of the Long View* by Peter Schwartz (who teaches at Berkeley's Haas School), *Control Your Destiny* by Noel Tichy (of the University of Michigan), *The Last Word on Power* by Tracy Goss, and other less prominent volumes. "Many businesspeople don't know how to convert their speaking insights to the printed page," says Kleiner. Similarly, the average consultant is adept at putting together a consultant-style report with lots of diagrams and analysis, and in giving a stirring end-of-project presentation. But when it comes to writing a book, consultants can come unstuck. Enter the ghost.

Academics are similarly limited. The tortured prose of academic journals is hardly likely to set the pulse racing. Real money comes from big sales and, even in the rampant business book market, dense academic treatises do not sell. So they too call for the ghost. Arie de Geus's *Living Company*, for example, was one of the most acclaimed business books of 1997. De Geus is now based at London Business School. "It took Nan Stone, then a senior editor at the *Harvard Business Review*, a week of her annual leave to coach me through the material and to help me arrive at the conclusion that, after all, it might be worth a try," de Geus says in the introduction.[7] "Nan Stone persuaded Art Kleiner, historian and author, to reshape the manuscript around its main theme of 'the living company'." It is up to the reader to determine whether the involvement of the editor of the *Harvard Business Review* and a well-known writer in his own right adds or detracts from the value of the book.

Ken Shelton believes that ghostwriting is an inevitable and useful editorial service. "Many *authors* can't or won't write. But they may be very gifted as thinkers, presenters, synthesizers, commentators, speakers, or entertainers," says Shelton. "I often use a track and field metaphor. If a person is world-class at the four-hundred-meter hurdles, does that mean that the same person should also be world-class at the hundred-meter sprint, the mile run, the high jump, or the marathon?"

The process that lies behind ghostwriting is far removed from the traditional publishing process where someone has an idea for a book and approaches a publisher. "There are parallels with the film industry. You get the star and build the project around the star," says Timothy Clark of King's College. "We are moving away from the origins of management books—the Peter Drucker–style academic—into the entertainment industry."

Indeed, the idea for a book can play a secondary role to the marketing plan. "It is very difficult for authors to break through," says literary agent John Willig, who represents over forty authors. "Publishers spend a lot of time discussing the author's marketing activities—they can spend as much time on that as on the actual contents of the book. The big change over recent years is that authors are communicators of their ideas whether through speaking engagements, Web sites, workshops. The book is just one part of supporting the message."

What happens once a ghost has been identified differs from case to case. "A ghost will interview the author and write a first draft of the material, possibly then writing a second or third draft as well, and then helping with final edits," says Art Kleiner. "But it varies. Different authors prefer different types of working relationships. Many times ghosts will not do research or vice versa."

The Wordworks approach is to allow the "authors" to concentrate on what they are good at. "A lot of the authors are very experienced speakers. Typically we outline each chapter and then ask the writer to give a presentation. It maintains the person's voice," says Wordworks's Donna Carpenter. "We are good at identifying whether lack of content is going to be a problem. It is much easier to edit someone who has a lot of material, shaping and pruning it." A typical Wordworks book will go through many drafts before publication—perhaps as many as forty—and the timescale for each differs from ninety days to the more usual one year to eighteen months.

While some, like Tom Peters, are noted for their willingness to generously spread the credit, others can be more reticent. The matter of how and where the ghost is credited is significant. Many get their name on the cover—though it is usually in much smaller typeface than the more famous name. This is understandable. Big names sell books. "There are very often two names on business books and often it's the first person who is primarily responsible for the promotion of the book—so much so that one tends to forget there was another person involved," says California-based book publicist Kathryn Hall, who represents the likes of Margaret Wheatley, Peter Block, and David Whyte. "I would prefer that the standard would be that if someone is going to be acknowledged as a writer that he or she deserve that recognition. I also know that there are successful collaborations in which someone is a good idea person and a great presenter, but not a writer. In this case I think a collaborative effort would be a win-win-win situation. We all win."

As professional writers, we would like to see greater transparency here. Surely it is not too hard to acknowledge the generation of original ideas and their packaging and presentation from different sources. (No one, after all, expects the stars of Hollywood to write their own scripts.) At present, however, while some ghosts make the cover but miss out on the promotional tour of Alaska, others have their name on the inside title page or buried at the bottom of the dust jacket. It is increasingly common to find ghostwriters included in lengthy lists of acknowledgments. There is therefore an art in discovering if a book has been ghostwritten. Euphemisms abound. "Most ghosts are acknowledged in the acknowledgments as consulting editors or some such. You can usually find them," says Art Kleiner. "Often ghosts take part in writing the acknowledgments about themselves, which is unfortunate because they often shortchange themselves. It's part of the ghosting personality to shortchange oneself since one has to be a bit self-effacing to take on the job in the first place." While most ghostwriters receive some sort of credit, others are forgotten completely—and their contract forbids their declaring their involvement.

It should be emphasized that there is nothing illegal with any of this. Ghostwriting is legal, yet another service in a service society. But is it decent? We would argue no—not in its present form. But we accept that the ethics of ghostwriting provide an interesting area for debate. To some it is merely a matter of providing a service. "Ghostwriting could be abused but, as practiced in business books, I think it's ethical," says bookseller and ghost Ted Kinni. "I don't know of an instance where the ideas, concepts, or story were not the listed author's. It is the presentation and readability that the ghost has created. Ghostwriting is unacceptable when the content of the book, the boiled-down thinking or story, is not the credited author's. If a ghost has good business ideas then he or she should take the credit." To Kinni, ghostwriting is commercial good sense:

"As a writer, if Intel's Andy Grove called me to ghost, I'd rather have his name on the book than mine. He's the message, I'm just the medium."

The obvious point of departure is whether the person credited on the cover is actually the author in any shape or form. Stories are recounted of so-called *authors* who have never actually read their book and of a well-known management academic who produced a book simply by dictating into tapes for twenty hours and then handing the tapes over to a ghost. Given such stories—and not all are apocryphal—some suspect that the point of no return has been passed. "The problem with ghostwritten books," says Tom Brown, who collates a top ten book list published on the Management General Web site, "is that they often camouflage or misrepresent the ideas of the author. In the best case, such books are often rhetorically enhanced, so that the name on the book cover sounds much more provocative, savvy, or deep than he or she really is. In the worst case, the book actually presents the ideas of the writer instead of the author—so whose book is it really? And which person should be making speeches around the world on its behalf?

"At least a book that lists a name on the cover *with* another name as writer makes it clear to the reader that, if in doubt, either person can be approached and interviewed. But a full-hidden ghostwritten book does a disservice first and foremost to the person who finds himself the author of a best-seller and is, because of that, tongue-tied in more ways than one."

Not surprisingly, those who have taken the trouble to write books by themselves feel slightly deflated. "I am absolutely appalled at the number of synthetic business books that, worse still, are labeled as organic," says Eileen Shapiro, author of *Fad Surfing* and *The Seven Deadly Sins of Business*. "Brands imply promises. If you buy a cereal from Kellogg's, you expect the product to meet the Kellogg's standards in all respects. The problem with ghosts is that they write well enough that they can make mediocre ideas sound compelling, even when the thinking is weak."

The genius of good writers is that they can disguise lack of content. They can make a silk purse out of a pile of tapes and thirty minutes in the great man's presence. It is worth looking closely at books that are supposedly based on research. The research can prove elusive. The ghost constructs a smooth edifice—uncluttered by such things as bibliographies or references—picking up ideas from here and there, crafting them into something that appears original and important. At best (from a literary standpoint), the ghostwritten business book is a smoothly written mirage.

Some may shrug their shoulders at concerns about the authenticity of business books. Does it really matter that a journalist honed the prose a little and dug around to find a few case studies? Probably not. But clearly if the ghost originates ideas it becomes more dubious. One of the great paradoxes of modern management is that a profession dominated by action should be so driven by theory. In business, books and the ideas they contain affect people throughout the world. "People do not read a John Grisham book and then change their company. Business books affect management actions," says Timothy Clark. "I know of companies where someone has read a book and then bought copies for everyone on the board. Then they have turned around and said let's do it. That then feeds into management education. Their work is reported on. It becomes a case study. Given this there must be some sort of ethical responsibility on publishers." Not surprisingly, publishers tend to argue that it is the quality of ideas that counts rather than the beauty of the prose. The quality of ideas, however, appears to be precisely what is missing.

6

Strings Attached?

Universities exist for learning and research. Business schools are geared to applicable knowledge. There has to be some responsibility for business schools to put what they say into practice, to stand on their own two feet. It is embarrassing to call yourself a business school and then go around fundraising. While charities are trying to behave more like businesses, business schools are acting more like charities.

—Eddie Obeng,
founder of Pentacle—The Virtual Business School

There is a long tradition of universities' being funded by donations from wealthy benefactors. In most cases, this largesse is inspired by a combination of philanthropy and ego. Most benefactors have wanted to make a contribution to society and to leave a lasting memorial to themselves. There is no harm in this. In fact, many important seats of learning have been built on such gestures. The same applies to former students who donate money to their alma mater when they are in a position to do so.

When it comes to business schools, however, fundraising has taken on new dimensions. Compared with other providers of education and even within their own universities, most business schools are wealthy institutions. Much of their money comes from donations from private citizens and corporations, or is income generated by selling services to corporate clients through executive education programs. To date, business schools have benefited from this additional source of revenue without compromising their integrity. In most cases, academic standards have been kept separate from the demands of customers, although, arguably, the flow into the already well-stocked business school coffers diverts money from other, more needy areas of education.

In the next few years, the water is likely to get muddier as more and more business schools become involved in consultancy-style relationships with corporate clients. This raises important issues. In particular, the current tax rules governing the activities that U.S. university business schools are able to engage in are out of line with those governing European schools—a recipe for trouble. Moreover, as more business schools are asked to provide executive development programs leading to accredited qualifications—a development that can already be seen in the growth of company MBAs—the pressures on academic standards are likely to increase. These issues require urgent clarification.

In this chapter we argue that greater transparency is essential in the future if business schools are to retain their independence of thought and action. At present, there are a number of areas where important issues are being fudged or simply ignored.

In particular, we believe that

- Fundraising from alumni and the companies they work for should be more transparent.
- The question of what benefactors receive for their money should be addressed directly.
- The way all business schools are funded should be a matter of public record.

- The more-is-better attitude toward spending that prevails in many business schools should be reevaluated and the value of projects balanced against other educational needs. (At present, business schools behave like hotels, competing on the basis of new facilities. This diverts limited funds from more important areas of education.)
- The tax status of business schools should be reviewed, and business schools made accountable through an independent audit process.

PAYBACK TIME

This is what happens when you go to business school. You pay a fortune for a high-quality business education. Perhaps you give up your job. Anyway, you make sacrifices. Your family is forgotten as you plow through Kotler on marketing, Porter on competitiveness, Drucker on everything. You drink a lot of coffee to keep you awake and then you emerge with an MBA. Suddenly, the world owes you a living. You get a well-paid job, which leads to an even better-paid job. Material wealth ensues. You start paying the business school back. Just to say thanks. You become active in the alumni network, make a few speeches, sign regular checks. Nothing too onerous. It's the least you can do. Look what they did for you. They took your money in exchange for their services. That's capitalism. Why turn it into charity?

London Business School is housed in a Georgian-fronted building on the edge of Regent's Park. If you cross the streams of traffic heading to Baker Street and walk fifty meters, you come to a building site. It is as dirty and as chaotic as any other such site. But here, hard-hatted workmen are erecting a building that, it is hoped, will give LBS resources fit for the new millennium. The four-year project will cost around £20 million ($32 million) and should be completed by

2000. It will bring the school a new library and a fully equipped health and fitness center, as well as thirty additional bedrooms and ancillary offices.

For any institution such a project would represent a substantial undertaking and investment. Twenty million pounds is a great deal of money. It is an awful lot of executive programs. To put it into perspective: during the financial year 1996–1997, LBS received £5.2 million ($8.32 million) from executive program fees. Indeed, the school's turnover in the last year was £33.4 million ($53.4 million), leaving it with £2.3 million ($3.68 million) to "transfer to reserve."

Compare this to the corporate world—the bottom company in the Financial Times Top 500 U.K. companies ranking is Time Products, with a turnover of £102.3 million ($163.68 million) and profits of £22 million ($35.2 million).

Finance for London Business School's new Taunton Place development has come from a variety of sources. Lord and Lady Sainsbury of Turville have given "in excess of £1 million." Lord Sainsbury is chairman of the school's governors. Corporate support has come from Andersen Consulting, the Wellcome Foundation (over £100,000—$160,000), the British Land Company, and Hanson and Midland Bank, among others. Individual backers include Mr. and Mrs. Ian Laing and Roger Carlsson. The curiously named "29th May 1961 Charitable Trust" has chipped in with a donation "in excess of £250,000" ($400,000).

According to a colorful brochure, the development also "offers a range of naming opportunities." For £5 million ($8 million) you can have the entire building named after you. The cheapest naming opportunity on offer is one of the sixteen seminar rooms, a bargain at £100,000 ($160,000) each. Even reception areas are available.

To some this is crass commercialism. To others it is straightforward good business. An unsurprising member of the second camp is Bill Conner, London Business School's director of development. The American Conner formerly raised money at the San Francisco Opera House, Boston University, and elsewhere. "The process in arts and education is fairly similar. You earn loyalty when the curtain goes up," says Conner. His last project prior to moving to London brought in $100 million. "It is all about philanthropy, supporting the community, giving something back to the community which has enabled you to succeed," he says, adding the important rider, lest you suspect it is a simple business—"Philanthropy becomes ever more competitive."

In addition, the appointment of a dean with American-style marketing experience is liable to put LBS alumni under even greater pressure. If you graduated from the London Business School and are now flourishing at the top of a profitable company, watch out. John Quelch, the new dean, is after you—and your company's money. When it came to choosing the successor to George Bain as principal of Britain's premier business school, the governors wanted someone who could hustle successfully for loads of money, in particular for the £20 million building extension program, and a strong leader with the marketing expertise to promote the LBS franchise around the world. In Quelch, they felt they had found someone to do both.

The competition to secure funding increasingly comes from other business schools. The issues facing LBS are common throughout the business school world. Schools believe that they have to invest in resources, faculty, facilities, technology, and infrastructure to keep ahead of the competition. If they are not in the market for the top professors, they are falling behind. If they do not have a state-of-the-art IT center, they will be quickly consigned to history. More is good.

As a result, all the major business schools are caught in a relentless cycle of fundraising and building. Some are better at it than others—one business school actually managed to spend more money on a particular fundraising campaign than it received.

In 1995, LBS's arch rival INSEAD launched the INSEAD Campaign, which aimed to raise 700 million French francs ($115 million) for a major expansion program at the school. When Don Jacobs became dean of Northwestern's Kellogg School in 1974, one of his first decisions was to build an executive center. Others have followed suit. Jacobs now laments: "It's cute to be emulated but it's a pain in the neck. Wharton has built an executive center; Columbia had an off-campus center. Harvard had an executive center. Now they're going to have to build a nicer executive center. Stanford's finished the Schwab Center." In the world of one-upmanship, the school with the biggest executive development center is king—for a while at least. The right facilities pay dividends.

Business schools compete as hotels and restaurants as well as academic institutions. Catering is important. A staggering 8 percent of INSEAD's income comes from catering and accommodation. At one school the food is so good that faculty tend to overindulge—to the extent that the heart bypass surgery rate is high. Too much rich food blocks arteries, but it is what pampered executives expect. Similarly, bedroom occupancy is increasingly a measure of how successful a business school is.

Choose Your Targets

The trouble with analysis is that sometimes it can run counter to that other important area of business life—common sense. Numbers can blind people. Goals can become detached from the real world. Even learned professors can make daft suggestions. At one business school, for example, there was a fraught meeting as the managing committee of academics contemplated performance. The problem was simple. The school was failing to meet its percentage targets for room occupancy. Too many of the residential bedrooms were lying empty. A silence fell over the brightly polished table. The assembled academics stared into the distance or at their notepads as they contemplated this thorny problem. How could they meet targets? Then one academic spoke up. Luckily he was a strategist, so there was high hope he would provide a carefully formulated long-term solution. "Why don't we close down part of the residential block. Then, I think you will find, we are meeting our targets." Silence resumed. It would be laughable if it wasn't for the fact that the same sort of b-school-inspired wooly thinking passes for strategy in other organizations too.

The merry-go-round continues. In 1997 Chicago announced it

was spending $4.3 million on refurbishing its four main classrooms and student lounge and cafeteria. This is par for the course. An extension here, improvements there. As we write, major investments in buildings are bearing fruit throughout the world. In April 1999, Harvard opened a new executive education housing facility, McArthur Hall (with 170 bedrooms). In February, HBS faculty gathered for a groundbreaking ceremony for its next project, the Spangler Canter, a multipurpose campus facility. Among others groundbreaking as we wrote were Weatherhead School of Management at Case Western Reserve University, Champam University School of Business and Economics, Claremont Graduate School, Middle Tennessee State University College of Business, University of North Carolina at Chapel Hill, Shippensburg University's Grove College of Business, and University of Texas at San Antonio College of Business. Many more could be added to the list.

Of course, there is no law stating that all business schools must compete in this way. But who is going to make the first move and declare that teaching is more important than bathroom suites and fitness programs? There are similarities with the airline business, in which, for decades, competition for business class passengers has concentrated on leg room, seat design, and providing a steady supply of peripherals—in-flight magazine, free drinks, boiled sweets. Business schools have sought to turn themselves into high-tech hotels with one added extra after another. As we have seen, for some, room occupancy is an important measure of success.

This means that low-cost niche operators have a multitude of opportunities to eat into the management development market. Over the last decade a huge number of smaller alternative providers have emerged with lower overheads, fewer thrills, and different approaches.

BANKING ON ALUMNI

The corollary of the competitive rule that more is better is that the better you are at fundraising the more resources and facilities you can afford. And, as a result, the more successful you will be. Fundraising therefore is the competitive lifeblood of the modern business school. (This explains why one school reputedly pays its chief fundraiser more than it pays its dean.)

The first stop for fundraisers is the roster of business school alumni. Most of the great and the good of the modern corporate world have attended a business school in some capacity or run companies that have strong links with a particular school. The begging bowl usually comes in thinly disguised form—the personal letter from the school's dean, the invitation to a speech by a famous alumnus or politician, the summer drinks get-together. It is about as subtle as any other method of extracting money from you.

The growth in numbers of MBA graduates mean that there is now a huge reservoir of alumni waiting to be tapped. France's INSEAD, for example, has 17,755 alumni, regarded as "INSEAD's ambassadors worldwide." Its International Alumni Association was formed in 1960 and in 1976 an Alumni Fund was created. There are now thirty national INSEAD alumni associations. Alumni were earmarked to raise 10 percent of the 700-million-franc INSEAD Campaign.

In the past, in Europe at least, alumni associations were generally seen as networking groups. Now they are regarded by the schools as potential sources of revenue. European schools increasingly have entire departments dedicated to meeting the needs of alumni. It is difficult to think of another industry in which ex-customers—who are often unlikely to return to the fold—are so assiduously courted. Or, for that matter, are so generous with their attentions.

The benchmark for European schools is the American system. In the United States, alumni are unashamedly tapped for every cent. American alumni associations are formidable networking and money-raising operations. Graduation is payback time. There is no escape—not that many are running. Entrepreneur Sam Wyly, for example, recently gave $10 million to his alma mater, the University of Michigan Business School in Ann Arbor, to help it expand its facilities. Wyly, who worked for IBM and Honeywell before founding University Computing Business in 1963, took his MBA at Michigan, graduating in 1957. His donation will go toward the cost of a new building to provide additional office and classroom space.

Private American colleges can typically raise money from half their alumni. "It is accepted. Every year you send in a check," says LBS's Bill Conner. "In Europe we have to earn loyalty in a more proactive way. At the moment only 13 percent of alumni from our two-year MBA program are donors and the figure is 6 percent for the one-year program."

The American emphasis is on mutual benefits. Networking is still important—and donations are the price you pay for a ready-made international network. Harvard is in the process of introducing personalized e-mail addresses so that 66,000 of its alumni can contact each other and find out about the school on the Internet. Typical news from Northwestern's Kellogg Graduate School of Management reports on alumni events in Australia, Canada, Hong Kong, Japan, the Philippines, and Singapore, as well as throughout the United States. Its alumni network covers eighty-three countries. Thanks to this network, Kellogg is now armed with endowments in excess of $200 million.

Or take six months in the life of the Wharton School of the University of Pennsylvania. When Tom Gerrity took over as dean, building up the school's endowments was one of his prime objectives. He has been outstandingly successful. In January 1997 the family of Jon Huntsman of the Huntsman Chemical Corporation gave $10 million to endow an undergraduate program in international studies and business. Jon Huntsman is an alumnus of Wharton's undergraduate class of 1959. At the same time, another Wharton alumnus, Leonard Lauder, weighed in with $10 million to further endow the Joseph H. Lauder Institute of Management and International Studies.

Despite their generosity, Huntsman and Lauder remain unconvinced about the usefulness of MBA programs. "We don't hire

MBAs. Most of the people who work here started out at lowly jobs behind the counter selling our products or working in the office as secretaries or assistants. These people are running the business now. They know what the customer wants," Leonard Lauder told *Forbes* magazine. Jon Huntsman said, "I went to night school to get an MBA. I should have utilized that time to set up more businesses. True entrepreneurs get out of school as fast as they can and get on with life."[1]

After these donations got the year off to a flying start, in March Ed Snider (chairman of Comcast Spectacor) donated $2 million to support the work of the school's Sol C. Snider Entrepreneurial Center, which he himself had endowed in 1985 to honor his father, a Russian immigrant who created a chain of supermarkets in Washington, D.C. Then, in June 1997, Wharton announced the creation of the Goergen Entrepreneurial Management Program, with a $10 million gift from Robert B. Goergen, chairman and CEO of Blyth Industries. Explaining his largesse, Goergen (a 1962 Wharton MBA graduate) said, "Wharton provided me with many of the tools and skills responsible for my business track record. Moreover, I'm a strong supporter of the entrepreneurial spirit in America, which creates business growth and increases employment and prosperity. Given Wharton's unrivaled reputation in fostering this spirit, the gift is intended to help the School prepare the next generation of business leaders by adding depth and breadth to its entrepreneurial management faculty."[2] With $32 million in headline-making donations—on top of its constant stream of smaller donations—the entrepreneurial spirit already appears alive and well at Wharton.

Not surprisingly given its reputation and resources, Harvard Business School has a smooth operation. HBS has categories of donor so you know where you stand—and, more important, how much others have given. The lowest rank is to be a "participating donor" (giving up to $249); then you progress up the scale—subscribing donor, supporting donor, sustainer, sponsor, patron, benefactor, leadership donor, leadership fellow, and finally entering hallowed ground and becoming a leadership associate with a gift of over $100,000. You can give to Harvard any number of ways. Charmed? You will be.

Harvard also has a sizable HBS Fund, established in 1949 under the leadership of Frank L. Tucker (MBA Class of 1930). Today the fund is headed by Thomas C. Theobald (MBA Class of 1960) and a volunteer corps of nine hundred alumni. During the 1996–1997 fund year, gifts and pledges exceeded $28 million, thanks to the generosity of over twelve thousand donors who participated as part of their class reunion gift campaigns or annual giving. (This makes for an average donation of $2,333.) Approximately 31 percent of MBA alumni supported the HBS Fund in 1997.

Names on Plates

Why do alumni give so generously? After all, many who study for an MBA are paying out of their own pocket. They are buying a product and a hefty endowment appears an overly generous tip.

First, there is a degree of snobbery. Alumni appear more willing to give donations to business schools—commercial ventures—than to universities, which are usually more needy. There appears more cachet in giving a donation to Harvard Business School than to Boston University even if the experiences that shaped your personality were at the latter.

Second, there is a self-perpetuating element to the matter of alumni fundraising. Alumni are almost obliged to continue to support their school. Inverse blackmail is at work. After all, the value of an MBA lies in where you took it rather than whether you covered global marketing in the second semester. By giving to your alma mater you are seeking to ensure that its standards remain high and that, as a result, your résumé resounds with intellectual gravitas. If your résumé boasts an MBA from a school that has since collapsed through lack of funds, its impact is lessened.

More cynically, some make donations as a statement of how wealthy they are and how seriously they take the education of the

FILLING THE COFFERS

The number of ways to leave your lover are more than matched by the number of ways you can give money to Harvard Business School.[3] The HBS Fund raked in gifts and pledges in excess of $28 million in 1996–1997. Its tactic is simply to give the donor as many ways to give money as possible. So many that the major decision is not how much, but how? They include the following:

- *Outright gift*. Tax efficient. "You may give cash, securities, closely held stock, real estate, and tangible personal property such as art." Monets welcome.
- *Life income gifts*. The Harvard Management Company manages the assets (minimum $10,000) and the donor receives an income. The Pooled Income Funds include the Harvard Balanced Fund, Harvard Growth Fund, International Bond Fund, and so on).
- *Charitable remainder trusts*. For $100,000-plus the donor can set up an individually managed trust.
- *Retained life estates*. For those who are extremely grateful indeed for their education. "With this plan, you can give your principal residence to HBS while retaining the right to live in it for the rest of your life." As an extra attraction, "a class gift credit is available for alumni who graduated 50 or more years ago."
- *The Cornerstone Society*. More appropriately the Tombstone Society. Membership is restricted to "all deferred-gift donors and those who notify the school that Harvard Business School is included in their estate plans."

next generation. Having a successful businessperson's name attached to a building or room or chair or program provides a constant message: join this program and you may end up as rich and as wise as the man who endowed it. But of all the needy causes in the world, a business school is not one whose need would place it high on the list.

For some, donations are memorials. For example, Michael Bloomberg, founder and president of Bloomberg Financial Markets and a member of the HBS class of 1966, gave the university a $3 million gift to establish the William Henry Bloomberg Professorship in honor of his late father.

The ultimate is to have an entire school named after you. This demands a great deal of money and an ego the size of a continent. There are no recorded examples of individuals endowing schools anonymously. There are a growing number of business schools with names attached. Cornell has its Johnson School of Management; Atlanta's Emory University boasts the Roberto C. Goizueta Business School, named after the late Coca-Cola chief. In 1979 the John L. and Helen Kellogg Foundation gave Northwestern University's School of Commerce a gift of $10 million. Mrs. Kellogg was curiously overlooked and the school was renamed the J. L. Kellogg Graduate School of Management. (Women are notable by their absence among the names of business school patrons.)

Strapped for Cash?

In courting benefactors business schools are merely following a well-established academic tradition. More than one Ivy League university, for example, would be short of a library without the largesse of some wealthy, public-spirited individual. But fundraising by business schools raises new issues and concerns.

First, there is the question of whether they really need all the money they suck into the coffers. After all, they are awesome cash generators in their own right. Second, their close relationship with business makes transparency and accountability much more important.

Are business schools really so desperate for cash that they need to hold out the begging bowl? A quick glance at the annual reports of the leading business schools shows that in fact they are perfectly able to generate a good income from the services they provide. (See the table captioned "In and Out" later in this chapter for a breakdown of the income of a selection of leading schools.) Chicago, for example, generates $22.5 million from its degree programs. You can buy a lot of computers with that. (Though one school we know of has already spent more money replacing computers that have gone missing or been borrowed by staff than it originally spent on updating its entire computing system.)

In fact, some people argue, not unreasonably, that it should be a test of a business school's competence that it should be able to manage itself in such a way that it is self-financing.

There are some, too, who object to business school fundraising on the grounds that it diverts cash from more needy causes. It is probably true that if you give a big donation to your old business school (which doesn't really need your money anyway) you won't give as much to your local college or school (which probably does). The same argument is also put forward by other academic disciplines, namely that the money flowing to business schools would otherwise be used for more useful purposes. Where a business school would invest in another new conference suite, another department might use the gift for something more mundane—books, for instance.

A note to alumni at Columbia, for example, recently reported: "Among the renovations in Uris Hall this summer is the Hepburn Lounge, which now has pale wood-finished walls with built-in large-screen televisions and a stereo." Lounge occupants, it said, could thank a 1955 alumnus for his generous support, and that of his family for several generations. Without that support, "the upgrade would not have been possible."

Paneled walls and built-in TVs are nice to have, but they have little to do with education. Sponsorship is more likely to be found for sexy projects. A state-of-the-art technology center full of the latest technical wizardry will grab media attention. An equally sophisticated internal network that provides on-line marking of assignments is unlikely to generate column inches. If sponsorship is used to raise the profile of the sponsor, it is prone to move with fashion rather than the long-term interests of the business school. The trouble here is that business schools appeal in a way that departments of medieval history do not. To what extent the money donated to business schools actually benefits society is questionable.

The second point is of more practical concern. In particular, there are some ethical issues—for example, what benefactors expect in return for their generosity. It's all very well for a university to take money from a software company to fund a professorship in the humanities. It is unlikely to affect either what is studied or the version of events that is reported. But when a business school takes money from the same company and then pontificates on the IT industry, things could become a little more gray.

One potential problem is that of control. "A company may say that sponsorship of a certain business school or a chair or even a room links with its brand image. It wants to be associated with developing people. But, in reality, it links you closely to a brand you have no control over," says Eddie Obeng of Pentacle—The Virtual Business School. The issue of control is two-sided. The business school has no control over its sponsor—the sponsor may go bankrupt, attract adverse publicity, or move into a business that many have ethical scruples about. Does the school really wish to be closely associated with an environmentally unsound company that issues profit warnings virtually daily and has just made tens of thousands of employees jobless? Equally, the sponsor has no control over the sponsored business school. What if the school gains bad publicity for the quality of its programs? Or what if the school accepts a larger donation from your arch rival?

Another minefield is that of independence. If a school names a conference center after a particular corporate sponsor, it may find it difficult to entice the sponsor's competitor to use the facilities.

Coca-Cola is unlikely to send its executives to sit at the feet of Pepsi-Cola-sponsored professors no matter who they are or where they are based.

A Gift Horse

In 1996, a donation of £20 million to Oxford University for creation of a new business school caused a furore. The donation, from Syrian businessman Wafic Rida Said, raises a number of issues about the funding of business schools in general. Some, though not all, of the debate at Oxford was to do with concerns about the influence Said would have over the governing body of the new school—the Said Business School, naturally. There were also concerns about his business activities. Some at the university questioned whether it was appropriate for a seat of learning such as Oxford to accept money from someone whose name had been linked to arms dealing. Student protestors carried a banner saying: "We don't want your bloody money." (If such moral judgments had been applied in earlier centuries, one suspects both Oxford and Cambridge would be short of a few colleges today.)

When the siting of the new school was discussed by the university's academics, several questioned the setup of the proposed foundation that was to run the Said Business School. They were especially concerned that the school's governing body would have six members appointed by the foundation and only four appointed by the university. Alexander Murray, doctor of medieval history at University College, opposed both the choice of site and what he called the university's "covert" procedures. "This was launched in the depths of the summer recess," he told the *Times*, "a favourite time for politicians to launch unpopular policies, as a fait accompli. Mr Said has insisted on secrecy, on speed, and on the central site for his foundation. I am struck by the degree we are beholden in this field to outside benefactors and this is why I find myself suspicious," he added. The constitution and the dignity of the oldest university in the English-speaking world were "more important than what we are told by potential benefactors."[4]

The objection that the university could be saddled with raising funds to match the donation was downplayed. Supporters pointed out that some £12 million had already been raised, and were confidently predicting that within six years the School of Management would be a net contributor to the university, bringing in something in the region of £300,000 ($495,000) a year.

Professor Mayer, who denied reports that Said had threatened to withdraw his donation if the proposed site fell through, added that occasional rumbling about management studies is not entirely unexpected as it takes most universities some time to accept new disciplines.

The motion to release the original site was defeated in Congregation by 259 votes to 215. Said subsequently relented on some of his demands, accepting less power over appointments at the school, and agreeing to an alternative site near the station. Construction of the Said Business School building is now under way, and is scheduled for completion in 2001.

Obviously, independence is integral to any worthwhile research. Research carried out to a preset agenda is the work of political think tanks. Research carried out by business schools needs to be untarnished by suggestions of bias or of an external agenda.

Sponsorship raises a number of other issues. If companies give a business school their money, do they receive the school's best research in return? Can companies dictate the research interests of faculty? The quick retort to this from business school academics is, "Of course not." But the reality is that business schools are pragmatic creatures usually willing to bite the ethical bullet when cash is on the table. Harvard Business School's leading thinker, John Kotter, is Konosuke Matsushita Professor of Leadership. He is also the author of *Matsushita Leadership: Lessons from the Twentieth Century's Most Remarkable Entrepreneur*. The title of Kotter's professorship and of his book may or may not be linked. Matsushita was undoubtedly an important and influential person worthy of such a study, but perhaps the two were best kept separate—they leave John Kotter, Harvard Business School, and business schools in general open to criticism. If you had enough money, could you make it a condition of giving $20 million to a school that the professor write a book about you?

The water around business school fundraising is getting murky. In 1996, *Business Week* reported, "Carnegie-Mellon University scrambled for a donor to create an endowed chair to keep a finance professor who was being courted by Northwestern University, according to sources close to the gift-giver. (The University denies a connection between Northwestern's offer and the chair.)"[5]

The waters will begin to clear only if the issues are addressed. Business schools need to clarify some points. Are they led by research or reality? Are they businesses or academic institutions? Is their brand for hire or does it aspire to be beyond reproach? The truth is that business schools exist in a never-never land. They are not universities with their strictly defined academic standards and fiercely guarded independent research. Nor are they businesses constantly looking to the bottom line. Indeed, most have tax-exempt status. They are awkward hybrids and confusion reigns.

The issue is particularly troubling at the present time because of two separate developments. One has to do with public accountability and the growing influence that business schools and their powerful alumni networks exercise on matters ranging from decisions about lucrative contracts to advice on government policy. The other has to do with the allocation of scarce funding from both the public and private sectors for university research across the board.

While there are many more issues raised by sponsorship, few are openly discussed by the schools. Some admit that there are no easy answers and that, sooner or later, the issues will have to be faced. "We have turned money down," says Henley Management College's principal, Ray Wild. When it comes to fundraising, Henley is among the most experienced European schools. Unlike some of its competitors it receives no central government money—and never has. For its fiftieth anniversary Henley raised £2.7 million, with the majority coming from companies rather than alumni. (INSEAD also prefers to target companies rather than individuals.) Henley has sponsored chairs and sponsored rooms, and also boasts ten thousand alumni worldwide. It even offers a Henley Visa Gold Card in association with Beneficial Bank—the Bank gives Henley a £10 donation for every new account and 0.25 percent of every card purchase.

"If people have conditions attached to a donation we would turn them down," says Professor Wild. "But we don't have no-go areas. The companies we would talk to would be the companies we are already working with. Ultimately, it has to be our decision."

Business schools generally appear willing to take the issue one step at a time. Asked if the school has a written policy on who it will and will not accept money from, London Business School's Bill Conner is honest: "There is nothing written down." Having spent six years fundraising in Miami, he is confident that donations are squeaky clean. The trouble with fundraising is that, however carefully you may tread, the mire is never far away.

In and Out

School (Total INCOME)	*INCOME source*	*Percent*
Chicago ($30 million)	MBA programs	75
	Sponsored research	5
	Annual fund	4
	Conference center income	4
	Endowments	5
	Other	7
Darden ($30 million)	Executive programs	48
	MBA programs	25
	Endowment income	20
	Other	7
Stanford ($44.2 million)	Gifts and endowment income	45
	Taught courses	55
IMD, Switzerland ($28.3 million)	MBA programs	9.5
	Corporate membership fees	18
	Executive programs	67
	Other	5.5
INSEAD, France ($49.5 million)	MBA programs	23
	Executive programs	49
	Gifts	9
	Accommodation and catering	8
	Other	11
London Business School, United Kingdom ($47.6 million)	Government grant	11
	Masters programs	29
	Accommodation and catering	8
	Sponsored research	15
	Executive programs	26

WHAT PRICE YOUR OWN BUSINESS SCHOOL?

The cost of having your name on a business school letterhead is rising. In 1979, you could have put your name on a small business school in Chicago called Northwestern for only $10 million. In 1980, your name could have adorned a nice southern business school at Duke University for $10 million. These were bargains.

In the mid-1980s the price rocketed. It cost Samuel Johnson $20 million to rename Cornell's b-school in 1986, and in 1988, it cost Leonard Stern $30 million to make NYU buy a new b-school letterhead.

For those prepared to look around, however, there are still bargains to be found. The Haas family gave their name to the business school at Berkeley—a real deal at $10 million in 1989. But they added another $8.75 million in 1992 for good measure. John Anderson's takeover of the UCLA name in 1986 cost a mere $15 million.

By the mid-1990s, prices had soared. In 1996, a donation of $33.5 million inspired the Owen Graduate School of Management at Vanderbilt University in Nashville, Tennessee. In that same year, a $30 million gift from the F. W. Olin Foundation ensured that the F. W. Olin Graduate School of Business went on the letterhead at Babson College, near Boston, Massachusetts.

And 1996 was also the year that Wafic Said paid £20 million (about $32 million) to have his name on the new business school at Oxford University. Sir Paul and Anne Judge, on the other hand, got a bargain, paying just £8 million ($12.8 million) to establish the Judge Institute at Cambridge University in 1990.

In 1997, Gordon Marshall gave USC $35 million for the pleasure of seeing his name in lights above the business school. An impressive $30 million-plus seems to be the going rate these days. But probably not for long—the once-obscure University of Arkansas College of Business Administration is now the Sam M. Walton College of Business Administration thanks to a $50 million donation.

Credit Cards Accepted: Major Donations to Business Schools

Year	Amount ($ million)	Donor	Recipient
1998	20*	J. B. Fuqua, founder, Fuqua Industries	Fuqua School of Management, Duke University
	40	Jon M. Huntsman, Huntsman Corp.	Wharton School, University of Pennsylvania
	20	Anonymous	School of Business, Penn State University at Erie
	50	Walton family	Sam M. Walton College of Business Administration, University of Arkansas
	30	Robert Emmett McDonough, founder and chairman, Remedy Temp	Georgetown University Business School
	20	Woodruff Foundation in recognition of achievements of Roberto Goizueta	Roberto C. Goizueta School, Emory University
	18	Larry Zicklin, managing principal, Neuberger & Berman, investment firm	Zicklin School of Business, Baruch College, City University of New York
	25	Darla D. Moore, president, Rainwater Inc., investment firm	The Darla Moore School of Business, University of South Carolina
	15	Robert H. Smith, president, Charles E. Smith Construction	Robert H. Smith School of Business, University of Maryland
	10	Karl Eller, chairman and CEO, Eller Media Co.	College of Business, University of Arizona
	10	Sam Wyly, Maverick Capital and Sterling Software	University of Michigan Business School
	10	Chen Fu Koo and sons	Wharton School, University of Pennsylvania
1997	35	Gordon S. Marshall, chairman, Marshall Industries	Gordon S. Marshall School of Management, University of Southern California
	30	Anonymous	University of St. Thomas Graduate School of Business

Credit Cards Accepted: Major Donations to Business Schools, continued

Year	*Amount ($ million)*	*Donor*	*Recipient*
1997	23	E. W. Kelley, chairman, Consolidated Products	Kelley School of Business, Indiana University
	18	Michael F. Price, mutual fund manager, Franklin Securities	Michael F. Price College of Business, University of Oklahoma
	10	Sam Wyly, Sterling Software, Sterling Commerce, Maverick Capital and Michaels Stores	School of Business Administration, University of Michigan
	10	Samuel Zell, financier and chairman, Equity Group Investments	Wharton School, University of Pennsylvania
1996	15	L. Lowry Mays, president and CEO, Clear Channel Communications	Lowry Mays College & Graduate School of Business, Texas A&M University
	15	Eric Gleacher, New York investment banker	Gleacher Center, Graduate School of Business, University of Chicago
	15	E. J. Ourso, businessman	E. J. Ourso College of Business Administration, Louisiana State University
	33.5	Ralph and Lulu Owen, founder, Equitable Securities Corp. and chairman, American Express	Owen Graduate School of Management, Vanderbilt University
1995	30	Franklin W. Olin Foundation	Franklin W. Olin Graduate School of Business, Babson College
	15	K. T. Lally, Niskayuna businessman	Kenneth T. & Thelma P. Lally School of Management & Technology, Rensselaer School of Management & Technology
1993	20	Max M. Fisher	Max M. Fisher College of Business, Ohio State University
1992	30	William Davidson, owner, Guardian Industries glassmakers and Detroit Pistons basketball team	University of Michigan School of Business

Year	Amount ($ million)	Donor	Recipient
1991	20	Eli Broad, chairman, president and CEO, Broad financial services; chairman, Kaufman & Broad Home Corp.	Eli Broad College of Business, Eli Broad Graduate School of Management, Michigan State University
	15	Emma Eccles Jones, schoolteacher (daughter of David Eccles, banker and industrialist)	David Eccles School of Business, University of Utah
1989	15	Family of Walter Haas Sr., president, Levi Strauss	Walter A. Haas School of Business, University of California at Berkeley
	15	Saul P. Steinberg, chairman and CEO Reliance Group, financial services company	Wharton School, University of Pennsylvania
1988	30	Leonard N. Stern, owner, the Hartz Group, pet supply company	Leonard N. Stern School of Business, New York University
	15	J. Willard Marriott Foundation (founder, Marriott Corporation)	J. Willard & Alice S. Marriott School of Business, Brigham Young University
	15	John M. Olin, industrialist	John M. Olin School of Business, Washington University (St. Louis)
1987	20	John Shad, former SEC chairman	Harvard Business School
1986	18	Curtis L. Carlson, chairman, Carlson Co.	Carlson School of Management, University of Minnesota
	15	John E. Anderson, lawyer and entrepreneur	Anderson Graduate School of Management, University of California, Los Angeles
	15	William E. Simon, politician and chairman, Westray Corporation	William E. Simon Graduate School of Business Administration, University of Rochester
1984	20	Samuel Curtis Johnson, CEO, SC Johnson & Co., Johnson wax products	Johnson Graduate School of Management, Cornell University

*Fuqua had already given Duke $17 million earlier.

7

Alumni Associations

The New Power Networks

The alumni are terrifically important. Former students are the greatest marketing opportunity that the school has—its own satisfied customers.

—John Quelch, dean of London Business School[1]

Networking has always been important in business as in other areas of life. The view you have of the traditional power networks—Ivy League, Oxbridge, Grandes Écoles, take your pick—probably depends on whether you attended one of these esteemed universities. More global in their reach, the leading business schools are creating new power networks. Again, your view of this development will depend on your affiliations.

The fact is that people don't go to the top business schools just for the learning; they go to join an elitist club, which has little to do with their ability as managers. Business schools encourage networking. They are right to do so. But we would make the following observation: management should not be an elitist activity. The interests of employees, shareholders, and customers are best served by creating a meritocracy among the management population. By all means reward talent—but don't elevate a diploma from a swanky business school above experience in the trenches.

The Ties That Bind

During 1997 London Business School wrestled with the thorny question of who was to succeed its departing principal, George Bain. From three hundred candidates selected by a leading headhunting company, the field was whittled down to three insiders (including Tom Robertson, who later departed for the Emory dean's job) and one outsider, Harvard's English-born John Quelch. On the selection board was Martin Sorrell, chief executive of advertising group WPP, who had met Quelch back in 1983 at Saatchi & Saatchi, where Quelch was a consultant and Sorrell, the company finance director. (Sorrell kept tactfully silent during Quelch's interview.) Eventually, Quelch was offered the job.

Surrounding this appointment are an array of connections and networks that are commonplace in the fraught political climate of academia. Before Quelch formally took over the post, London announced a new management team. This included Quelch (now reincarnated as dean rather than principal); Martin Sorrell (a Harvard Business School alumnus); Robert F. White (a Harvard Business School alumnus and managing director and founder of Bain Capital); and Jonathan Ledecky (entrepreneur and man behind US Office Products and Harvard Business School alumnus). We asked John Quelch if he planned to convert London Business School into a mini-Harvard. He replied: "No, that would be inappropriate." Quelch has also been a non-executive director of US Office Products and WPP Group.

DOOR OPENING TIME

Educated to the hilt, well networked, with contacts in high places, an army of business school graduates is on the march. They span the globe, and their influence extends far beyond the world of business. Forget the freemasons and other traditional business networks, the business school alumni associations are the new networks of power, influence, and affluence.

Of course, life is like that. We all use contacts and networks. It is just that some networks open more—and more lucrative—doors.

Part—some would say a big part—of the reason for going to business school is to make the right contacts. Belonging to a powerful professional network can be very advantageous to someone looking for a fast route to the executive suite. Along with the promise of a big salary at the end of it, graduates of the world's top business schools also get another benefit. The cherry on top of the business school cake is access to their school's alumni network. This is a network to die for.

According to the *Financial Times*, no fewer than a quarter of the directors of the Fortune 500 companies are Harvard alumni. That's a lot of doors.

Companies can come to resemble alumni outposts. The famous Wall Street doyen Morgan Stanley Dean Witter recruits heavily from nearby Columbia Business School. At the last count, the firm had no fewer than a hundred Columbia graduates at senior management levels—including fifty vice presidents, thirty principals, and twenty managing directors—Terry Meguid of Morgan Stanley & Co. and Brad Evans of the mergers and acquisitions division among them.

And the networks of power are continuously expanding as business school graduates move out of their corporate offices into other spheres. A number of leading politicians have MBAs and other business school qualifications tucked in their back pockets. Among them are INSEAD alumnus and ex-McKinsey man William Hague, now leader of the United Kingdom's Conservative party. Archie Norman, chairman of the supermarket chain Asda and deputy chairman of the Tory party, got his MBA from Harvard. On the other side of the British political divide is another INSEAD old boy, David Simon—now Lord Simon—the former chairman of BP who cashed in his shares in the company to become a leading light in Tony Blair's Labour government.

When President Clinton designated Janet Yellen, a professor of international trade at the Haas Business School at the University of California at Berkeley, to chair the President's Council of

Economic Advisers, it was the twelfth time he had appointed a Berkeley faculty member to a senior economic policy position. Yellen had been serving as a governor of the Federal Reserve System in Washington, D.C., and had been on leave from Haas since 1994. Her new role is an influential one, with responsibility for advising the president across a "vast array of economic policy areas."

Yellen follows in the footsteps of Laura Tyson, Bill Clinton's former chief economics adviser, who was recently appointed dean of the Haas Business School. Tyson was the president's first chair of the CEA. Other business school–educated politicos include former Senator William Proxmire, who earned his MBA at Harvard.

Officially, the business schools' alumni clubs help graduates develop their careers, update skills, make new contacts—and generally open doors in the world of business, politics, and beyond. At the bigger and better-known schools, the alumni networks are worldwide fellowships. From Boston to Beijing, and most cities in between, there will be a member of the alumni network who is only too pleased to make them feel at home. A couple of phone calls, and a graduate of Harvard Business School or one of the other top-tier schools can be sure of a friendly reception in most parts of the world. This makes life a lot easier than scrabbling around desperately for contacts.

THE INSEAD WAY

To understand the influence of the alumni networks of the top business schools, consider the French school INSEAD, among the best in the world. The influence of INSEAD's alumni association is legendary. In the beautiful forest of Fontainebleau, the former hunting ground of French kings, alumni meet at the famous châteaux. (Not one château, but five châteaux—although the school insists they are "small ones.") Introductions are made. Doors are opened. Deals are done. It is civilized, urbane, and integral to possessing an INSEAD MBA.

With 18,000 members, the INSEAD Alumni Association wields great power. Its members are drawn from the MBA program (9,700) and from executive programs (8,300). More than 12,900 of INSEAD's alumni are based in Europe, making the European network twice as large as that of any other business school. INSEAD alumni live in 120 countries throughout the world.

The 1997 INSEAD Alumni Reunion Survey shows that twenty years after graduating, 36 percent of MBA alumni are company chairmen or CEOs. International mobility and an entrepreneurial outlook are also highlighted, with alumni spending around 30 percent to 65 percent of their careers abroad, and 42 percent of alumni running their own businesses twenty years after graduation. These are successful people, and successful people who keep religiously in touch with INSEAD. Indeed, alumni make up 30 percent of INSEAD's International Council and hold ten of the twenty-three seats on the Board of Directors.

In 1996, more than a thousand INSEAD alumni made the journey back to the school to attend reunion events. To celebrate the Alumni Association's thirty-fifth anniversary, over a thousand alumni and partners returned for reunions on campus in France from as far away as Buenos Aires, São Paulo, Santiago, Cape Town, Abidjan, Seoul, Ho Chi Minh City, and Suzhou. The MBA classes of 1966, 1976, 1986, and 1991 achieved 55 percent to 65 percent attendance.

The geographic distribution of alumni present was nearly as broad and global as that of the promotions themselves: 25 percent France, 20 percent United Kingdom, 10 percent Germany and Austria, 8 percent North America, 8 percent Southern Europe, 8 percent Benelux, 6 percent Switzerland, 5 percent Scandinavia, 3 percent Australia and Asia, and 2 percent South America.

Eight hundred alumni volunteers worldwide serve in various capacities on national alumni association committees, helping organize reunions and international speaking events as well as interviewing MBA candidates in their home countries.

In 1997, a new alumni association was established in Argentina and the founding of further associations is under way in Ireland, Brazil, Indonesia, and Mexico, which will bring the total number of IAA national associations to thirty-four worldwide. Alumni contact networks are also present in another thirteen countries. Management Update events have been organized with alumni in London, Vienna, New York, and Utrecht. They attract between a hundred and two hundred alumni, drawing 25 percent of them from INSEAD's worldwide population, to hear faculty speak and to have opportunities to network.

Other major schools are similarly well organized, with connections stretching throughout the world like tentacles. Switzerland's IMD has twenty-five thousand alumni in 140 countries, including Peter Wallenberg, head of the famous Swedish industrial empire, and the CEOs of Lego and Nestlé. Members of London Business School's alumni association number more than twelve thousand, of which some five thousand are MBA graduates (some schools count only graduates, others include anyone who has taken an executive program).

But when it comes to power networks, the Americans make their European cousins look like amateurs. True, they've been at the business school game longer. Their alumni networks span the globe like empires. Armed with their MBAs they march into overseas territories with the school badge as a standard. Northwestern's Kellogg holds alumni events all over the world. Its network extends to over 80 countries around the globe. Wharton's alumni network amounts to over 69,000 alumni in more than 130 countries—making it the largest business school network in the world, so the school says. Wharton alumni have organized seventy-six U.S. and international clubs and regional representatives.

The Graduate School of Business at the University of Chicago counts some thirty thousand alumni, including the CEOs of RJR Nabisco, Harley-Davidson, and Revlon. Columbia has twenty thousand—with eleven thousand based in New York, New Jersey, and Connecticut and another nine thousand scattered around the globe, including one well-known citizen of Omaha—the sage himself, Warren Buffett.

But in terms of pure networking muscle Harvard Business School is in a class of its own. Take its 1997 Global Alumni Conference, held in Hong Kong. The organizers reported that more than eight hundred alumni and guests from over forty-five countries gathered in the former British colony on the eve of the handover of power to China. "A once-in-a-lifetime opportunity" is how one HBS alumnus described the event. "Three days of lively discussions among alumni, twelve HBS professors, and a distinguished group of Asian business and government officials, focused on the June 30 transfer of Hong Kong to the People's Republic of China and the expected impact on business in the region."

That's some serious networking. It's Harvard's calling card. As HBS dean Kim Clark observed in his address to those present: "This is a historic time. It is important to recognize that what we are doing here in Hong Kong is a hallmark of the school. We bring together important people to work on important problems. This is an opportunity to build relationships."

Tours to Shanghai and Beijing gave participating alumni plenty of opportunity to make contacts. In China, they also had a chance to visit a number of joint ventures between Western companies and their Chinese partners, and to learn how those relationships were developing in the climate surrounding the handover of Hong Kong. The changeover from one regime to another seemed to strike a chord with the HBS dean, who talked of a three-pronged defense of the school's empire.

"We're really at a turning point," Dean Clark told a gathering convened on the Sunday afternoon. "To stay ahead in an increasingly competitive, global economy, the business school has to continue its tradition of excellence. That means ensuring that the faculty are close to practice, the school cultivates its powerful alumni network, and new technologies are incorporated into teaching and student life."

Those new technologies also play an increasing role in the activities of the alumni networks. In recent years, the leading business schools have been investing in more and more sophisticated IT infrastructures, enabling members to leverage even more from the already powerful alumni associations. For example, e-mail addresses were integrated in the 1997 INSEAD Address Book, now in its thirtieth year of publication. A designated alumni area has grown up and has now merged with the INSEAD Web site.

But alumni networks aren't just about business. They also give business school graduates a helping hand with their other interests. The program for Harvard's 1998 alumni event in Chicago boasted: "Private visits with senior management at some of the top venture capital companies in the city. And, depending on playoff dates, a behind the scenes tour of the United Center (home of the Chicago Bulls and Blackhawks) and a certain well-known locker room, led by Blackhawks owner Bill Wirtz." Sports and business. Who could ask for more? And there's always that $100,000-plus starting salary to get you on your feet, of course. It all makes perfect sense. After all, what's the point in going to Harvard Business School unless you can leverage the hell out of the brand?

CAREER ELEVATORS

Alumni networking has become something of an industry. Alumni make use of the networks by reading the school newsletter and directories, which contain up-to-date information on ex-students. Schools also operate their own databases which, like exclusive dating agencies, can help put former students in touch with other old boys and girls around the world. So if your company wants you to drum up some business in Miami or Malaysia, the database will help you find out who might be there already to help you.

Whether it's making the odd introduction to government ministers or other dignitaries or recommending suppliers, alumni are usually only too pleased to help. As management commentator Joshua Jampol notes: "If the firm wants you to open a market in India, the database will tell you who on the ground can help you meet ministers and other heavyweights. Calls between graduates almost always get results. They share a bond and enjoy lending each other a hand."[2]

The power of networking is a career safety net. But the system rarely fails—for every MBA who is bankrupt there are a lot of millionaires. While others use the career ladder, business school graduates go by the career elevator. First stop is a bachelor's degree at a good university (Oxbridge, Ivy League, Grandes Écoles are all good), second stop is an MBA program at a top business school. Quality counts. In the United States that means one of the top ten: Harvard, Stanford, Wharton, Chicago, Kellogg (Northwestern), Michigan, Darden, Columbia, MIT, Tuck (Dartmouth). In Europe, it means one of the top five or six: INSEAD, IMD, LBS, IESE, SDA Bocconi, Cranfield.

Third stop is a well-paying job at a prestigious management consultancy—McKinsey, Boston Consulting Group, or Andersen Consulting are popular haunts with MBA graduates. The head of Andersen Consulting is an alumnus of London Business School. The head of McKinsey went to Harvard. Bain, BCG, Booz•Allen, Mercer, and KPMG are hallowed names. Or alternatively, they go straight to Wall Street (or London's Square Mile) to work in an investment bank.

In your first job after graduating from business school, you can expect a six-figure starting salary and quite probably a large "joining bonus" or "golden hello" just for signing up. These days, if you go to the right company you'll get stock options thrown in for good measure. In a couple of years, you should have repaid any student loans—and probably the mortgage, too. At thirty-five, you should be ready to get on with the serious pursuit of the blessed trinity of power, influence, and affluence.

Fourth stop: just about anything you want, really. By now, if you've played the game well, you should be wealthy enough and sufficiently well connected to launch a second career in almost any direction that takes your fancy. Politics is popular with business school graduates.

Business schools themselves like to put an educational spin on the activities of alumni associations. They talk about "lifetime learning" and "updating skills," arguing that alumni associations can help members take advantage of both.

Access to new research and the latest management thinking, say the schools, is another benefit to be gained from an ongoing association with your alma mater.

Alumni are also used by business schools to market their courses to potential students. Many use former students based in other countries as their ambassadors in new markets, or as their eyes and ears to spot new opportunities. Schools use graduates to talk to applicants who have received offers and persuade them to regard theirs as the "best" school. In some cases, especially where distance is a problem, they will even ask alumni based near an applicant to carry out an interview and report back prior to making an offer.

As the business school market has become more mature, employers have become much more selective about which schools they recruit from—a fact that students are only too aware of when they apply. Choosing an MBA course is a bit like choosing a car. Much depends on how fast you want to go, how much money you have to spend, and what you plan to do with it later. As with cars, too, other people—especially employers—put great store in the badge on the hood.

An MBA from a top school carries more clout with employers and peers than one from a lesser-known institution. The cost tends to reflect that. Just as cars have the same basic components—four wheels, engine, and steering wheel—the same is true of MBAs. Programs consist of core management subjects including finance, marketing, economics, IT, and organizational behavior, and a choice of optional extras called electives. Finally, there is usually a dissertation or an in-company project. The business school brand is the added extra that can make the difference.

An MBA from a top-name business school may not be intellectually superior to one from somewhere less renowned. You may know marketing theory inside out. But it doesn't matter. An MBA from Harvard, Wharton, Kellogg, or another top school is an elite qualification. And herein lies the opportunity for business schools: their alumni rely on the high standing of the school to bolster their own careers and are, as a result, prepared to help in maintaining the high standing of the business school's brand. It is win-win. The business school gets money and support; the alumni maintain the luster of their qualification and have access to a powerful network.

REAL-LIFE NETWORKS

For a quick look at the extent of MBA networks, we gathered the names of the companies in the 1998 Fortune 50 and their CEOs. We then spent an hour surfing the Internet to see how many personal and organizational links to b-schools we could find. The results are presented in the table.

THE MBA NETWORK

The list of those who have reached prominent positions in their industries grows longer each year. High-profile MBAs, for example, include Harvard graduates Scott Cook, founder of Intuit; Michael Bloomberg, the business news and technology tycoon; IBM CEO Louis Gerstner; and former Northwest Airlines CEO Al Cecchi. Peter Lynch, the renowned stock fund manager, and American Airlines CEO Robert Crandall both earned their MBAs at Wharton, and David Johnson, CEO of Campbell Soup Co., went to the University of Chicago. Investment sage Warren Buffett is an alumnus of Columbia.

Famous European MBAs include Simon Critchell, president and CEO of Cartier; Ronaldo Schmitz, a member of the board of Deutsche Bank; Helmut Maucher, chairman of the board and CEO of Nestlé; Barbara Kux-Parein, vice president of Nestlé; Lindsay Owen-Jones, president, director general of L'Oréal; Robin Field, CEO of Filofax. The list goes on.

Martin Sorrell, founder of the advertising agency WPP, has an MBA from Harvard and is a big noise at London Business School where he is governor. He is also on the advisory board of the Judge Institute, the business school at Cambridge University, and IESE, the famous Spanish business school based in Barcelona.

Sir Paul Judge, whose name adorns the Judge Institute at Cambridge, received his own MBA from Wharton. Another influential Wharton MBA graduate is Richard Koch, the consultant turned would-be management guru, and a non-executive director at Filofax. John Neill, CEO of Unipart, got his MBA from Strathclyde. Greg Hutchings, chairman of the conglomerate Tomkins, picked his up from Aston in the United Kingdom. David Sainsbury, now Lord Sainsbury, who recently stepped down from the helm of the family supermarket chain J. Sainsbury, is former chairman of the governing body of LBS, but received his MBA from Columbia in New York.

Links Between CEOs of Fortune 50 Companies and Business Schools

Fortune 50 Rank	*Company*	*CEO*	*B-School Links*
1	General Motors	John F. Smith	Smith has a Boston University MBA (1965)
2	Ford Motor Company	Alex Trotman	Trotman has an MBA from Michigan State; is a lead investor ($50,000 or more) at Stanford; Boston University dean Louis Lataif is former president of Ford Europe
4	Wal-Mart Stores	David D. Glass	Glass set up two seven-figure endowments at Southern Methodist University's College of Business Administration
5	General Electric	Jack Welch	Chairman emeritus Reg Jones is an alumnus of Wharton and Harvard; Harvard Business School professor James I. Cash is on the GE board
6	International Business Machines	Louis V. Gerstner	Gerstner has a Harvard MBA (1965); IBM is a "principal" of Duke's Fuqua School ($1 million in cumulative giving)
7	Chrysler	Robert J. Eaton	Eaton is a member of the Industrial Advisory Board at Stanford University; Chrysler is an associate of Chicago ($15,000–$19,999) and a "managing partner" at Fuqua ($100,000-plus every year)
8	Mobil Oil	Lucio A. Noto	Mobil is a managing partner of Cornell ($50,000 plus annual donation); Duke dean Rex D. Adams is an ex-Mobil VP
10	AT&T	C. Michael Armstrong	Armstrong is on the advisory board at Yale School of Management; AT&T is a "principal business partner" at Duke's Fuqua School (giving over $1 million in total); Carnegie-Mellon GSIA dean Douglas Dunn is an ex-AT&T VP

Links Between CEOs of Fortune 50 Companies and Business Schools, continued

Fortune 50 Rank	*Company*	*CEO*	*B-School Links*
11	Boeing	Philip M. Condit	Condit recently received the Award for Business Excellence from USC's Marshall School
12	Texaco	Peter I. Bijur	Bijur has an MBA from Columbia (1966)
14	Hewlett-Packard	Lewis E. Platt	Platt is an alumnus of Wharton; Hewlett-Packard has given over $1 million to Cornell's Johnson School; Platt has also received an Award for Business Excellence from USC's Marshall School
16	Sears, Roebuck	Arthur C. Martinez	Martinez is a trustee of Northwestern University; University of Illinois dean Anthony Rucci is a former executive VP at Sears
20	Procter & Gamble	John E. Pepper	P&G is an associate of Chicago ($25,000–$29,999), a managing partner of Cornell ($50,000-plus annual donation), an affiliate benefactor to Kellogg ($50,000-plus during 1996–1997), and a managing partner ($25,000-plus) at UCLA's Anderson School; Chairman Edwin Artzt is a member of Anderson's Board of Visitors
21	Citicorp	John S. Reed	Citicorp is a senior partner (donating $25,000–$50,000 every year) at Cornell, a lead investor ($50,000 or more) at Stanford, and a managing partner ($25,000 or more) at UCLA's Anderson School
27	Chase Manhattan	Walter V. Shipley	Company is a senior partner at Cornell ($25,000–$50,000 per year)
29	Motorola	Christopher B. Galvin	Galvin is a Kellogg alumnus

Fortune 50 Rank	*Company*	*CEO*	*B-School Links*
31	Pepsico	Roger Enrico	Enrico applied to b-school—but joined the Navy instead
33	Fannie Mae	James A. Johnson	Johnson is an alumnus of Wharton
38	Intel	Andrew S. Grove	Grove has lectured at Stanford Business School since 1991 and is on the school's Advisory Council; Intel is a "managing partner" at Cornell, giving $50,000 and up annually
42	Compaq Computer	Eckhard Pfeiffer	Chairman Benjamin Rosen has an MBA from Columbia
46	Merck	Raymond V. Gilmartin	Merck is a corporate associate of Pennsylvania State's Smeal College
47	BankAmerica Corporation	David A. Coulter	Coulter has a master's degree in industrial administration from Carnegie-Mellon
48	GTE	Charles R. Lee	GTE is a senior partner at Cornell (giving $25,000–$50,000 per year)

8

Rankings on the Line

Some deans refer to John Byrne, the Business Week *journalist responsible for compiling the rankings, not altogether jokingly as "the most important man in North American management education."*

—George Bickerstaffe, business journalist[1]

The interest in business schools has spawned a secondary industry in providing information about the top schools. This includes the publication of a host of guidebooks, Web sites, and other comparative data targeted at potential students and corporate clients. The best-known examples are the business school rankings that are compiled by a variety of sources—including a number of newspapers and magazines.

As a general principle, journalists like rankings. They make good copy. Articles that analyze the latest league table to see who's up and who's down make for good reading. If those rankings provide useful information to consumers, so much the better. But it is in the nature of rankings that they will always be flawed. Much depends on the criteria you use, the data you collect, and the way you collect that data. Inevitably, some rankings apply more rigorous methodologies than others. We assume that students are smart enough to read the small print and make their own judgments.

There is nothing intrinsically wrong with business school rankings as long as they are seen for what they are, a sideshow, and are not allowed to dictate the agenda of either the business schools or the corporate recruiters. In other words, when it comes to business school rankings, the tail should not be allowed to wag the dog.

At present, rankings raise these issues:

- Reputational concerns have spawned an industry in business school rankings, which detracts from more serious matters.
- Rankings, despite their flaws, have been elevated above their true significance (this is partly the fault of the business schools, which take them too seriously).
- The way most rankings are compiled is fundamentally flawed.
- Business school rankings are now spreading to Europe, with similar consequences.
- Quality control (business school accreditation), a much more important issue, has not been properly addressed outside the United States.

REPUTATIONS TO DIE FOR

Business school reputations are all-important. It's the same with all branded products—and make no mistake, it's branded products that the top business schools sell.

It takes time to establish your brand proposition with consumers. The top schools talk about quality and internationalism as if they are a magic dust sprinkled on their products to differentiate them from other providers. They tell a good tale. What you see isn't always what you get. But that's business schools for you.

If the business school experience was just about the learning, then a student could go to one of the many up-and-coming business schools in Europe, Asia, or the United States. In terms of the teaching, some are probably as good as their more famous brethren. But to get the luster of real business school gold, you have to go to a school with a big name. If there's a mantra for the business school applicant who wants to ride the career elevator it has to be an update of the old real-estate adage: reputation, reputation, reputation.

The top schools put a great deal of effort into their marketing. Lavish brochures (conversion rate of brochures to clients 0.01 percent) and showcase events are just part of the pageantry. The trouble is that the wrapping can sometimes get in the way of the content. The top schools attract the top faculty. That's a fact of academic life. They also confer stature on their alumni.

As a result, the famous business schools are sensitive about what is written about them. Deans have been known to call journalists to petition for more coverage. They have been known to turn nasty if they don't like the coverage they do get. Business schools live on their reputations more than most organizations. They know that it's the school's credibility (and the size of its MBA program) that will bring the top recruiters onto campus—recruiters like to fish in well-stocked rivers. But the process starts well before graduation. The top schools attract the brightest applicants. They also offer the key to the killer networks.

It is reputation, too, that will ensure the investment lasts. What really matters with a business school qualification is that it keeps its currency. No one wants to pay all that money, go through all that pain, all those late nights, to find a few years down the road that the treasured qualification isn't worth the paper it's written on. What alumni really want is a business school that treats its own brand like gold. One that guards its good name.

The problem for business schools is knowing how best to safeguard their reputations. Here they face another dilemma. The more prestigious the school, the more difficult it is to change direction. But failure to keep up with the pace of change in today's business world inevitably leads to obsolescence. So what schools tend to do is to tinker but not really change anything much—until they face a crisis. Continuous improvement is something they talk about in class but rarely discuss in their planning sessions. It took the recession of the 1990s, for example, plus widespread and increasingly vocal criticism from the business community, before the leading U.S. schools recognized they had to do something to become more relevant and more responsive.

Even the famous Harvard halo slipped for a while. By the late 1980s, its failure to change with the times and its bureaucratic systems meant that HBS looked in danger of sleepwalking off the edge of a cliff. It took the appointment of an energetic new dean in Kim Clark to shake things up. Clark was an insider. He knew what needed fixing. In his first six months he invested more than $11 million in IT, an area where HBS was slipping behind its rivals. He also initiated a major overhaul of the school's flagship programs, including the MBA program.

In this, Harvard was just playing catch-up with other U.S. schools. Wharton and Columbia had already taken the decision to overhaul their curricula. The other leading schools followed. Reputations were at risk.

In Europe, too, there was a period of soul-searching at the start of the 1990s, with all the major schools introducing changes to their MBA programs.

But beyond these seismic changes in the marketplace, individual business schools are also vulnerable to what corporate brand managers call the "salami process."

Over the years, successive generations of brand managers have discovered they could make some slack in their budgets by asking consumers to compare two products of brand X. One has 100 percent of its key (expensive) ingredient and the proposed innovation has only 95 percent. Lying below the threshold of detection, the difference is likely to escape the consumer's notice. A year or so on, depending on how the budget looks, another 5 percent gets sliced off, again below the threshold of detection by research. Eventually sales and brand reputation start to fall apart. The fault is traced to the shortage of the key ingredient, which is now far below the original specification.

In business schools, the expensive ingredient is often the time of the top faculty or the quality of materials. The point is that for a while no one notices that the product has lost its edge. Then one day, people start noticing. The reputation takes a knock. Bad press follows. But word of mouth does the real damage. Working against this is the full might of the alumni network. Alumni have an investment to protect. They have no intention of seeing their brand stock drop in value. That's why rankings are so important. That's also why they cause so much trouble.

THE POWER OF JOHN BYRNE

Business schools have a love-hate relationship with rankings. Whenever the topic comes up, deans say they hate, loathe, and detest them. They add that the methodology used for compiling them is flawed, and that comparing schools and programs from different countries and traditions is like trying to compare apples with pears. But there is a much more deep-seated reason for this distaste. They don't like losing.

Whenever a new ranking is threatened the deans of the top business schools are fearful that their school will slip a few places. Once the results are published, it's often a different story. The schools that come out well have been known to rave about the rankings and to spend the next two years bragging that they beat their rival in this or that important area, whether it's the size of their graduates' starting salaries or the number of teachers with Ph.D.'s. Any glimmer of a competitive advantage is seized upon and used to bolster the school's image. Kenan-Flagler, for example, sent out reprints of a *Business Week* report on executive education to journalists and corporate clients. The report ranked the school fourth in America. The position was highlighted.

We recently noticed that a leading American school and a top European school both reported strong showings in a ranking published by the *London Times*. This despite the fact that the *Times* has never compiled its own ranking of business schools, preferring to report the findings of others. A genuine mistake, perhaps. But the point is that such overenthusiastic claims are inevitable—business schools crave media validation.

The fascination for rankings is not unique to business schools, of course. American law schools have been the subject of unofficial league tables for years. In fact, the top U.S. law schools and the leading business schools have much in common. Both offer gateways to enormous wealth and power. Choosing the right school is vital.

The problem here is that there is no officially sanctioned league table or pecking order for business schools. Given the highly competitive nature of the market, and the American obsession with who is number one, this has inevitably created a vacuum that magazines and newspapers have been only too ready to fill. Today, there are literally dozens of these.

Among the best known is the annual ranking published by *U.S. News & World Report*. But without a doubt the most influential is *Business Week* magazine's ranking of the top twenty-five U.S. schools. What is remarkable is the clout these media-based rankings carry. The very idea that a magazine or newspaper should be the arbiter of quality in this sector is faintly ludicrous. Yet publication of the *Business Week* rankings is a cause of sleepless nights for the deans of America's leading b-schools. Deans often think only of rankings in the six-month run-up to publication. (Pedants inevitably also have sleepless nights poring over the methodologies—"It is a sad reflection on business magazines that *Business Week* and *U.S. News & World Report* do not seem to grasp even the most elementary aspects of a basic tool of their subject, namely statistics," one methodology freak wrote to *The Economist* in complaint.)

Updated every two years, places in the *Business Week* ranking are based on the responses of students and corporate recruiters to a survey questionnaire. "Let the customer speak. That is the philosophy behind *Business Week*'s rankings," noted the editorial that accompanied the 1998 results. For a magazine, it is a massive undertaking. Among U.S. schools, the results are awaited with bated breath. The poll is the magazine's cover story and boosts circulation massively—the b-school issue is reportedly the year's biggest seller.

The practice is now spreading to Europe. There is some unease at this. "The problem in the U.S. is that people try and please the rankings, instead of doing right by their students," says one European placement director. "Deans shouldn't report to magazines, but to their programs," adds a former director of placement and admissions at IMD. "The whole thing has got out of hand."

Early attempts to rank European schools failed to produce a credible equivalent to the best-known American versions. Several were sabotaged by business schools' either threatening legal action or refusing to participate. Published for the first time in January 1999, new global rankings by the *Financial Times* may change the gentlemanly game. This follows an earlier attempt by the *FT* to get a ranking off the ground in 1998. On that occasion the attempt was undermined by European business schools' getting their retaliation in early. Letters were sent from at least two of Europe's best-known schools to the editor challenging the methodology used and the validity of the ranking concept. The newspaper, wisely, put publishing a full-blown ranking on hold while it talked to people in the b-school world. In the intervening period it set about spiking their guns. (Curiously enough, less than a week after the—watered-down—results were published, one of the same schools was quoting the survey findings to other journalists to promote its MBA program. None of this should come as any great surprise. The people who market business schools aren't there to see the reputation of the school get tarnished. They are there to keep it highly polished.)

Newspapers, however, don't give up that easily. Having consulted with the leading schools about the fairest way to compile rankings, the *FT* went ahead and published its ranking, including an attempt to rank schools on the quality of research. The *FT* asked schools for eight journal articles written by faculty members. However, the *FT* ranking did not include employers. It may be no coincidence that some schools included their top statisticians in the consultation process.

RANKING THE RANKINGS

Our research did not need to be exhaustive to find no fewer than thirty-four different business school rankings. These gave rankings for the top American b-schools across a range of criteria. Categories included popular rankings, academic quality rankings, reputation with recruiters and CEOs rankings, graduates' return on investment rankings, and specialized degrees rankings. GMAT percentile and MBA resources were also ranked.

The other side of the rankings question is, whose figures are they based on, anyway? It depends on which criteria you look at. But in one critical area at least, number of job placements and starting salary, the answer is less than reassuring. The figures fed into the highly sophisticated statistical methodologies come from that most reliable of sources—the business schools themselves. But no one audits the numbers.

While some people may not have a problem with this, including many of those who compile the rankings, others do. This has led to the creation of an organization dedicated to ensuring the figures in the great job placement race are accurate.

The MBA Career Services Council was created to keep everyone on the straight and narrow. Funded mainly by eighty-two or so U.S. business schools, it is currently engaged in the worthy task of evaluating and refining a set of standards its constituent schools can use to report salaries, total compensation, and job offers for graduates. This is of more than academic interest.

As *Business Week* itself admitted in an editorial in May 1998, these placement figures influence the rankings—including its own ranking of the Top 25 Business Schools. There's little doubt, the article said, that the high stakes involved have led to creative arithmetic at many schools—and engendered no small degree of cynicism.[2]

The fact is that schools with the most attractive statistics are likely to attract the best and the brightest students, and also the biggest donations from alumni. Selecting a school with the best job placement record can make a difference of thousands of dollars in the first job.

Rankings are, in our view, fundamentally flawed. It is not that we question the math. It is simply that any methodology will be unable to produce an accurate ranking of business schools—or any other such diverse group of institutions, for that matter. There are some specific problems with the way the *Business Week* rankings are arrived at, too. In particular, we question whether asking students—soon to become alumni—to rate their own school provides an accurate picture. Not only do they have no way of comparing their school with other business schools, but they have a vested interest in rating their school highly.[3] (It's a bit like asking someone who has spent a lot of time and money on a luxury car to tell you that he's made a mistake.) To us, the ranking also seems disproportionately to favor schools that have introduced changes to their programs in recent years, which could penalize a school for sticking to what it's good at.

These points aside, the *Business Week* rankings in particular generate a great deal of interest. They stimulate discussion and give applicants some sort of benchmark. This is a very valuable service to its readership—just as long as no one takes the published rankings too seriously.

RANKING FILE

For its 1998 rankings Recruiter Survey, *Business Week* polled 350 companies, all "active recruiters of MBAs," and got answers from 259. These companies may do the most MBA recruiting. But does it follow that they are the same firms who represent the majority of MBA employers? Lists of companies polled are rarely presented with the rankings, so it's hard to judge. Many MBA groups report that, in fact, MBAs are found in greater concentrations in smaller organizations, which are rarely, if ever, asked to contribute to the rankings.

What do employers who rank business schools know about academia? Probably as much, or as little, as any other outsiders—including reporters conducting surveys for their magazines, who don't take the courses, don't know how schools grade, and are generally ignorant of day-to-day campus life. What an employer can judge, however, is the ability of a business school to turn out the kind of employees it needs. The danger is that recruiters are simply reporting on whether or not they liked a school's admissions process—the people it offered places to.

Business Week ranks about ten different factors, then pools the average. The more criteria you rate, the more potential winners there are. But might it not also follow that the more you judge, the more movement you create? This could lead to volatile findings, such as: "School Drops 20 Points." Such a headline might help sell magazines.

What is undeniable is that the *Business Week* rankings do generate a lot of interest. So do those carried by *U.S. News & World Report*, which also has a reputation for sound methodology. Its rankings for America's three hundred accredited MBA programs are based on measures of academic quality, which include reputation, placement success, and student selectivity.

In the magazine's 1997 rankings, reputation was based on two surveys. In one, deans and directors of accredited programs were asked to rank each program. In the second, corporate recruiters selected the nation's top twenty-five schools, based on a program's reputation for academic excellence and its ability to produce top leaders, effective managers, consultants, and analysts, and successful entrepreneurs.

Placement success was based on four indicators for the full-time class that graduated in 1997: median starting base salaries, excluding bonuses; proportion employed three months after graduation; proportion employed at graduation; and the ratio of the number of firms that recruited on campus to the number of graduates.

Student selectivity was based on three indicators for full-time MBAs entering that year: average Graduate Management Admission Test scores, undergraduate grade point average, and the proportion of applicants accepted by the school.

Both *Business Week* and *U.S. News* stimulate discussion and give potential candidates some sort of benchmark. This is a valuable service to readers. They also give employers an idea if they are targeting the right schools. But it's only one element. "They give some guidance, but not all," says Michel Van der Mooter, director of human resources at Eli Lilly. Rankings provide one tool for selecting the right school. But you can't build a house with a hammer.

In Europe, the rankings issue is complicated by diversity. The fact that American schools and programs are more homogenous makes judgment easier because you're comparing like with like. The fare on offer from European institutions is far too diverse for the U.S. method to apply. Should a European Top 20 compare one-year with two-year programs? National or international courses? Modular versus open learning? English-language and French-language degrees? It's hard enough equating programs in the same country, much less across borders of fifteen different countries, all with varying educational systems.

If rankings are viewed as a slightly frivolous diversion rather than a prospective source of competitive advantage, they provide endless amusement—and make good copy for journalists. They can even provide some information for consumers.

We are indebted to John E. Wehrli, who produces the definitive diversion for ranking enthusiasts: a composite of all the other rankings. Further details as to how these rankings are composed are included in the Appendix.

Composite Rankings of Business Schools

Rank	*Actual*	*School*
1	2.65	Stanford
2	2.69	Harvard
3	4.1	University of Pennsylvania, Wharton
4	5.0	MIT, Sloan
5	5.1	Northwestern, Kellogg
6	6.4	University of Chicago
7	9.1	Columbia
8	9.4	University of California, Berkeley, Haas
9	9.9	Dartmouth, Amos Tuck
10	10.8	University of Michigan
11	11.8	University of Virginia, Darden
12	11.9	UCLA, Anderson
13	12.2	Duke
14	15.1	Cornell, Johnson
15	15.9	New York University
16	15.9	University of Texas
17	15.2	Carnegie-Mellon
18	17.3	University of North Carolina, Kenan-Flagler
19	17.9	Indiana University
20	20.1	Yale
21	20.4	Purdue
22	24.3	Georgetown

23	25.0	Washington University, Olin
24	25.4	University of Rochester, Simon
25	26.2	USC
26	26.6	Emory, Goizueta
27	26.8	University of Illinois
28	27.1	University of Wisconsin
29	29.0	Vanderbilt, Owen
30	29.1	Ohio State University, Fisher

The following schools are ranked 31 to 55 according to the average of published rankings only and are not part of composite ranking. Schools ranked 55 and above are subject to significantly greater variance and higher averages.

Rank	*Actual*	*School*
31	30.8	Minnesota, Carlson
32	32.7	Pittsburgh, Katz
33	33.6	Case Western Reserve, Weatherhead
34	33.7	Washington
35	33.9	Pennsylvania State
36	35.2	Michigan State, Broad
37	37.1	Georgia Tech
38	38.6	Tulane, Freeman
39	39.9	Iowa
40	40.8	Notre Dame
41	40.8	American Graduate School of International Management, Thunderbird
42	41.4	Southern Methodist, Cox
43	42.2	Texas A&M
44	42.8	Florida
45	43.9	Brigham Young, Marriott
46	45.4	Maryland
47	47.1	Arizona State
48	48.6	Wake Forest, Babcock

Rank	*Actual*	*School*
49	49.7	Claremont, Drucker
50	50.1	Arizona
51	50.8	Georgia
52	51.9	Babson
53	53.0	Tennessee
54	55.1	William & Mary
55	60.0	University of California, Davis

For the top thirty schools, the "Actual" column consists of average composite ranking based on all published rankings (70 percent) and ratings for student caliber, placement, and selectivity (30 percent). For the next twenty-five schools, "Actual" consists of the average of all published rankings.

RETURN ON INVESTMENT

What many business school applicants really want to know is what the payback will be on their qualification. Ronald Yeaple, a professor at the Simon Graduate School of Business at the University of Rochester in New York, tried to oblige. While other rankings tied themselves in knots about the quality of teaching, in true MBA spirit Yeaple went for the jugular: Return on Investment.

In doing so, he may have been the first person to take a hard-headed look at the value of a business education. In 1994, he wrote a book called *The MBA Advantage: Why It Pays to Get an* MBA, in which he ranked twenty top U.S. business schools according to the financial return they gave their graduates. It represents perhaps the best attempt to come to grips with the whole business school phenomenon.

The so-called MBA advantage of each school was the cumulative amount that a typical member of the class of 1992 could expect to earn in the five years following graduation, after subtracting tuition fees and what the student would have made without the MBA.

The ranking that emerged presented a very different view of business schools. Certainly it was an alternative to the more righteous rankings such as those produced by *Business Week*. This was a ranking for those with their eyes on the dollar signs.

Northwestern University, for instance, achieved only sixth place in Yeaple's book, despite being top in the *Business Week* rankings at the time. Yale University, which hadn't even made the *Business Week* list, rose to fifth. Yeaple's calculations didn't pull any punches. All that counted was just how big—or small—the payback from an MBA was. It confirmed what many already suspected.

Five years after graduating from b-school, a typical Harvard graduate (Yeaple's number 1 school) had an MBA advantage of $133,647, while a typical graduate from New York University—Yeaple's lowest-ranked school—had one of only $4,121.

Once adjusted for taxes and the return on the extra money over time, and the differences were even more stark: five years after graduation, the Harvard MBA was up by $148,378, while the NYU graduate actually lost $3,749 by attending business school. Game, set, and match to Harvard.

QUALITY CONTROL AND SELF-REGULATION

The United States may be obsessed with rankings, but at least in the American Assembly of Collegiate Schools of Business (AACSB) it has something approaching quality control. The AACSB accreditation scheme, which is the dominant accreditation system, is not perfect, not by any stretch of the imagination. Nor is it truly comprehensive, as some schools prefer not to play ball. But it is a lot more effective as a means of ensuring the quality of business school products than anything currently in place in Europe.

Europe is really just beginning to come to grips with the accreditation issue. Until very recently the best it could muster was a system of national accreditation bodies, with assessment criteria and processes that were often as different as their agendas. Today, the long-running debate about an accreditation system for Europe's schools rumbles on. The need for a recognized body to provide a watermark for European MBA providers is now widely admitted. But there are several contenders for the role.

In the past two years, competition among front-runners has heated up, with the AACSB signaling its global ambitions by changing its name (outside the United States) to International Association of Management Education.

In Europe, the Brussels-based European Foundation for Management Development (EFMD) and the United Kingdom's Association of MBAs (AMBA) have both been setting up their stalls. In 1997, the EFMD launched its own accreditation system, EQUIS (European Quality Improvement System)—Europe's answer to the threat of colonization by the AACSB. EQUIS aims to audit institutions, rather than simply MBA programs.

In March 1998, the first group of six European business schools received the EQUIS seal of approval. Another ten followed, taking the total of EQUIS accredited schools to sixteen by the end of that year. To date, the list is as follows:

- École Européenne des Affaires (EAP), France
- Escuela Superior de Administracion y Direccion de Empresas (ESADE), Spain
- École Supérieure de Commerce de Paris (ESCP), France
- HEC School of Management, France
- Helsinki School of Economics and Business Administration, Finland
- INSEAD, France
- Instituto de Empresa, Spain

- International Graduate School of Management (IESE), Spain
- International Institute for Management Development (IMD), Switzerland
- London Business School, United Kingdom
- Scuola di Direzione Aziendale (SDA Bocconi), Italy
- Ashridge Management College, United Kingdom
- École de Management Lyon (EM Lyon), France
- École Supérieure de Commerce de Nantes Atlantique (ESCNA), France
- Rotterdam School of Management, the Netherlands
- WHU Koblenz, Otto Beisheim Graduate School of Management, Germany

Others are expected to follow. The acid test of any accreditation scheme, however, is whether those in charge are willing to enforce high standards. In EQUIS's case, this remains to be seen.

The "pioneer schools," as the schools in the first wave were called, were supposed to play an active part in the accreditation process, providing feedback on what standards should be established and helping pay to set up the scheme. According to Gordon Shenton, who was recruited from France's EM Lyon to be EQUIS's project manager, fears that the scheme could lead to a "European business school super league" are unfounded. "You have to start somewhere," Shenton says. "The system has to establish its legitimacy. At the same time, the idea is not to limit it to an elite. In time, we aim to audit all schools with a claim to this standard."

The EFMD approach to accreditation is also an inclusive one. Bernadette Conraths, EFMD director general, admits that the different accreditation bodies haven't always seen eye to eye, but believes that over the long haul, cooperation is the best approach. "There was some distance between the AACSB and us when we resisted their offer to cooperate on a joint approach to European accreditation," she says. "We were happy to cooperate but only as equal partners. We wanted to get a European system up and running first, otherwise we couldn't expect to be equal partners."

"Tensions cause temporary problems," she adds. "In the long term I don't think it's useful to have lots of accreditation systems as it is confusing for the market. Globally speaking, we should do what we did in Europe and sit around the table with the regional accreditation bodies, so that evaluation takes account of the local environment and culture."

East and Central European schools will be happy to hear this. Business schools have sprung up across this region in the last five to eight years, and some sort of benchmarking is necessary. Though East and Central European schools feel they have a lot to learn from the West, they know (and smart Westerners agree) that their situation is unique, and the West can't teach them everything about economies in transition. This may make assessment hard, for most of the auditors who will visit the new campuses to assess their attributes will come from the other side of the Danube. Schools in ex-Communist countries want to join the EQUIS club, but they don't want handouts. They have a lot to offer, too.

So far, all the schools that have been audited have passed. It will be interesting to see what happens when a school presents itself that doesn't meet the letter of the standards. Will EQUIS prefer to enforce the standards or accommodate a new client by finding ways to reinterpret them?

The whole history of European accreditation is littered with distrust and rumor. EQUIS is just the latest in a string of schemes to emerge in recent years. The original EFMD plan, which was based on the subsidiarity principle or mutual recognition among national accrediting bodies, was dealt a severe blow by the British when the Association of MBAs (AMBA) pulled out.

In 1997, AMBA also pulled out of negotiations with the Association of Business Schools (ABS) and announced its own ambitions to become the internationally recognized MBA accreditation body in Europe.

Where EQUIS scores over the others, however, is that—unlike the current AMBA scheme, which accredits individual MBA programs—it will accredit entire schools, and will be administered under the auspices of the EFMD by a separate agency already established to oversee the process. Nonetheless, it seems likely that accreditation nightmares will continue.

EMPIRE BUILDING

Meanwhile, rumors that the American accreditation body—the AACSB—ultimately intends to foist its own accreditation on Europe persist. Some European schools, keen to appeal to U.S. applicants, have already applied to the AACSB for accreditation, and the U.K.-based AMBA is also believed to favor a strategic alliance with the U.S. body.

The news that a number of European schools have applied to the AACSB suggests that the battle of the accreditors is just beginning. In 1997, the French school Groupe ESSEC (École Supérieure des Sciences Économiques et Commerciales) became the first European business school to gain the U.S. accreditation. The news has encouraged others to follow suit.

There are good reasons why the French college would want the U.S. quality stamp. ESSEC has a high profile at home yet is virtually unknown abroad. Like most schools, it is keen to access new markets, and can use the well-known U.S. standard to lure overseas students. Maurice Thévenet, ESSEC's director, says the American accreditation will help recruit foreign students (who currently make up a slim 10 percent of ESSEC's programs), and build links with global firms and universities.

Rotterdam, Warwick, the Instituto de Empresa in Madrid, and others have followed. Rotterdam earned the AACSB stamp in early

1998, while Warwick adopted a two-in-one approach, aiming for simultaneous accreditation from the Americans and AMBA. (The school already held AMBA accreditation but—with programs periodically reaccredited—hoped the combined exercise would streamline the process.) Henley Management College is the latest to go for the U.S. quality seal.

In the past, the AACSB has been criticized for its "inflexible" requirements, more geared to American business schools than to the diversity of approaches found in Europe. But the U.S. body has promised to keep an open mind about European differences, a change of attitude that is music to European ears, more used to rigid rules from the United States.

"Some of the American attitudes remind me of the person who says cooperation means leadership," observes Bernadette Conraths, director general of the EFMD. "That causes a reaction from those who want to cooperate but don't want to be led. Some of the big U.S. b-schools will always adopt a leadership role in partnership situation. They would be well advised to listen a bit more and understand what the local environment tells them."

The AACSB recognizes that its accreditation will not appeal to every European school. "We're engaging only those schools that show interest," says managing director Milton Blood. He puts this number at "dozens."

The Association of MBAs, too, reports growing interest from overseas schools, with enquiries from Continental Europe, Latin America, Australasia, and China. "The market for MBAs is truly global now," Dr. Robert Owen, who heads up accreditation at AMBA, says. "Students want more information about whether programs they are considering are worthwhile. We are currently the only body that accredits MBAs worldwide."

Back in Brussels, meanwhile, the EFMD is convinced that EQUIS will become the standard for Europe. The focus with EQUIS is on the quality of internal processes, providing a framework for schools to improve themselves across the board. There is also a strong commitment to involve corporate members, thereby strengthening the link between what business schools offer and what companies require.

However, question marks remain over whether the EFMD has the resources to cover the European continent. Gordon Shenton agrees that the arrival of the Americans makes getting EQUIS up and running quickly all the more important. "It is clear that they have international ambitions," he says. "But with or without the Americans, we need a process in Europe. Certainly there is now a sense of urgency in putting our system in place. There will always be competition. But Europe needs a system that is adapted to the diversity of schools in this market. It needs to be a system which is flexible enough to cope with different approaches but at the same time has quality standards built into it. From that point of view, there is a feeling that our approach is innovative and that it is designed to add value to business schools."

While some commentators believe the competing accreditation systems confuse potential applicants and make extra work for the business schools, other observers such as Edward More O'Ferrall, whose company Edition XII publishes *The Directory of MBAs*, claim the current situation is unavoidable. "You can say, Wouldn't it be nice to have just one accreditation system, but the way business is taught varies from country to country and even within countries. All these systems are trying to help. They are a sign of how the business world is globalizing. By providing quality standards they offer useful benchmarks not just for consumers but for the schools themselves."

Some European schools, however, think that the accreditation industry has too many players. Privately a number of deans claim that with growing pressure on them to apply to different accrediting bodies, the whole process has already got way out of hand. In the United Kingdom, where schools already have to endure government-sponsored assessments for research and teaching, many say that accreditation is becoming a distraction from the real issues facing their institutions.

Some sort of international system for quality control for business schools makes sense. The schools will argue that it is just not feasible. Companies have been resolving similar issues ever since markets started to become global. That is what ISO 9000 and other quality standards are all about. But that is to ignore the political nature of academic institutions. In many ways, the current accreditation debate is simply about American imperialism, which is being resisted by Europe. It could be a long fight. Universities have largely contented themselves with national standards. If you want to get an American education, then you go to an American university. If you want a French or British education, the same applies. It's that simple. All have national standards in place. The problem the business schools have created is that they want to sell themselves globally. They want to behave like international businesses, but they can't help behaving like academics.

In the end, however, the squabbling over accreditation and the disproportionate importance placed on rankings dreamed up by journalists are a waste of time and energy.

9

The New Competition

The big consultancies have not been slow to move into areas such as leadership and organizational transformation where we work and where we would like to work.

—Ian Tanner, Manchester Business School

Business schools have had it all their own way for a long time, but competition in their markets is increasing. Companies are creating their own executive development centers—there are now more than a thousand so-called corporate universities. Along with these in-house providers new external suppliers are entering the fray. The executive education market is just too tempting for the management consultancies and others to resist. Companies are starting to demand executive programs that include an element of organizational transformation. As a result, a new market is developing in tailored programs—a market that is part exec ed and part consultancy. U.S. university business schools, in particular, are unsuited to meeting this demand. The question is, How do they plan to respond?

In the future, we expect to see many more partnerships between exec ed providers, designed to take advantage of their strengths. These may involve joint ventures between two or more business schools, combinations of business schools and corporate universities, business schools working with management consultancies or educational providers with strong IT or publishing capability—just about any permutation you care to think of. The impact on business schools could be profound, not just in their exec ed markets but in qualification programs as well.

A number of points are already clear:

- New competition is likely to come from a number of sources, including corporate universities, consultancies, and new players—software and media companies, for example.
- Delivery is all-important—an array of new delivery possibilities are now available.
- The exec ed map will be redrawn—this has wider implications for the future of b-schools.
- Business schools cannot afford to rest on their laurels; many rely on income from exec ed to support academic programs. Partnerships will be critical.

THE COMPETITIVE FRENZY

Hardly a day goes by without another important announcement from a business school. A new building, a revamped program, the recruitment of a star academic. All are trumpeted from the rooftops as schools desperately attempt to stay one step ahead of the competition.

This frenzied activity is just one indication of the vitality of the executive development market—not to mention the huge corporate budgets that are up for grabs and the ferocity of the competition. Surging demand has brought with it a wealth of new providers. The days when executive education was the sole preserve of business schools are over. Today, although business schools still dominate, new players are entering the market, contributing to an ever wider range of programs.

The diversity of the market means that managers in all sectors and at all levels are catered for. Whether just starting the first job after university or settled in as CEO, they will find a program to meet their needs. Prestigious programs such as Harvard's Advanced Management Program and its many imitators in the United States and Europe remain popular with senior executives. At the same time, these general management programs are being joined by courses that focus on specific roles.

In recent years, senior management programs have been added by the top schools, including courses aimed specifically at chief executives—such as IMD's "Seminar for Chief Executives" program. For less senior managers there are programs on the key management disciplines, including everything from programs in finance for managers through to programs on the manager and the media. And as one might expect, there is a profusion of other programs—from marketing on the Web to managing a multinational enterprise, and from teamwork to TQM.

Business schools have sought to give the market what it wants through an array of programs. Once again, more is regarded as better. As we have noted, however, the general trend is toward organizations' taking more control of executive training—witness the emergence of custom and other corporate programs.

Nowhere is this more evident than in the growth of corporate universities. Like it or not, they are one of the new faces of executive education. In the 1980s, Bill Wiggenhorn—head of Motorola's Training and Education Center—addressed a meeting of business school deans. They asked if he and the Motorola University were competing with business schools. Wiggenhorn was unequivocal. Absolutely, he said, we are directly competing with you. The deans probably shook their heads at the sheer effrontery of this. Now, they are not so sure. (Indeed, an admirer of Motorola's management is Kellogg dean Don Jacobs.)

Today, the most explosive source of competition for business schools comes from this source. When they were first established, corporate universities raised a few academic eyebrows. There were sniggers at the thought of McDonald's Hamburger University in Oak Brook, Illinois, or Disney University in Florida (which sports a coat of arms featuring Mickey's eponymous ears rather than rampant lions and the obligatory Latin motto).The mirth has subsided and suspicion has taken over. If corporations can train their own executives, their reliance on business schools is reduced.

The trend toward do-it-yourself management development is strongest in the United States, where over a thousand corporate colleges are now operating. They come in all shapes and sizes, and cover virtually every industry. The Ohio automotive-parts manufacturer, Dana Corporation, has Dana University; Ford has a Heavy Truck University in Detroit; Intel runs a university in Santa Clara; Sun Microsystems has Sun U; and Apple has its own university in Cupertino, California.

The scale of the corporate universities is, in many cases, impressive. Hamburger University may not have a great deal of academic credibility in some circles, but it is celebrating its thirty-fifth anniversary and boasts over fifty thousand graduates. It has thirty resident professors, suggesting that its programs go a little beyond the art of frying. Indeed, the McDonald's educational empire has spread in parallel with the growth of its business—there are now ten international training centers in the United Kingdom, Japan, Germany, and Australia—and technology enables programs to be delivered simultaneously in twenty-two languages. Disney University is similarly successful, though its success is built on training managers from external organizations. The Disney approach is simple: Disney is a successful global company with a unique culture; this is how we do it. Basically, Disney University presents its own corporate case study concentrating on corporate culture, motivating and coaching employees, teamwork, and customer service. It has no pretensions to a broader approach, but argues that its success is built on universal managerial skills. As case studies go, it is impressive. Walt Disney World may not be a hallowed hall of academia but it does employ over forty thousand people ("cast members" in Disney jargon).

Perhaps the best-known corporate university is that run by Motorola. The Motorola University ("an instrument of renewal," according to the company) supplies 550,000 student days a year and costs $170 million. Every single Motorola employee—and there are 139,000 of them—is expected to receive at least forty hours of training per year. The company has also developed its own international MBA program. Motorola calculates that every dollar invested in training reaps $33.[1] The only difference between Motorola U. and a conventional university is the absence of a football team.

The growth in corporate universities can largely be attributed to three things. First, critics of traditional business schools have accused them repeatedly of being too far from the pulse of the business world. This is a widely perceived weakness that corporate universities are keen to capitalize on. In response, many business schools have moved to bring more reality to their programs through project-based work, and have developed custom programs. To a large extent the debate about their being distanced from reality is now a spurious one, but stereotypes linger on.

The second impetus behind the growth of corporate universities is the realization that developing people is key to future survival, something that is too important to be delegated to an external organization. American research found that companies with their own universities spent 2.5 percent of payroll on learning—double the U.S. national average.

The third impetus has come from technology. It is notable that many of the corporate universities are based in or near Silicon Valley. Through employing the latest in technology, companies can economically and effectively deliver distance learning and virtual learning. And, crucially, learning can become both continuous and immediate.

Corporate universities are not for the fainthearted. They are highly expensive. Research in the United States by Jeanne Meister calculated that the average operating budget for a corporate university was $12.4 million (though 60 percent reported budgets of $5 million or less). Typically, National Semiconductor University, opened in 1994, occupies 22,000-square-foot premises with nine classrooms and room for 430 students. Such facilities—as business schools have been pointing out for years—are costly. Running Intel University cost the company $150 million in 1996—Intel offers 2,600 courses, which drew forty thousand participants. Little wonder that corporate universities are largely the domain of multinationals.

Corporate universities are not solely an American phenomenon. IBM has a business school in the United Kingdom, and one of the leaders in the field is the General Electric Company's Dunchurch—which first opened its courses to outsiders in the 1960s. After decades honing the skills of civil servants, the U.K.'s Civil Service College now offers over five hundred courses, attracting managers from the public and private sectors.

In April 1998, British Aerospace, one of Europe's biggest defense and aerospace companies, unveiled plans to create its own virtual university in partnership with outside academic institutions. The move, which goes much further than other emerging corporate universities, comes after twelve months spent developing the concept—which is seen as important for securing the company's competitive place in the next millennium. Called the British Aerospace Virtual University, the initiative involves a massive financial commitment by the company. In the next decade, it has pledged to invest more than £1.5 billion on building up the company's all-important "knowledge base" for the future. The new organization will be headed by a leading academic, Dr. Geraldine Kenney-Wallace, recruited from the University of Toronto.

The chief downside of corporate universities has been that they often do not offer anything other than an internal qualification. In an effort to broaden their appeal, corporate universities are establishing partnerships with a wide range of organizations. Courses are increasingly affiliated to those of more traditional academic institutions. At National Semiconductor University, for example, people can earn associate's, bachelor's or master's degrees from various universities.

Herein lies a major threat to business schools. Some corporate universities are attempting to develop degree-awarding powers themselves. Consulting firm Arthur D. Little has already pursued the degree route at its Boston-based school. A survey of a hundred corporate university deans carried out for the AACSB by Corporate University Xchange found that 40 percent of corporate universities now plan to offer degrees in partnership with higher education institutions, mostly in business administration, computer science, engineering, and finance.[2] It is up to business schools to decide whether they believe this constitutes an opportunity or a risk.

It is also doubtful whether corporate universities can produce meaningful or useful research. Their close allegiances preclude thoughts of objectivity and independence. "There is a difference between training and development. Corporate universities should handle training. Universities aren't good at training. It is skill-based while development is really giving you the knowledge. You don't know when you will need that knowledge. It is an investment in tomorrow while training is about today," says Kenan-Flagler's Jean Hauser. "The danger of developing yourself is that you end up talking to yourself. There is often a corporate line, which means that it is hard to generate the necessary debate."

Whether the growth in corporate universities will continue is a matter of some debate—most obviously within business schools. In their review of worldwide executive development, *Crafting Competitiveness*, Al Vicere and Robert Fulmer sound a note of caution. "While the corporate university movement has to be viewed as a positive affirmation of an organization's commitment to lifelong learning, a slight danger looms on the horizon," note Vicere and Fulmer. "The commitment to learning which leads an organization to establish a corporate university must be carefully monitored, kept flexible, and focused on the strategic imperatives of the sponsoring organization if maximum benefit from the investment is to be reaped."[3]

Motorola must remember that it is in the semiconductor business, not the executive education business. The latter supports the former—for the time being, anyway. If corporate universities are to succeed in the long term they must maintain their difference from alternative training providers. Seeking out affiliations and partnerships may be attractive but in the long term could be self-defeating. Hamburger and Harvard would be wise to discard any notions of an unlikely alliance. The more corporate universities resemble traditional universities and business schools, the less their appeal is likely to be.

CONSULTANTS TURN TEACHERS

There are a range of other new competitors for business schools to contemplate. Among them are offshoots of global management consultancies. Providers such as the Arthur D. Little Management Education Institute, established by the eponymous Boston-based consultancy as long ago as 1964, and Sundridge Park in the United Kingdom—an offshoot of PA Consulting—provide a growing range of short courses aimed at senior and middle managers.

Newcomers include other familiar names such as PriceWaterhouseCoopers and KPMG, which offer management development as part of consultancy packages.

At Cranfield School of Management, chairman of executive development Martin Christopher sees competition to the business schools coming increasingly from consultancies. "There are a number of specialist firms providing courses in personal skills and leadership," he says. "But it's often the bigger consultancies who can offer a bundle of projects and executive development that have the biggest impact."

In many cases, too, the big consultancies are stealing the clothes of business schools by providing proprietary brands of executive development based on original research, or tried and tested methods developed from working with clients. Increasingly, they see themselves as in the business of knowledge creation, and are keen to position themselves as the originators of new research and ideas. As we have seen, "thought leadership" is now a battlefield with the leading consultancies and business schools seeking to occupy the higher ground.

Early in 1998, for example, Andersen Consulting launched "The Third Millennium Forum," which it claims as a "new generation of business school designed to assist multinationals identify the key business capabilities their organizations must possess in order to survive into the next millennium."

What traditional business schools have on their side, Martin Christopher believes, is their specialist knowledge of executive development, plus an academic heritage. "A consultant is a consultant at the end of the day. We have teaching skills—we're full-time academics and management developers."

The different roles of business schools and consultants is pithily summed up by Kenan-Flagler's Jean Hauser: "The sole purpose of universities is the creation and dissemination of new knowledge. In contrast, consulting firms help companies to implement. Consulting firms are hired hands; they can't do the thinking. Companies often tell us they wish they had debated the issues with us before they hired consulting firms."

It is interesting that a number of business school deans have consulting links—in the U.S. alone there is Wharton's Tom Gerrity, who was there at the inception of CSC Consulting; F. David Fowler of George Washington University and KPMG; William Hasler of the University of California and KPMG; and Tom Sarowski of the University of Kansas and Andersen Consulting.

There is a degree of irony in the fact that another source of competition to business schools comes from professional institutions.

Corporate Universities

Location	*Company-Sponsored Schools*
Arizona	American Express Quality University, Phoenix
Arkansas	Walton Institute, Bentonville
California	Amdahl University, Sunnyvale Apple University, Cupertino Chevron Technical University, Richmond Disney University, Anaheim Intel University, Santa Clara National Semiconductor University, Santa Clara PeopleSoft, Pleasanton Schwab University, San Francisco Sun U, Mountain View Viking University, San Jose
Connecticut	Aetna Institute for Corporate Education, Hartford ITT Training & Education, Hartford Mashantucket Pequot Academy, Mashantucket
Georgia	Coca-Cola Company Learning Center, Atlanta The Home Depot University, Atlanta Southern Company College, Atlanta Transcend University, Atlanta
Illinois	Amoco Management Learning Center, Downers Grove Arthur Andersen Center for Professional Development, St. Charles Hamburger University, Oak Brook Hart, Schaffner & Marx University, Chicago Motorola University, Schaumburg
Kansas	Sprint University of Excellence, Westwood
Maryland	Land Rover University, Lanham
Massachusetts	Fidelity Investments Retail Training Services, Boston Arthur D. Little School of Management, Boston Polaroid Leadership Institute, Cambridge Reebok Center for Training & Development, Stoughton Thomson University, Boston
Michigan	Dow Leadership Development Center, Hillsdale General Motors University, Detroit

Location	*Company-Sponsored Schools*
Minnesota	Target Stores University, Minneapolis
New Jersey	AT&T Learning Center, Basking Ridge
	KPMG's Center for Leadership Development, Montvale
	Prudential Center for Learning & Innovation, Newark
New York	Corning Education & Training Center, Corning
	General Electric Management Development Institute, Croton-on-Hudson
	NYNEX Learning Center, Marlboro
Ohio	Banc One College, Columbus
	Iams University, Dayton
Tennessee	Federal Express Leadership Institute, Memphis
	Saturn Training Center, Spring Hill
	Tennessee Valley Authority University, Knoxville
Texas	Dell University, Austin
	Shell Learning Center, Houston
	Texas Instruments Learning Institute, Dallas
	University for People (Southwest Airlines), Dallas
Virginia	PTO University, Arlington
	Xerox University, Leesburg
Washington	Eddie Bauer University, Redmond
	Microsoft University, Bellevue
	Seafirst University, Seattle
Canada	CIBC Leadership Center, King City, Ontario
Cyberspace	IBM's Global Campus
United Kingdom	Cable & Wireless College, Coventry
	IBM Business School
	Dunchurch College
	Civil Service College
	British Aerospace Virtual University

After leading the charge toward the professionalization of management, business schools find themselves fending off the unwanted advances of a posse of professional groups keen to get into the management development market.

In the United Kingdom, for example, the Institute of Directors runs courses to help managers make the transition to directors (some of them in conjunction with leading business schools), while the Institute of Chartered Accountants and the Chartered Institute of Management Accountants both offer programs to enhance the wider contributions of their members to business success. The Institute of Personnel and Development offers a wide range of programs focused on HR issues, and the Industrial Society claims to offer the widest range of training and development programs in Europe.

Such limited endeavors may appear to pose little threat to the business school monoliths. But recent years have also seen the rise of a profusion of general providers of management development and training across a wide spectrum of issues and disciplines.

There are upstarts and start-ups everywhere you look. Students across North America can take courses through Executive Education Network, a tele-learning program created by Westcott Communications of Carrollton, Texas. The company finds top faculty at universities or executives in industry and offers interactive sessions by phone, modem, and video. Students can choose from twelve programs a month, from project management at George Washington University in Washington, D.C., to negotiations from the University of Southern California. Other classes come from Pennsylvania State University or sessions with executives like Lars Nyberg, CEO of NCR Corporation.

Among the more interesting examples are the Body Shop's New Academy of Business. This was established by the chief executive of Body Shop International, Anita Roddick, in 1995 and aims "to bring together the best in values-led business practice with progressive management thinking." There are also various technology-led bodies, such as Pentacle—The Virtual Business School, that use the immediacy of technology to cover their lack of traditional resources.

Then there are the specialist training companies. Companies such as GBS Training, Hawksmere, and Fielden House, for example, offer a wide range of courses covering everything from leading a sales team to conducting a negotiation, and from benchmarking to appraisal interviewing. More specialized still are organizations such as the Center for International Briefing, which offers intensive language courses and cultural sensitivity programs to help prepare managers for overseas assignments. Then there are a whole host of niche organizations that address specific developmental needs such as mentoring and coaching.

GURUS INCORPORATED

Among the more eye-catching new competitors to business schools are providers of a particular proprietary brand of management development often based on original research or a particular philosophy of management. These are now frequently vehicles for an individual thinker or management guru. Here, the growth is particularly explosive.

Typical of these is the Covey Institute, the corporate giant that has emerged from Stephen Covey's self-improvement books. The Covey Institute began life in 1986 with a staff of two. It is based not on the latest technology but on imaginative and remorseless marketing. Based in Provo, Utah, it now employs seven hundred people and is part of the Franklin Group. Covey's institute is a child of its times and yet Covey is a conventional child of yesterday—he has an MBA from Harvard Business School and spent the bulk of his career at Brigham Young University, where he was first an administrator and then professor of organizational behavior. He could have joined the ranks of tens of thousands of other moderately successful academics. Covey's doctoral research looked at "success literature." Having examined it in detail, Covey created his own (or, as we have seen, employed Ken Shelton to help him create it).

Covey reached a huge global audience with the success of *The Seven Habits of Highly Effective People* (1989), which has sold over six million copies. Along the way, the devout Mormon transformed himself into an end-of-the-century Dale Carnegie. "He has sold himself with a brashness that makes the overexcited Tom Peters look like a shrinking violet," noted *The Economist*. Another commentator observed, "Mr. Covey has a knack of dressing up spiritual principles in pinstripes." In fact, Covey's "principles" are a mixture of the commonsensical and the hackneyed—be proactive, begin with the end in mind, put first things first, think win-win, seek first to understand then to be understood, synergize, sharpen the saw. Yet it is their very simplicity and accessibility that partly explain Covey's astonishing success.

In 1984, Covey founded his Leadership Center, aiming to "serve the worldwide community by empowering people and organizations to significantly increase their performance capability in order to achieve worthwhile purposes through understanding and living principle-centered leadership." Whatever you think of the man or his ideas, Stephen Covey is no rocket scientist. He is simply a very astute marketer of himself, his company, and his ideas.

Whether other gurus can follow in Covey's footsteps is open to debate. Most prefer the lucre of consulting to the trials and tribulations of the mass market of executive education. Covey has proved highly successful, but others with similarly high profiles have fared less well. Tom Peters established the Tom Peters Group at the height of his fame in the 1980s, but the company never fully exploited the strength of his brand name.

BEAUTY PAGEANTS

As the market has become crowded with new entrants, the number of business schools has continued to rise. A combination of innovative approaches and keen pricing by these new entrants has put pressure on the more established business schools. They have to fight harder to get the work.

At the same time, increasing levels of sophistication and knowledge among HR professionals means that even at the top end of the market companies are more inclined to shop around, often holding discussions with several providers at the same time.

As Ian Tanner, director of the executive center at Manchester Business School—one of Britain's oldest and best-known business schools—observes, "The proliferation of suppliers means there's a lot more choice now. It isn't uncommon to find yourself up against two or three or even half a dozen other providers. There's no doubt that HR professionals have become a lot more knowledgeable and are more likely to compare what different schools are offering. There's an element of beauty contests going on that wasn't there before." He confirms that as a result prices, especially those for tailored programs, are increasingly negotiable. "There is certainly price sensitivity. Some of the new providers—the new universities in particular—came into the market with very different price structures. It's a question of differentiating between the quality of providers, but within the broad bands of similar offerings there is some negotiation. There are one or two courses where demand is so high that price is nonnegotiable. It's a bit like trying to get a discount on a new Mercedes Benz, some schools take a similar view with their leading programs."

Geographically, too, the market for executive education has been transformed in recent years. Where the top U.S. schools and the American model of executive education once dominated, the leading European schools are a force to be reckoned with—not just in their home markets but throughout the world. "There are some very strong European schools now," says Wanda Wallace, managing director of executive education at Duke University's Fuqua Business School in North Carolina. "Our clients talk about INSEAD, IMD, and LBS, in particular. We're hearing less from the Asian schools, but we expect that to change in the next few years. They will come up the learning curve very quickly. Companies are very keen to have an Asian presence on programs and will no doubt partner schools in the region. We're already using a lot of faculty from Asian schools on our programs."

TIGER POWER

The currency crises in Asia of early 1998 have undermined the market for executive education in that region, with a ripple effect on U.S. and other Western business schools. In time, however, assuming Asia's Tiger economies recover their confidence, demand from this quarter will exert a new influence on executive programs both in this region and in the more mature markets of Europe and North America. The *Far East Economic Review* recently carried a headline that would have inspired hope and optimism in all Western business schools. It simply read: "Wanted: 3 million managers for Asia."

In these and other emerging markets there are already a growing number of local providers, offering programs that cater to the demands of multinational companies operating in the region. A number of Asian business schools, influenced by the U.S. model but also reflecting local knowledge and business practice, are rapidly earning a reputation as quality executive education providers in their own right.

When it started in 1968, for example, the Asian Institute of Management in Manila, the region's first Western-style business school, used materials only from Harvard. Now 60 percent of case studies for its MBA program are written in-house or come from other Asian schools.

The Sasin Graduate Institute of Business Administration, Bangkok's top business school, offers a graduate program in cross-cultural management that focuses on neighboring countries such as Vietnam. It also offers weekend training for midcareer Thai executives. The Hong Kong University of Science and Technology has recently added electives in Mandarin and Chinese economic reforms to its MBA syllabus.

Moreover, many Western companies, which see these markets as increasingly important to their business, recognize that such schools can provide a gateway to local markets, while companies from the Tiger economies look to executive programs to help them sustain performance. Observes Narayan Pant, deputy chairman of executive programs at the National University of Singapore: "Levels of sophistication among purchasers of executive education are rising in the Southeast Asian market as there are few even medium-sized companies where senior managers have not been to some high-profile executive program."

Private management institutes are also springing up in these regions, offering courses in everything from time-management to teamwork. Increasingly, too, today's managers must know how to function across cultures. Human resource directors in top multinationals say executive programs provide big-picture views of the global economy while breeding leaders with transnational skills.

Globalization of the economy is also prompting firms that operate internationally to ask schools from different parts of the world to get together on their behalf. "Business schools would like to think they are setting the agenda," says Cranfield's Martin Christopher. "But the reality is that it's being set on a global stage now, with ideas and issues coming from many sources. This can work to the advantage of schools that stay closer to practice than theory."

But, as ever, U.S. schools are keen to explore new business opportunities. The University of Michigan's William Davidson Institute is developing special training programs to turn Communist managers into capitalist competitors, retraining hundreds of managers in Vietnamese state-owned industries that are customer companies of Citibank.

In the coming years, demand from the emerging markets of Asia and Eastern Europe will exert a powerful influence over the way that executive programs evolve, not just in these regions but in Europe and the United States.

The skills and disciplines companies demand from management education providers are also changing. Where once business schools sought only to teach the hard functional areas of management such as finance and marketing, today companies are demanding programs that foster the softer skills, including interpersonal skills, communication, and leadership.

The growth of business in Asia is also likely to have an impact on the content of traditional programs. There is a growing acceptance that simply transplanting Western-style management techniques and approaches is not enough.

The hire-and-fire, short-term-profit-maximization ethos of many U.S. companies, for example, is inappropriate to the paternalistic business cultures of many Asian countries, where workers still expect their loyalty to be reciprocated. Not surprisingly, downsizing and business process reengineering do not play well in the Asian cultures.

Nor do traditional Western programs prepare managers for the rapid-fire deal-making style that characterizes Asian transactions, where personal contacts and extended family are often more important than cold logic. In particular, Asian business leaders are underwhelmed by the West's elevation of analysis to something bordering on obsession.

The chief of one of Hong Kong's leading property developers was reported recently as saying he had fired every one of the Western-trained MBAs he had hired straight out of business school because they weren't responsive enough to the Asian environment. Now he looks for MBAs with a minimum of five years' experience in the region. "If you analyze too much," he says, "you can't make money."

Users of executive programs—and more enlightened providers—will welcome the new competition. Over time, it is likely to have the effect of ratcheting up the quality of programs across the board.

In the short term, too, the emerging economies of these regions offer an opportunity for European and American providers who are fleet of foot. Those that take advantage of the opportunity to establish themselves are likely to gain an important strategic advantage over their competitors not just in terms of selling their services today but also in their ability to import new perspectives and approaches into the products they offer in their home markets.

The management training boom in Asia in recent years has attracted the interest of the leading U.S. business schools and academics. *Business Week* reports that faculty from schools such as Columbia, Northwestern, and Michigan have taken up temporary residence at campuses across Asia, drawn no doubt not simply by lucrative contracts but with a view to enhancing their own knowledge of the local business culture.

At the same time, the top schools from the United States and Europe are using their international reputations as a platform for selling programs in the region. In the first wave, this tended to be short courses and one-day seminars, using local universities or hotels as a temporary base. But increasingly they are ramping up their activities, establishing campuses in the region or forging partnerships with local institutions to offer longer programs.

As a result, many of the differences between these national markets are already blurring as management development becomes a global business in its own right. Companies expect to send their managers on high-quality executive programs wherever they happen to be in the world, an expectation that is accelerating the growth of business schools and other providers in regions as diverse as Eastern Europe, Asia, and Latin America.

Elsewhere, the opening of markets previously closed to trade is also prompting the growth of a whole new network of executive education providers from the Czech Republic to the Baltic States, many of them working in partnership with established American and European providers.

China is beginning to stir and yawn and stretch its muscles, attracting interest to executive program providers in Hong Kong and new institutions springing up throughout the vast nation as Western companies seek a business interface with the largest domestic market in the world.

10

Uncertain Futures

We believe that university business schools, in particular, are at a crossroads. They can choose to respond to critical challenges and new customer demands as they stumble upon them. Or, they can harness the energy of emerging market trends in executive education/leadership development by revitalizing and transforming themselves into the kinds of educational providers now demanded by their corporate constituency.

—*Albert Vicere and Robert Fulmer,*
Crafting Competitiveness[1]

For many schools, exec ed is the cream in their coffee. They rely on corporate clients' sending managers to exec ed programs to subsidize research and degree programs. They will be badly affected if the exec ed business dries up. The American university business schools face a problem with customized programs. Their tax-exempt status forbids them from providing consultancy. But what a growing number of corporate clients want are programs that provide an element of organizational transformation as well individual development. How will the schools respond? Partnerships and other arrangements are one possible solution, or something more radical, involving a break with their universities. (Independent schools such as INSEAD and IMD have fewer restrictions.)

Is Harvard Business School ready to go it alone as a business? Is Wharton, or Stanford? In the future, they may have to take the option seriously, or accept a smaller role in the overall executive development market. Either way, it is clear that the future will be different. Business schools are at a crossroads:

- The good news is that demand for all types of executive education is increasing and is likely to continue to do so in the foreseeable future.
- The bad news is that the rules of the game are changing as corporate clients demand demonstrable impact on their organizations, and as new competitors enter the market.
- Content and delivery mechanisms are both critical—new technology, in particular, will transform the exec ed landscape in the next few years.
- Despite what they teach, many business schools appear complacent about their market (a quick refresher of their core competencies would not go amiss).
- New competition is eroding their grip on the exec ed market.
- In time, this could undermine their other roles (if the income dries up, they will need to work harder to justify their existence if they are to retain corporate funding).
- The future of the top-flight schools is assured in the immediate future. (In the long run, corporations will be loath to fund irrelevant research and exec ed programs. In the next few years, the schools will have to get real and demonstrate value. The best strategy may be

to occupy the academic high ground at the expense of corporate work.)

- Second- and third-tier schools need to decide which market they are in.

WELCOME TO THE FUTURE

The trouble for business schools is that the future has already arrived. Their lucrative markets for exec ed—which traditionally generated a large part of their incomes—are already being eroded. While they were busy squabbling about who should ride in the front carriage, others boarded the education train.

They may, for example, have never heard of the Apollo Group. Based in Phoenix, Arizona, Apollo has recorded average growth over the last five years of 29 percent. Its 1997 sales were $266 million, from which its net income was $30.2 million. It has a market value of over $2 billion.

Apollo was the brainchild of John G. Sperling, still its CEO and owner of just under 20 percent of the company (stock valued at $415 million). Now in his late seventies, Sperling started the company twenty-five years ago. Working at San Jose State University, Sperling was refused support for an adult degree program. Undaunted, he started his own business in adult degree programs. Long before the idea was fashionable, Sperling believed that lifelong employment with a single employer would be replaced by lifelong learning and employment with a variety of employers. (Sperling wasn't alone. No less a figure than Milton Friedman observed: "There are many activities that have very little to do with higher education—namely, athletics and research. Institutions are run by faculty, and the faculty is interested in its own welfare, the question is why competing institutions have not grown up which are private and for profit."[2])

Sperling's first contract came from the University of San Francisco. Now his educational business is highly profitable and expanding rapidly. Apollo more than doubled its total enrollments and revenues between 1993 and 1997. Its businesses include the University of Phoenix (40,000 students at fifty-one campuses in thirteen states plus 2,600 students through virtual classrooms), the Institute for Professional Development, the College for Financial Planning, and Western International University. All in all it has one hundred campuses in thirty-two states and activities in Puerto Rico and London.[3]

Sperling is just more farsighted than most. Others are boarding the educational bandwagon. Michael Milken's new venture is not on Wall Street, it's in education and training: Knowledge Universe. Milken founded the company at the beginning of 1996 partnered by his brother, Lowell Milken, and by Oracle CEO Larry Ellison. Targeting the "education products market," Knowledge Universe now has majority interests in seven computer training companies as well as owning Symmetrix, a Boston technology consulting company, and Children's Discovery Centers. Milken, partnered by Donaldson Lufkin & Jenrette, narrowly missed out on buying Simon & Schuster in early 1998. Media group Pearson won that auction, where the prize was Simon & Schuster's educational publishing. (Pearson has created a distance learning company targeted at management training—already the company has offices in the United Kingdom, the United States, and Malaysia. "Lifelong and distance learning in management skills and development is one of the fastest-growing sectors of the education market," says Pearson CEO Marjorie Scardino.)[4] Education, Knowledge Universe and others have decided, is where it's at. Initially focused on the IT training marketplace, Knowledge Universe aims to build a substantial, broad-based business in education.

The future is here. In 1993, Peterson's guide to American colleges detailed 93 cyberschools. By 1997 there were reputed to be 762. The future is here. It won't wait for the laggards. They will be left at the station or shunted into sidings.

The key to distribution is the new technology. The key to the economics is faculty salaries. Part-time faculty cost less—the University of Phoenix spends $46 per credit hour of education on teaching salaries and benefits; Arizona State spends $247.[5]

Some b-schools have embraced the new technology with something approaching abandon. Duke's Global Executive MBA is now available on-line—though you pay a premium price ($86,000 against $50,000 if you are actually there). Carnegie-Mellon offers an MBA and MS via videoconference and computer. Michigan has beamed in its professors to provide customized MBA programs via videoconferencing to managers at Daewoo Corporation in Korea and Cathay Pacific Airways in Hong Kong. Harvard, on the other hand, has spent millions of dollars wiring up its campus and creating its Intranet so that students don't have to be in the lecture theater to watch the gurus perform—what one business school insider calls "cable guru."

SLEEPWALKING THROUGH A REVOLUTION

The new rules of the game are about leverage. Some business schools are so busy talking about intellectual capital that they aren't leveraging their own. After years of trying to corner the market for the best business teachers in the world, they don't seem to know what to do with them. Most have a strategy that's little more than a motherhood statement. To say you want to be the best is fine—but as a game plan, it's a nonstarter.

Whatever the future holds for business schools, we are unlikely to see their demise. But what we will see is changes in the way they are organized, changes in the way they deliver their services, and continual changes in their offerings. How business schools employ and manage technology is key to all these issues. The marriage of technology and education is the future.

The trouble is that it is a future for which business schools seem singularly badly equipped. With a few notable exceptions, they have embraced technology with a level of enthusiasm that could be best described as tepid. No matter how much they talk about it, in practice most business schools either don't get it, won't get it, or can't afford it.

"When it comes to technology, business schools are in catch-up mode," admits Kenan-Flagler dean Bob Sullivan. "Technology needs to permeate the learning experience. Technology enables us to get to the individual level. We are not good practitioners. There is tremendous inertia in the system. Classroom processes don't think the way Michael Dell is thinking."

The common conclusion is that business schools are so steeped in the past and internally focused that they are too blinkered to realize what is happening. In some cases this may be the case. What is more damning, perhaps, is the way in which some have *appeared* to embrace technology. If you walk around a business school you will find the hardware in abundance. There are PCs, networks, computer centers, and the like at every turn. It is notable that they often lie unused or are used only by students.

Those that proclaim their technological credentials tend to take an inside-out view of technology's potential. They use videoconferencing, for example, to extend the reach of the traditional classroom. As a result, you can find supposedly high-tech programs with videoconference links featuring an academic going through a well-worn slide presentation. Harvard Business School, for example, is using CD-ROM. This simply involves transforming a conventional Harvard case study into an interactive CD-ROM package.

"Such an approach can hardly be termed progress. The key to effective use of technology does not lie in automating the past. By regarding videoconferencing as the bright new technological age, organizations are deceiving themselves and their clients," says Paul Turnbull of Ashridge Management College. "Harvard's CD-ROM is better seen as the end of the product life cycle for the Harvard case study rather than an entrance into a technologically driven world."

Turnbull is critical of some U.S. and European schools for using IT simply to put their "gurus on-line." "We had some people come over from Wharton recently who said that what we're doing is two years ahead of the U.S. market," he says. "The technology is mature now. It has the capability to be transformational, to change the rules of the game."

It would have seemed unthinkable just a few years ago, but the stakes are so high that even America's biggest brand business schools are beginning to cut deals with private sector partners that can provide the technological backup to reach a mass audience.

Robert S. Hamada, dean of the Graduate School of Business at Chicago, is sanguine about what's around the corner. "There's no question that there'll be more technology involved," he says. "Microsoft has contacted all the major business schools, as has Knowledge Universe, Larry Ellison and Michael Milken's company, and the *Financial Times*. They all see a pot of gold here. I think they are probably right. They can provide the technology. But a Microsoft MBA may not sell so well. What they'd like to do is to tap into some equity branding and some real expertise from the top schools. They see an important role for business schools to partner with.

"I don't know how this is going to shake out. Harvard has set up its own operation to look into the opportunities. We're talking to everyone, so are Columbia and Stanford. I think the top tier of b-schools are pretty safe. But they will need to maintain their campus MBA to keep their reputation and flagship product. Who should be worried? I think maybe the second tier schools, and maybe the part-time programs."

Wharton is testing the water. The scheme is called Wharton Direct. It involves a joint venture between the Wharton School at the University of Pennsylvania and Caliber Learning, a company spun off from the private sector education provider Sylvan Learning Systems. Wharton recently ran a distance learning program for executives, transmitting the same lecture simultaneously to twenty-nine cities across the United States. Technology allows professors from Wharton to reach 260 students scattered in different locations. A spokesperson from the business school described the hookup between Wharton and Caliber as "a natural alliance." The logic is clear: Wharton has the content, providing the professors and curriculum; Caliber has the technology and infrastructure, having invested heavily in recent years to install well-equipped lecture rooms throughout the United States and to develop software that allows a higher level of interaction than was previously possible.

Pursuing the radical model, too, are Europe's distance learning providers. Michael Pitfield, director of marketing at Henley Management College, for example, believes the arrival of the Internet and other communications technologies could "liberate executive education." In a paper presented to the International University Consortium for Executive Education (UNICON), Pitfield set out his vision for the year 2002. The Internet and other communications media, he said, would mean information—including course materials—was widely available, switching the emphasis from provision of knowledge to the interpretation of information. Pitfield anticipated that providers would no longer sell course materials and content as they do now. Rather, they would charge fees for additional support such as mentoring, assessments, and qualifications, plus electronic contact with alumni peer group. Under this model, the role of faculty would change from teaching and presenting to coaching and guiding.

Others, however, believe technology is no substitute for the human touch. Among them are some exec ed providers who see the Internet and videoconferencing not as delivery mechanisms in their own right but as tools to support more traditional program delivery. "Everything is changing," acknowledges Professor Carlos Cavallé, dean of the Barcelona-based business school IESE. "IT will have a great impact on the transmission of knowledge, but it cannot replace the exchange of experience. We are using IT as something to complement but not to replace face-to-face teaching." Commenting on the technique of beaming lectures from top members of faculty to company sites, he adds: "When you want the top faculty you don't want to see them on TV. You want to have the chance to meet them, especially at very senior management levels. You want to see the real animal and touch the real person."

If it is worthwhile, technology must enable an organization to satisfy the needs of customers in different and better ways. Innovative technology is only as good as the innovative uses to which it is put. Videoconferencing, for example, offers a myriad of possibilities beyond repeating now historical methods. More of the same is no longer acceptable.

NO BUSINESS IS AN ISLAND

The challenge facing business schools is to marry the needs of corporations and their executives with the potential of the mature technology. The starting point must be the demands of corporate clients. Business schools need to get wired, and quickly.

Companies are increasingly realizing that they compete on the basis of the competencies of those they employ. Companies are using technology—through knowledge networks and expert systems—to enhance these competencies. Many publicly proclaim their faith in knowledge and learning as the future of their business. PriceWaterhouseCoopers has identified "learning capability" as one of the core competencies it wishes to develop; Skandia has a director of intellectual capital; Ernst & Young and others have created a new job title: chief knowledge officer—"Part of a growing trend by organizations to manage institutional intelligence as they would any other precious asset," explains the company; the Canadian Imperial Bank of Commerce has a vice president of learning organization. Inventing job titles is, of course, the easy part. But it is a start and represents a clear statement of values.

In contrast, business schools have been slow to clearly and unequivocally commit themselves to developing knowledge and learning as core competencies both internally and among their clients. This is, perhaps, understandable. Traditionally, business schools thought of themselves as the sole preserve of knowledge and learning. Knowledge and learning were then distributed to those prepared to pay. Now the rules have changed. Instead of being isolated and occasional occurrences, knowledge and learning are the lifeblood of any organization. An occasional infusion is not enough; companies require a constant transfusion, with continuous distribution and implementation of skills and ideas. As a result, business schools can no longer consider themselves as citadels of learning. Instead, they must become part of networks of learning, creating their own extended communities. Here they have a valuable advantage—they already have well-developed alumni networks.

Within organizations, the identification of core corporate and individual competencies owes much to the HR function. In their championing of competencies and in their identification of knowledge and learning as the keys to the future, HR managers are not only shaping the organizations of tomorrow but recasting their own roles within these organizations. Increasingly HR is a strategic issue. Its preoccupation with management training is moving toward organizational development. The awareness and perspectives required of HR managers are now broad and strategic rather than narrow and operational. Instead of being concerned with the present, HR is looking to the future. This marks a fundamental change.

Traditionally, the solution to questions of competencies was to dispatch senior managers to executive training programs. This solution was limited to the managerial elite, the movers and shakers of the present and future. Now there is a pressing need for companies to develop the competencies of the entire cadre of management. If they are to compete successfully, training and development has to be all-embracing rather than the preserve of the chosen few.

The need for training for all is easily espoused. Politicians, management thinkers and commentators, and business schools frequently express it. In practice, companies face the daunting prospect of enormous training bills. As a result, they are left in an untenable and unwinnable dilemma. On one hand, they recognize the need to develop the competencies of all their employees. On the other, the figures involved in doing so are impossibly high. Shell, for example, has forty thousand managers; Unilever has twenty-two thousand.

WIRED FOR LEARNING

Technology enables learning to be more personalized and immediate. The classroom approach, orchestrated by a resident expert, is no longer appropriate for many types of development experience. Managers want to access learning from their desks and to relate learning to an issue that confronts them in their business. Development must be managed by them rather than being based on an unbending program. The increasing regularity of job changes highlights this particular need. After the flurry of downsizing and delayering in recent years, managers find themselves frequently changing positions. As their responsibilities alter, so too do their immediate training needs. In such circumstances, development planning is difficult, if not plain unrealistic. Learning needs emerge rapidly and need to be met with the same speed. It is little use sending a manager on a course covering ten subject areas when only three or four are of immediate use. Far better to supply individual subject areas if and when they are required.

Instead of being a separate activity, training is being reincarnated as "performance support," helping people do their jobs more effectively. And part of this support will come through greater use of mentoring—on-line mentors can ensure that learning is effectively translated into improved performance. Research by the American Society for Training and Development found that 84 percent of human resource executives thought that by the year 2000 there will be a new balance between training as we know it today and performance support. Ominously, 73 percent thought that current training managers and staff are ill-prepared for performance support.

This has broad repercussions. Organizations demand well-rounded and multitalented people who are able to respond to strategic and operational initiatives. They must be competent in a range of business, personal, and teamworking skills. For managers to respond to changes in organization and responsibility requires access to learning resources as and when required. Learning must be continuous and continuously accessible. With these parameters, learning is a process rather than, as traditional business schools continue to suggest, a product.

Some schools seem to be getting the message. Schools now must answer each executive's personal management problems. Content can no longer come from books, or from participants' combined work experience. Learning is more individualized, content participant-oriented. "From knowledge to process," is how Thierry Grange, dean of ESC Grenoble, puts it. "From capital to speed."[6]

This is having a profound effect on what schools teach, even on who teaches. In Europe, French and British institutions are leading the region's exec ed into the new millennium. Henry Mintzberg believes the most interesting developments in exec ed are occurring in Europe. "The sector is ripe for really interesting change," he says, "and almost all of it is happening in the U.K. There is tons of innovative activity there. That's where the real rethinking is being done."[7]

And, at the most innovative schools, thinking is linked directly and explicitly to action. At Lancaster University's School of Management, John Mackness, director of the management development division, explains, "Today's managers want programs that start with an analysis of the issues, so they can manage them. That's the approach we take. We look at issues people face in their organizations."

In France, ESC Grenoble's project management course used to teach how to organize project management. It included basic core knowledge from faculty writings or company white papers. Now the course jumps right in with a diagnosis of participants' problems. "We begin creating, not knowledge sharing," says Thierry Grange. "Direct solutions for identified participants. The whole thing is personalized and customized."

"The biggest change in our programs," declares Terry Campbell, former dean at the Theseus International Management Institute on the French Riviera, "is an emphasis on making lessons learned applicable the first day you're back at work. This has been the biggest improvement in exec ed I've seen." It's an approach that seems to be in tune with corporate thinking. The message from companies to exec ed providers is "give us knowledge, but make it knowledge we can use."

There is a growing interest, for example, in programs that break out of the classroom to make use of action learning and other experiential techniques.

The Theseus Institute specializes in what it calls "strategic executive development." Dedicated to project-based action learning, it runs programs for the likes of GE, Johnson & Johnson, and Volkswagen. Aimed at very senior managers, the approach is based on creating programs that address key strategic issues facing the company. In effect, the programs combine personal development with a form of internal consultancy. Faculty act as coaches and facilitators. As Dr. Yury Boshyk, director of executive development, explains: "This is not the traditional business school approach. Programs are tied to a big strategic issue: 'How are we going to grow the business by 30 percent by the year 2000?' for example. Participants working on these strategic projects develop internal consultancy and teamworking skills. They report their findings back to the board. In GE's case, recommendations go directly to Jack Welch. Companies say it saves them millions with consultancies like McKinsey."

A typical class on financial analysis for shareholder value twenty years ago, Campbell recalls, taught the concept of shareholder value, and encouraged participants to use it at work. "Now we make them convert it to an action plan: change the concept to an operating language they can use in decision making. Not only that, but they have to coach others. We're trying to create *cascade learning*, so lessons learned don't stop with the course participants but are shared with colleagues."

THE MEDIUM IS THE MESSAGE

Technology enables learning to be delivered in different ways: "Business schools have been too concerned with content—what they deliver in their courses," says Henley Management College's principal, Ray Wild. "In future, their effectiveness will be as much, if not more, a function of delivery—how well and how appropriately do they deliver their services to busy, mobile, preoccupied managers working in turbulent organizations."

Wharton MBA and technological guru Peter Cohen says: "I think that one area that will be more important for managers to understand in the future is . . . technology. In the future, managers will not be able to hide behind a CIO or CTO when it comes to matters of technology. And I think business schools will have to change in order to prepare managers to deal with matters that take place at the intersection of business and technology. Part of it is a generational thing. Tomorrow's MBA students will have grown up with computers. But they will still need models for helping them deal with issues that are at the intersection of technology and business. Examples of such issues include how to use technology in some way to tilt the playing field in a company's favor, how technology can be used to help hire and retain the best people, how technology can enhance a company's relationships with suppliers and customers, etc."

But it may already be too late. The lack of enthusiasm of business schools for technology has opened the gates to other providers.

Eddie Obeng is founder of Pentacle—The Virtual Business School. It is located not in Silicon Valley but in Beaconsfield, England, within striking distance of London and Heathrow. Obeng argues that the concept of the virtual organization is readily transferable to the business school model. He contrasts his current virtual organization with his previous employer, Ashridge Management College. Pentacle has three employees and a turnover of £1 million and rising; Ashridge has substantial overheads with over two hundred employees and an array of buildings.

"To be virtual is to have the same effect without the traditional form," says Obeng. "In a reengineering exercise at Ashridge I identified thirteen major processes. Only three had anything to do with delivering learning, so I set out to create an organization which concentrated on and delivered the three processes. It is an experiment to see if the theories work, but I am experimenting with myself."

The basic premise behind the virtual business school is that there needs to be a continuous link between learning and implementation. Such an ongoing relationship can be better served by an organization built around networks of experts with low fixed overheads and constant communication with its clients. "As a strategy moves forward, objectives will change so people need to learn at the right stages. You can't simply dispatch them on a week's course beforehand," says Obeng. Course members use Lotus Notes, virtual reality simulations, and short modular "learning events" to update their knowledge continually. This allows them to apply what they have learned directly to their jobs rather than to theoretical case studies that don't address real-life issues.

The theory is undeniably neat, as tidy as the consultant's solutions Obeng enthusiastically derides. But fall in love with the technology at your peril, warns Obeng. "The technology is simply a flexible means of delivery and should not be allowed to cloud the objective: implementation. The virtual organization is one way of creating flexible structures which are strategic," he says. "Companies may say that they need a grand strategy when what they desperately need is a better means of implementation. To work out what's best, go into the future and look back. Companies must either use rapid analysis followed by rapid implementation or match high levels of innovation with creative implementation. The new world demands new approaches, new ways of thinking. The old ways aren't working."

"Changed times demand new approaches to development. People now have to manage multiple strategies. They are dealing with great complexity. Bringing in a consultant who stays for a brief period, offers insight on a small number of issues to a small number of people, and then disappears, is not useful."

If managers can't be sitting in the same classroom, the traditional response has been to use some form of distance learning. While classroom-based and distance learning are clearly valuable, they cannot avoid being formulaic or relying on a one-best-way approach. The emerging need therefore is for local learning—learning that is continuously adapted and fitted around the immediate needs of managers. If access to learning is immediate it becomes a far more valuable managerial currency.

Pentacle uses technology for mentoring. "The constant interaction allowed by networking on the information superhighway turns mentoring into a far more dynamic, customer-focused, and practical exercise," says Obeng. Senior executives without typing skills are spared—they can use voice mail and now relatively inexpensive desktop videophones.

Enthusiasm for such approaches appears to be growing. Demand for computer-based simulations and needs analysis software for management development has skyrocketed as multimedia has finally become a practical reality for many businesses.

Skeptics might suggest that while the world is full of talk of virtual reality, virtuality is generally far from reality. The virtual organization still retains a ring of Californian management thinkers anxiously scanning the dictionary for new buzzwords. "In the past people had to be brought together because they couldn't do things for themselves," says Laurence Lyons, coauthor of *Creating Tomorrow's Organization* and cofounder of the Future Work Forum. "Now, technology is giving more power to individuals. The implications for management development are phenomenal. Managers will have to organize, manage, motivate, and develop themselves in a world where organizations and individuals become atomized. But they will not do so in isolation. They need to be linked to the organization and to interact with the other people in it."

Eddie Obeng believes that the "v" word is misunderstood. "There is nothing grandiose about the concept. Managers are adept at using networks and, increasingly, at working in teams. It should never be forgotten that technology enables managers to work more effectively and to learn new skills cost-effectively. The virtual concept is a label, what matters is making it work."

Pentacle now offers a virtual reality simulation exercise. From a practical viewpoint, this doesn't take up huge amounts of room on a PC and can be sent down phone lines quickly and cheaply. However, it is highly traditional in one respect—as the manager progresses through the program, success is measured by the size of the dollar sign displayed.

THE THREE-TIER BUSINESS SCHOOL SYSTEM

Technology is revolutionizing education. It will inevitably revolutionize exec ed. The second major trend which will shape the business schools of the future is the development of three tiers of business schools. It is easy to envisage the development of a hierarchy topped by an elite of business schools continuing with high-quality research while the remainder follow behind as interpreters and translators.

At the top would be the elite: probably no more than fifty business schools throughout the world carrying a premium brand and filling a traditional academic role. "Ninety-five percent of business schools are in follower mode. The remaining 5 percent defines what is professionally acceptable," says Kenan-Flagler dean Robert Sullivan.

"Schools like ours have to decide not to play the games of other schools. We have to do what we are good at and add value to the profession. It takes a network and a willingness to take risk."

The elite schools will be international in their outlook, centers of excellence for their areas of research—much more narrowly defined specialties, offering real depth of knowledge rather than breadth. They will compete globally. "Place of delivery will still matter but you must have a capacity to deliver elsewhere in the world, indeed anywhere in the world," says Fuqua's Blair Sheppard.

The second tier would consist of national competitors providing general executive education. These schools would serve as a training ground for managers and faculty alike, feeding people into industry and into the first-tier schools. Their horizons, aspirations, and resources would be more targeted than is currently the case. They would no longer aim to be the biggest but would concentrate on the knowledge and expertise necessary to become the best.

Below the national schools, there would be a variety of small niche providers serving local demand for executive education. These schools would be in competition with local training firms and also with the coursework offered by professional bodies.

It is also possible to foresee far greater movement between the worlds of consulting and business schools than ever before. This could be mutually beneficial. Under continual pressure as they shuttle from project to project, consultants would benefit from being given the space, time, and opportunity to study the implications of their work more thoroughly and systematically. Similarly, research academics could benefit from closer contact with the immediacy of consulting work. The result could be a more balanced output of ideas, with business schools reclaiming their place as factories of ideas rather than becoming producers of programs.

For the elite business schools, brand management will be high on the agenda. Brand expert Chris Lederer of Chicago-based Helios Consulting argues that only the best brands will survive. "American schools such as Harvard, Wharton, Amos Tuck, Northwestern, the University of Virginia's Darden, and MIT's Sloan School have successfully created brands which are separate from their universities," says Lederer. "With the proliferation of schools and the MBA now almost generic, business schools have to develop brands which differentiate them from the competition."

According to Lederer, sound brand management is one feature of Harvard Business School's success. "The benchmark is Harvard. It recognized the importance of branding early on—even by having its own coat of arms. It has been very careful in extending its brand. Harvard's onus is on cultivating alumni through relentless communication. It has controlled its brand and prices its products accordingly."

With branding preeminent, Lederer presents an intriguing scenario: "A quarter of Harvard Business School graduates receive job offers from consulting firm McKinsey. So think of the potential of the Harvard Business School–McKinsey MBA. With the blurring of divides between consulting firms, corporations, and business schools it could make sense. Students could spend a year learning through the case study method at Harvard and the following year working on McKinsey assignments. It would be a powerful coupling of brands."

While the Harvard-McKinsey dream ticket remains a dream, the elite schools will increasingly attempt to leverage their brands. This will be achieved in a number of ways: international expansion, franchising, and networking with other schools and organizations in the business.

International Expansion

Schools recruit international faculty to give the impression of global perspectives. Some have gathered an impressive array of international academics to prove their global credentials. But such an approach does not make a business school global. Academics soon become isolated, out of touch with the local environment and culture they are hired to be knowledgeable about.

"We're not going to expand into Europe in the foreseeable future," Fuqua's Blair Sheppard told us when we spoke to him a couple of years back. Fuqua has joint ventures with a number of European providers, including London Business School. "We don't and cannot know Europe the way a European business school knows it. To think you do is hubris. We would rather LBS, INSEAD, and others regarded us as an asset rather than a threat." How schools manage their international development will be key to their future success. As we write, we understand that Duke is to open the Fuqua School of Business Europe—probably in Frankfurt—with others to follow, possibly in China, India, or South America.

Franchising Their Programs

Picture this. In the year 2006 a graduate of Harvard Business School's MBA program graduates not through the ivy-covered portals of Harvard but at the University of the West Indies. The graduate emerges with a bona fide Harvard MBA without ever setting foot in Boston.

Depending on your perspective, this is either wishful thinking, a nightmare scenario, or a logical development for business schools. Acceptance of the franchised MBA—where an established provider allows another institution to deliver its MBA program—may not be far away. Making the franchised MBA a reality may, however, take a little longer.

Trends in the MBA marketplace point to the possibilities. Franchising is, after all, another means of leveraging a brand. Business schools are, for example, establishing links and alliances with others throughout the world in an effort to establish their global credentials. Typically, the University of Rochester in the United States works in partnership with Nijenrode University in the Netherlands and the Universität Bern in Switzerland. The University of Chicago offers an International Executive MBA at Barcelona with all courses taught by Chicago faculty and has plans to open a campus in Singapore. With a network of such alliances and the growing use of the Internet and IT to deliver MBA programs, the place of delivery is becoming less important than what is actually delivered.

The Chicago-Barcelona initiative is probably the nearest a major business school has got to an MBA franchise. At the moment, it cannot be categorized as a franchise as Chicago faculty carry out the teaching. This has the advantage of widening the international perspectives and experience of the faculty. The trouble is that, with limited faculty, such an initiative is restricted to a single location. With plans to open a branch office in Singapore, how will it service the needs of all three locations?

Other trends also point to the possibilities of a big name offering a franchise to a provider in another country to provide its MBA program. Distance learning, for example, is highly popular—led by the United Kingdom's Open University Business School, Henley Management College, Warwick and Herriot-Watt. Henley has six thousand distance learning students in a hundred countries, with local support in thirty-five of those countries. It is not, as programs director Colin Carnall makes clear, in the franchise business. "We are not running a franchise. Our MBA is networked with all assessment being carried out by Henley faculty. This provides its own complex challenges and demanding quality assurance issues," says Professor Carnall. "Running a full franchise is very difficult indeed and fraught with grave risks."

But Carnall agrees that the concept of the franchised MBA is tempting. With intense competition in the worldwide exec ed market, it provides a relatively easy means of boosting revenues. This is particularly true for relatively recent arrivals on the MBA scene, which are furiously competing for credibility and cash. If a big name business school franchises its MBA elsewhere in the world there would undoubtedly be willing recruits, enticed by the Western brand. "Schools which franchise their MBAs run the risk of undermining the value of their own program," warns Carnall. "There has to be a concern that if programs are offered as a franchise outside the U.K. they will not be of the same standard as those in the U.K. No one can offer that assurance."

Quality is the key. The franchising business school must exercise control over the quality of what is delivered. Running an MBA program is a complex operation. Handing over your program lock, stock, and barrel and then walking away is the route to mayhem.

Though there are clearly drawbacks and a variety of potential pitfalls, some are already taking the plunge. The Open University Business School (OUBS) is one of the first to move franchising beyond mere debate. It has licensed its MBA program to the Open Learning Institute in Hong Kong. Launched in October 1995, the program captured one-third of the local MBA market in its first year. OUBS plans to develop its licensing in Singapore through the Singapore Institute of Management and is eyeing other opportunities in South Africa, India, and China.

OUBS stops short of labeling its licensing agreement as a franchise—though the program in Hong Kong uses its materials and it trains the tutors and provides advice on assessment, the end result is not an Open University qualification. As the initial success of the OUBS venture suggests, the rewards are potentially lucrative. In spite of the pitfalls, it is probably only a matter of time before a big name enters the franchising fray.

Establishing Networks and Alliances

As we have seen in the area of international development, leveraging brands requires the establishment of a variety of networks. Schools will need to form alliances:

With Other Business Schools. Kenan-Flagler is developing distance learning programs with Aoyama Gakuin University in Japan. The programs are developed for Fudan University in Shanghai. The development is funded by Toshiba.

In February 1997, five European schools launched PRIME (Program for International Managers in Europe), an executive course with an emphasis on doing business in Europe. PRIME is a global development program offered by Copenhagen Business School, Erasmus University in Rotterdam, ESADE in Barcelona, HEC in Paris, SDA Bocconi in Milan, and WU-Wien in Vienna. It is tailored to provide insights into the diversity of European cultures, including week-long stays in five of the schools' home cities.

As Jean-Loup Ardoin, associate dean at HEC (the Grande École outside Paris that participates in the program), explains: "Educators have seen the big push to go global in the last five years. One way to do that is to join forces with other schools."

With Corporate Universities. British Aerospace is to spend a staggering $2.4 billion on developing its own virtual university with partner institutions. Partnerships for the design and delivery of a new British Aerospace Certificate in Management are with two U.K. business schools—the Management School at the University of Lancaster and the Open University Business School.

With Corporations. Custom programs will continue to increase in popularity. Open programs will be delivered by local-based business schools. IBM has established partnerships with several leading business schools, including Manchester Business School in the United Kingdom, which provides a comprehensive range of management education programs for IBM staff.

With Consulting Firms: The Rise of the Giant. In their search for partners and alliances, business schools will no longer be able to overlook the most obvious source of partnership: consulting firms. Big name consulting firms have the advantages of being in a parallel ideas-based business, being staffed by business school–trained professionals, and operating through established international networks.

For most schools, the nightmare scenario is a link between a big consulting firm and a top business school. Consultancies already use business school faculty to teach in executive programs. For tailored courses, it will become more commonplace. When Tony Blair's office set up a training program for the government-in-waiting, for example, Templeton College Oxford worked side by side with Andersen Consulting.

Alternatively, a link between a top business school and a major media firm, or a company like Microsoft with on-line media channels, could present an entirely different scenario.

WHERE DOES THIS LEAVE THE MBA?

If current trends continue, the MBA qualification will be devalued. This will happen for three reasons.

First, there are simply too many MBA programs out there. In the future, only a qualification from one of the elite schools will be worth anything in the employment marketplace. "The MBA degree itself doesn't mean the same thing in all schools," says Harvard's Kim Clark. "Schools are quite different; the types of education you get are different and the standards by which you evaluate and judge the schools are quite different."[8]

The second reason for the devaluation of the business world's premier qualification is that it is at odds with idea of lifelong learning. "Though MBA students may take a few specialized courses in their second year, the fact is that these so-called citadels of professional learning turn out dilettantes (would the degree better be called PBA, for Pastiche of Business Administration?) who walk away with an acceptable technical vocabulary but little in-depth knowledge and, worse, because of the abiding focus on finding jobs, little taste for perpetual learning and true mastery," says Tom Peters.

The value of qualifications as passports is declining. It is no longer good enough to have known what was going on five or six years ago. In the future, top-off training won't be enough. It will have to be drip-fed training—probably using a variety of delivery mechanisms. The spoon-fed, shove-it-down-your-throat approach of the traditional MBA is out of step with this. The MBA will be seen for what it is—a training ground for analysis-retentive consultants.

The third problem is that the MBA delivers traditional functional skills. Increasingly CEOs need softer skills that MBA programs do not provide. Silo organizations are on the way out; silo-style training is no longer appropriate. What is needed now is integrative coursework—learning that is driven by issues, rather than issues that are driven by learning.

"In reality, few are genuinely challenging the well-established notion of what a business school actually is and what it should provide," says Ashridge's Paul Turnbull. "To respond to corporate needs and take advantage of the technology now available, the center of gravity of business schools must shift. Traditionally, the core of business schools has been their expertise in the functional areas of marketing, finance, and so on. Interpersonal skills such as teamworking have only recently attracted the attention of some business schools. In the future it is likely that the once-core functional areas will be delivered outside the business school." Interpersonal skills, by their very nature, require feedback and interaction, and they will become the focus of business school programs. New courses on offer at Harvard reflect the changing emphasis—the doyen of tradition now offers electives in social entrepreneurship and field studies in social enterprise.

It is also likely that the structure of courses will change. Sessions will be shorter—half a day or a day rather than two weeks. Tutors will spend time in client businesses. Business schools will become responsive to the needs, requirements, and aspirations of individuals—most notably through self-managed learning.

Already the next-generation MBA is being shaped. Characteristically, Henry Mintzberg has put his imagination where his mouth is. He has masterminded the launch of the International Masters Program in Management (IMPM), which he hopes will become "the next-generation program in management education."

Professor Mintzberg argues that there is more to business success (and life) than MBAs. "To be superbly successful you have to be a visionary—someone with a very novel vision of the world and a real sense of where they are going. If you have that you can get away with the commercial equivalent of murder. Alternatively, success can come if you are a true empowerer of people, are empathetic and sensitive." These, he makes clear, are not qualities conventional MBA programs are likely to nurture. "MBA programs generally attract neither creative nor generous people and the end result is trivial strategists."

The IMPM may or may not be the program of the future. But it is certainly an antidote to much of the moribund sterility of other business school programs. As described in Chapter Two, the classroom activity takes place in five modules of two or three weeks each, spread over almost a year and a half, and the content is structured around specific ways of looking at the world. As Lancaster University's program director, Jonathan Gosling, points out, "The question is not just how people act economically or politically or creatively, not just how economies function or social ethics develop, but how these different perspectives interact to create the behaviors we see around us." Clearly, such notions are a world away from the functional emphasis still pursued by most MBA programs.

Thoughtful, international, innovative, and built around alliances, the IMPM has many of the characteristics necessary for the business school programs of the future. Few others reach its imaginative standards.

11

Where Now for Business Schools?

> *We are living through a time of extraordinary change, with changes in technology, in the geopolitical framework of the world, in capital markets and all the rest of it. These are driving significant developments in business and I think you really have to bring about some substantial changes in the way business education works in order to prepare people well for what lies ahead.*
>
> —*Kim Clark, dean of Harvard Business School*[1]

It will seem odd to some in the business school world that at a time when the future looks especially rosy we should be harbingers of doom. It is hard, though, to avoid the conclusion that the institutions that were so successful in the twentieth century are now at a crossroads. They have come as far as they can within their current confines. Already, the inherent tensions within them are showing. The dissonance between the academic world and the business world will only become louder.

So what does the future hold for business schools? Overall, we would suggest that for those schools willing to grasp the challenges, the future looks bright. For the leading schools the real enemy is complacency and arrogance. There are fundamental issues that need to be addressed. Cracks caused by the tensions between commercial pressures and academic standards, in particular, cannot be papered over forever. Academic rigor will always be an uncomfortable bedfellow of pragmatic business.

For some university business schools, it may be necessary to give up the pretense at firewalls and spin off the exec ed operation from the academic institution altogether, creating a new brand. Other schools may prefer to part company with their universities or give up some of their commercial activities. Independent schools will have to create new partnerships to maintain their independence. These are far-reaching changes, too radical for many schools to contemplate at present. But unless they are prepared to think the unthinkable, they risk extinction down the road.

The great challenge for business schools is to follow their own advice: to reinvent themselves for the twenty-first century. With that in mind, we offer some points that seem to follow logically from the best business school thinking. Some will say that using their own sticks to beat them is unfair. But it seems to us that it is simply a case of practicing what they preach.

GAME UP OR GAME ON?

An astute brief history of the development of business schools comes from Ray Wild, principal of Henley Management College. Wild contends that there have been three stages in business school development. During stage one, "schools were largely driven by faculty. Debate within schools and between them and other academic areas was extensive. Faculty concerns about their roles, their creation of research territories, and the search for significance were important dynamics. This, coupled with business schools' efforts to secure financial security and appropriate treatment from parent universities, ensured that the main influences on schools' attitudes and behaviors were internal."

The second stage saw schools "coming to terms with the relevance issue whilst preserving substance, recognizing the prerogatives of clients but still largely driven by faculty, seeking a balance between internal and external influences but avoiding compromise."

Now schools are teetering on the edge of the third stage. "Schools and their faculty must learn to reverse the traditional direction of their work. Instead of conveying information to recipients they will work in the opposite direction—back up the supply chain. They must design and provide learning opportunities for their markets—and provide directed access to relevant information, whatever its source, to support that learning. Certainly academic work will give rise to new information—but for most schools, for most of the time—information, ever increasing in quantity and perishability, will be outsourced as they focus on their distinctive role of creating real-time learning opportunities and on-line support."

The reality is that business schools must change if they are to survive and prosper in the new millennium. Those that fail to do so will fall by the wayside—abandoned by their universities, cut off by their sponsors, or bankrupted through lack of business. Change or die is the reality.

Listen to what Doug Lamont, visiting lecturer at Northwestern's Kellogg School, has to say: "You can draw a parallel with the 1970s. Remember the oil crisis and the effect it had on the U.S. automobile industry? It made large U.S. models obsolete almost overnight. There will be a shock to the system for business schools when the U.S. schools suddenly wake up. At that time their products will have to be radically redesigned. What worries me is that no one is thinking radically at the top U.S. schools or at the accreditation bodies. No one is doing any radical thinking. To use a management term, no one is thinking out of the box. That's very worrying."

Business schools as they stand are fatally flawed. Unless they do something about it, and quick, the institutions that rode the education gravy train so effectively in the twentieth century risk being shunted into a siding at the start of the twenty-first century. They have to reform themselves or they are in severe danger of becoming marginalized.

Business schools need to address the issues raised in this chapter. Not all need to be tackled by each and every school. Different schools will have their unique priorities and circumstances. For many it will be a case of targeting a particular niche in the marketplace. For all but a very few schools, the days of total executive education provision are over.

COMPETITION

Change the Rules; Don't Follow

Business schools may teach the latest strategic thinking. In practice, they ignore it. Gary Hamel argues that there are three kinds of companies. First are "the real makers," companies such as British Airways and Xerox. They are the aristocracy—well-managed, consistent high achievers. Second, says Hamel, are the takers, "peasants who only keep what the Lord doesn't want." This group typically has around 15 percent market share—such as Kodak in the copier business or Avis—whose slogan "We try harder" enshrined the peasantry in its mission statement. "Harder doesn't get you anywhere," says Hamel dismissively.[2]

Third are the breakers, industrial revolutionaries. These are the companies Hamel believes to be creating the new wealth. They include the likes of Starbucks, which is coining money in the coffee business. "Companies should be asking themselves, Who is going to capture the new wealth in our industry?" he says.

When Hamel talks of change, he is not considering tinkering at the edges. "The primary agenda is to be the architect of industry transformation, not simply corporate transformation," he says. Organizations that view change as an internal matter are liable to be left behind. Instead, they need to look outside their industry boundaries. Hamel calculates that if you want to see the future coming, 80 percent of the learning will take place outside company boundaries. This is not something companies or business schools are very good at. Bastions of learning remain generally reticent about proactively learning from other organizations. One comfort is that they are mostly as bad as each other. "The good news is that companies in most industries are blind in the same way," says Hamel. "There is no inevitability about the future. There is no proprietary data about the future. The goal is to imagine what you can make happen."

Business schools are not natural revolutionaries. Yet that is exactly what they need to be if they are to reinvent themselves.

Identify What Business They Are In

Business schools seem curiously confused as to what business they are actually involved in. Is it management development? Development for senior executives? Is it research? Degree or executive programs? Unable to reach a definitive conclusion, most believe they are involved in all these businesses. Too often they follow the money. "Management must think of itself not as producing products but as providing customer-creating value satisfactions," said marketing guru Ted Levitt over thirty years ago. Levitt observed that production-led thinking inevitably led to narrow perspectives. He argued that companies must broaden their view of the nature of their business. Otherwise their customers will soon be forgotten. "The railroads are in trouble today not because the need was filled by others . . . but because it was not filled by the railroads themselves," wrote Levitt. "They let others take customers away from them because they assumed themselves to be in the railroad business rather than in the transportation business. The reason they defined their industry wrong was because they were railroad-oriented instead of transportation-oriented; they were product-oriented instead of customer-oriented." The railroad business was constrained, in Levitt's view, by a lack of willingness to expand its horizons.[3]

Levitt went on to level similar criticisms at other industries. The film industry failed to respond to the growth of television because it regarded itself as being in the business of making movies rather than providing entertainment. Business schools need to clarify what business they are in.

At present what exists is a fudge, with business schools wanting to be seen as academic institutions or businesses depending on which suits them at that particular moment. "I agree schools will have to make up their minds about some of these issues," says Bernadette Conraths, director general of the EFMD, the European accreditation body. "Business schools have to decide what they're good at. And what their core competencies are, and stop trying to be all things to all men.

"The executive education market is where it really will be quite tough. There are so many providers. Business schools will have to decide if they want to take a scientific or academic approach or simply be training providers. They will have to ask: do we have enough research critical mass to provide this thought leadership role, or should we simply concentrate on training and development?"

Understand Their Competitive Advantage

What have business schools got that other providers haven't? This is a matter little considered by many schools. With intensifying competition, they will have to identify their competitive advantages. Among the more obvious advantages possessed by business schools are their capacity to award degrees (though corporate universities will increasingly also be able to do so), their broad range of activities and expertise (though this can be a weakness), the long-term perspectives of their tenured staff, their academic independence from corporate control, their alumni networks, and their strong brands (reputations).

In particular, the ability to award nationally (sometimes internationally) recognized qualifications is important. Companies are looking at how their development programs can be externally accredited to provide meaningful, portable qualifications. They are in need of academic partners who can provide external quality control to management training activities. This is already happening. Warwick School of Business, for example, works with British Steel as part of its Accelerated Management Development Program. Participants can take examinations after the program, which parallels the first part of an MBA. EM Lyon in France has a modular program so participants can get certificate or diploma validation for short programs. Another advantage of such relationships is that externally validated qualifications add to an employee's employability.

Move Beyond Rankings

"The sports world has a lot to answer for—league tables have become a national (and even an international) obsession," says Henley's Ray Wild. Competing on the basis of rankings compiled by a team of journalist researchers is an indictment of the business school industry. At best, it is based on a lowest common denominator view of schools. At worst, it encourages schools to cheat.

Don't Compete on Catering and Accommodation

Another sad reflection on the development of business schools is that catering and accommodation facilities have become so important to the schools in terms of finance and to students and course participants in terms of comfort. Hotels do it better. One past student at Ashridge Management College was moved to poetry, such was the splendor of the college's food:

> Business athletes who run the economy
> Seeking "mens" and "corpore" agronomy
> Know that Ashridge in Herts
> Reaches all of the parts
> And their chefs are the stars of (g)astronomy.[4]

Lavish catering is a hangover from the days when executive education was corporate R&R. It encourages the atmosphere of a gentleman's club. Offering an extensive wine list does not constitute a competitive advantage. For many schools it poses a distraction from their core activity.

PHILOSOPHY

Become Learning Organizations

Harvard's Chris Argyris has revealed that those we expect to be good at learning are often very poor at learning. This applies to business schools. "In the simplest sense, a learning organization is a group of people who are continually enhancing their capability to create their future," explains MIT's Peter Senge, who brought the concept of the learning organization to a mass audience. "The traditional meaning of the word learning is much deeper than just *taking information in*. It is about changing individuals so that they produce results they care about, accomplish things that are important to them."[5] Business schools remain committed to traditional concepts of learning.

Senge suggests there are five components to a learning organization:

• *Systems thinking:* Senge champions systems thinking, the recognition that things are interconnected. (Business schools largely prefer to view things in vacuum-sealed isolation—as the case study approach does.)

• *Personal mastery:* Senge grounds this idea in the familiar competencies and skills associated with management, but also includes spiritual growth—opening oneself up to a progressively deeper reality—and living life from a creative rather than a reactive viewpoint. This discipline involves two underlying movements: continually learning how to see current reality more clearly, and using the ensuing gap between vision and reality to produce the creative tension from which learning arises. (Business schools have proved ill-equipped to respond to the personal development movement leaving the way open to self-improvement gurus like Stephen Covey and Anthony Robbins.)

• *Mental models:* This essentially deals with the organization's driving and fundamental values and principles. Senge alerts managers to the power of patterns of thinking at the organizational level and the importance of nondefensive inquiry into the nature of these patterns. (Why are business schools organized as they are?)

- *Shared vision:* Here Senge stresses the importance of co-creation and argues that shared vision can only be built on personal vision. He claims that shared vision is present when the task that follows from the vision is no longer seen by the team members as separate from the self. (How many business school deans have effectively mapped out visions for their organizations?)
- *Team learning:* The discipline of team learning involves two practices: dialogue and discussion. The former is characterized by its exploratory nature, the latter by the opposite process of narrowing down the field to the best alternative for the decisions that need to be made. The two are mutually complementary, but the benefits of combining them only come from having previously separated them. Most teams lack the ability to distinguish between the two and to move consciously between them. (How many business schools develop groups or teams of academics?)

For the traditional organization, the learning organization poses huge challenges. In the learning organization managers are researchers and designers rather than controllers and overseers. Senge argues that managers should encourage employees to be open to new ideas, communicate frankly with each other, understand thoroughly how their companies operate, form a collective vision, and work together to achieve their goal.

"The world we live in presents unprecedented challenges for which our institutions are ill prepared," says Senge.[6] Among these institutions are business schools.

Invest in Intellectual Capital

France's INSEAD has reasserted its commitment to research—"If you're not a knowledge creator you don't have any advantage over your competition," says Dean Antonio Borges, echoing the words of leading businesspeople. And the only way to create knowledge is to invest in intellectual capital.

Deliver Lifelong Learning

One notable advantage possessed by corporate universities is that they can provide continuous long-term development. They are there when people need them. Business schools need to develop means by which they can be there for executives throughout their careers. Their role will become more one of supportive partnership than of supplier to clients. Forming direct relationships with managers rather than training directors will be essential.

"It's becoming clear that the notion of lifelong learning is not just a cliché—it's reality. So an MBA program like ours, where we try to attract young people in the early stages of their career, has to be seen as the beginning of a professional learning experience and as the foundation for a lifetime's learning," says Harvard dean Kim Clark.[7]

But how can business schools tie in lifelong learning to a two-year or one-year program? The first school to do so—to sell true lifelong learning as a product or service—will secure a major competitive head start.

Link Learning to Workplace Achievement

Business schools have tended to sneer at workplace demands for instant rewards from training. It just can't be done, they say. Of course, they are right. Management development should deliver long-term benefits. Companies today have higher expectations from executive programs than ever before. Whether they are sending a small number of managers to open programs to learn new skills or putting large numbers through a tailored program, they expect to see a clear return on their investment. This has the welcome side effect of ensuring a higher level of support for managers attending courses than was once the case.

As executive development becomes more embedded in the culture of many companies, there is an increasing recognition of the importance of study and finding ways to consolidate what has been learned when the manager steps back into the workplace. Most companies see such measures as enlightened self-interest.

"No one can afford to just hand out executive programs as rewards or holidays for good behavior," says Vivian Dunn, manager of executive and international development at the telecommunications giant British Telecom. "I think there was an element of that in the 1980s. But today we invest a lot of time in preparing people for programs and trying to ensure that what is learned is passed back to the organization."

Gale Bitter, director of executive programs at Stanford Graduate School of Business, agrees: "Companies have been saying their people are their most important assets for a long time. But I think the change is that they are now acting on it by sending people on executive programs. They expect what participants learn to be used when they get back into the workplace. These courses are no longer a perk."

The level of support from the company will typically depend, however, on the seniority of the participant and the type and purpose of the program. Open programs have traditionally been the mainstay of the executive education market and represent the more traditional experience.

Providers also recognize the importance of finding ways to support learning. Says Colin Carnall of Henley Management College, "There is a clear push for greater definition of the value added by a program. Often, this is linked to definitions of the competencies the company needs. Follow-up, including the use of mentoring and support for in-company mentoring, is increasingly important."

Develop Expertise in Soft Skill Areas and Appraisal

Business schools have generally shied away from the softest of soft skills. Few offer coaching and mentoring services. Even fewer have the capacity to deliver 360-degree feedback. If they did so, they could more convincingly position themselves as lifelong partners in learning.

Learn from Other Cultures

The American business school model has proved notably resistant to input from other cultures. Western business schools largely remain preoccupied with conquering the world. The colonial impulse remains strong. Witness the University of Michigan's William Davidson Institute's activities in Vietnam, where it claims to be converting Communist managers into capitalists. Isn't it time to reverse the polarity of some of this learning?

"The American schools think that because they invented the MBA they have all the answers," says Doug Lamont. "U.S. business schools have been a great success story over the past twenty years. Although they are looking out into the rest of the world more now, they don't look with a view to learning anything from Europe or Asia. The twin roles of business education in the global market are understanding of cultures, tradition, history, etc., and understanding of technology and science. The U.S. schools have been very good at the latter but they struggle with the former."

Get International

There is a great deal of hype and hyperbole about how business schools have globalized themselves. Asked by George Bickerstaffe what Harvard Business School will look like in five or ten years' time, Dean Kim Clark replied: "HBS is going to be global. We are in the process of building research centers in different parts of the world where some of our faculty will be located. We will also have research and case writing initiatives underway all over the world. We are expanding our educational programs and our faculty will be more multinational."[8]

U.S. schools are now trying to recruit more foreign faculty. They will make much of this in coming years. But according to IESE's dean Carlos Cavallé, "Internationalism is an attitude, not a statistic." This is a fair point. But part of the attitude is to do with what participants bring into the classroom. European schools have a natural advantage here.

At present, fewer than half of the participants in Harvard's executive education courses are from outside the United States. In this department, the European schools appear to lead. IMD boasts that 84 percent of participants are from outside Switzerland. INSEAD has 81 percent from outside France. The fact is that if you operate in smaller countries like Switzerland you have to be international. What makes the Europeans look good, however, is the generally lamentable performance of U.S. schools. Duke manages just 7 percent, Chicago a paltry 6 percent of foreign participants in executive programs. This is not international by any stretch of the imagination.

Forget Fads and Fashions

If business schools are genuine thought leaders they have to provide intellectual leadership rather than tamely following in the insubstantial footsteps of charlatans and opportunistic consultants. Most of the management fads of recent years have failed to deliver on their promises. "I think we will increasingly recognize that it is not healthy for managers and organizations to get into a flavor of the month kind of thing. We need to go deeper into problems," says Harvard dean Kim Clark.[9]

There are those, however, who argue that the content of the idea is often unimportant anyway. What matters is that organizations receive regular electric shocks to wake them up, to galvanize managers into action and dispel complacency. London Business School assistant professor Liz Mellon is dismissive of the idea. "The electric shock view comes from the same school of thought that says the only way to change an organization is to manufacture a crisis. It's a corrupt philosophy. If that's the only way you can motivate people then it indicates a failure of management."

Mellon points to business school research carried out over a twenty-one-year period, asking organizations what they wanted from their managers. The same three messages keep recurring: they want them to be strategic, to be decisive, and to care about the organization. "Those three ideas haven't gone away," she says. "They come back again and again."

This is, or at least should be, the big difference between the business schools on one hand and the consultants and quack doctors (two categories, not one) on the other. Business schools exist to advance the science of management. Their methodology is academically sound. Their research involves rigor. (At present, some would say rigor mortis is setting in.)

TEACHING METHODS

Move Beyond the Case Study Method

Case studies are the fodder of consultants. Even with the latest technology, case studies remain a limited and superficial method of teaching tomorrow's business leaders. Interactive they may be, but case studies bring students up-to-date with yesterday rather than allowing them the scope to imagine and create the future. Worse, they foster a climate of arrogance—MBA graduates learn to solve case studies rather than manage real people. Real life is not a case study.

Consign the Guru-Teacher to History

Gurus are entertaining. They attract useful attention but the good ones are at their best when challenged rather than deified. They also breed jealousy and lead to imitation. Use them wisely and in conjunction with other viewpoints. No one professor ever has a lock on the truth. "There's more to executive education than one person's take on reality," notes Fuqua's Wanda Wallace.

Monitor and Measure the Impact of Training

Business schools have often been accused of having little idea of how, where, and why management training benefits organizations.

Increasingly now, the emphasis is on linking training to performance. Companies want to see with their own eyes how their investment in training and development has affected their bottom lines. Training has to make a difference—and be able to prove that it has made a difference. "Management training will become increasingly results-oriented. Learning processes that lack concrete relevance to a commercial organization's business goals are simply not justifiable," says Matthias Bellmann, charged with top management development at the electronics giant Siemens. "We have to find a consistent balance between decentralized learning needs and integrated learning structures."[10]

FACULTY ISSUES

Change Begins and Ends with People

Business school faculty are fond of telling organizations that any program of change has to begin with employees. Yet business schools cling to a studied reticence about changing working relationships with faculty. Look, for example, at the difficulties encountered by Rene McPherson during the 1980s as Stanford dean. McPherson was a highly experienced CEO—with Dana Corporation—who found that academics are about as keen on change as turkeys are on Thanksgiving.

Once again, for insight into what they need to do, business schools should learn from one of their own. Sumantra Ghoshal argues that few companies have an ability for self-renewal. "You cannot renew a company without revitalizing its people. Top management has always said this. After a decade of restructuring and downsizing, top management now believes it. Having come to believe it, what does it really mean?"

Ghoshal contends that revitalizing people is fundamentally about changing people. The trouble is that adults don't change their basic attitudes unless they encounter personal tragedy. Things that happen at work rarely make such an impact. If organizations are to revitalize people, they must change the context of what they create around people.

Fire Faculty—Then Rehire Them

"The nature of faculty will change. We need professionals who really understand. Faculty need to be encouraged to look forward," says Kenan-Flagler dean Robert Sullivan. We then asked Sullivan whether, in the future, he thought business schools would sack faculty. "Yes, I do," he replied. The faculty system remains largely free of the performance pressures experienced by people in virtually every other profession. Preaching from comfort zones is no way to encourage innovative thinking. Schools should fire their faculty and then rehire them as freelancers.

End Faculty Moonlighting

Faculty either are or are not full-time employees. End the anomaly that allows professors to feather their own nests with consulting arrangements while collecting a regular monthly paycheck (and sometimes more than one). At present, both students and business schools are being shortchanged. If business academics need to get in touch with reality, business schools should start here.

Change the Ways in Which Faculty Are Rewarded

Manchester Business School introduced a performance-related element in 1997. London Business School has had performance-related pay since 1990. Assessment at London Business School is made up of five areas—teaching, research, good citizenship, external visibility, and academic administration. Faculty are assessed individually and are all on contract rather than being tenured. Indiana University School of Business now has performance-related pay. "When I first got here I asked the faculty what were the principal issues facing all of them, and they said the compensation scheme didn't reinforce what we needed to do strategically," says Indiana dean John

Rau.[11] Indiana has now identified six constituencies that academics have to satisfy—representatives of the undergraduate, postgraduate, and doctorate programs; the placement office; executive education; and the dean. Hierarchy is not dead at Indiana, though—the dean's vote is worth twice as much as anyone else's.

At the heart of this issue is the entire business of academic tenure. Measuring academics by their publications is limited and limiting. Yet it remains the dominant system. We asked Frank Morgan, director of executive programs at Kenan-Flagler, what made for a successful academic career at a business school. He responded: "Unfortunately at 95 percent or more, a publication record that isn't relevant to the practicing manager and doesn't advance knowledge very far."

Faculty Should Engage in Constructive Confrontation

Business schools pride themselves on fostering a competitive attitude among students—they say it mirrors the cut and thrust of corporate life. The reality is often very different. The last thing a professor wants to do is to annoy a student who has paid tens of thousands of dollars to attend a program (and who may give the school many more thousands of dollars as an alumnus).

A recent article in a student publication at Kellogg asked: "Is Kellogg too nice? The hallways of Leverone echo with complaints from students who claim their professors are too quick to praise class comments. Other students mourn the absence of argument and confrontation in class and group meetings." Teachers who don't challenge the thinking of their students aren't doing their jobs.

Recruit from a Broader Base

Business schools recruit from a narrow base. A large percentage of Harvard faculty studied at Harvard for their Ph.D.'s. This breeds an insular climate. (A climate that may have cost it dear. "The school suffers from more than the usual amount of internal competition. This internal orientation makes it difficult for Harvard to encourage the kind of interdisciplinary work that has made Wharton so effective," says consultant Peter Cohan.) The shortage of high-caliber business academics means that in the future business schools will have to cast their net wider. Bringing in deans from outside academia must be healthy for the long-term development of business schools. It helps create a bridge between the otherwise all-too-separate world of the classroom and business reality. (Consultancy is not the same as running a business.) This links to the next point.

Involve Real Executives in Teaching

At most schools real business executives are notable by their absence. Of the big names in corporate America, for example, only Andy Grove of Intel teaches at business school. This is a damning indictment. CEOs and chairmen visit business schools to give speeches about how successful they have been. They are also more than willing to sign checks. But this does not constitute involvement in the learning processes. The nuts and bolts of business need to be introduced into classroom teaching. It would be good to see lower-ranking managers involved in the classroom, too. Managerial wisdom is not the sole preserve of middle-aged senior managers—even less business school professors.

One school that has experimented in this area is Columbia Business School. It has its own executives in residence—nine in all—who lecture, offer advice to students, and help with fundraising. The executives are retired or semiretired and include the former vice chairman of Booz•Allen & Hamilton, John Rhodes, and Robert Callander, ex-president of Chemical Bank. According to one of the nine, Ehud Houminer (late of Philip Morris and a Wharton MBA), "We represent continuity; all the rest is a moving show out there. When a student comes to me with a problem I remember 20 similar conversations I had with former students and I know what happened to each of them." Columbia's Meyer Feldberg says, "These men and women have no agenda. Their only aim is to help the students."[12]

When at Harvard, John Quelch was known for his ability to seek out unusual real-life examples. He brought in the founder of

El Salvadoran company Hilasal, which has become the premium manufacturer of beach towels. The founder lectured to Harvard students on how he got his foot in the door of big U.S. department stores. This is not a case study, this is real life from someone who has been there and done it.

Involve Alumni in Teaching

John Kotter of Harvard has tracked the careers of Harvard MBA graduates. He found that the average net worth of the 115 graduates in the class of 1974 was $1 million by 1992. They are successful—but over one-third had been dismissed or been made redundant at some time.[13] Schools make little effort, at the moment, to tap into this reservoir of real-world corporate experience and knowledge. Instead of simply treating alumni as a cash cow, business schools should seek to maximize their intellectual capital.

Adapt to Succeed

Strangely, for business school faculty who are prepared to adapt and apply technology, the situation couldn't be brighter. They are working in a growth market and one in which there is a fundamental shortage of skilled people. The point that they haven't fully grasped yet is that many of them no longer need their business schools as much as their business schools need them.

Already, the number of experienced senior business school faculty is proving inadequate to meet the demands of the marketplace. Faculty shortages are likely to be exacerbated by the continuing growth in the executive education market.

Their roles will fundamentally change: "If you could start a virtual university and have Lester Thurow and Michael Porter and other gurus to teach, why would you want anybody else? What it means is that a faculty member at Acme State will increasingly be, not a subject expert, but a learning facilitator, a mentor, a coach," predicts Charles Hickman of the American Assembly of College Schools of Business.[14]

STUDENTS AND ALUMNI

Increase the Number of Women in Programs

Until 1967, when it moved to its current location, INSEAD refused to admit women to its programs on the grounds that its MBA course was taught in the local monastery. Over thirty years on and business schools remain dominated by male WASPs. This is not an accurate reflection of business reality. Until this balance is redressed—through affirmative action in some way—business schools cannot claim to be developing tomorrow's business leaders.

Make Programs Customer Friendly

Business school programs must be built around the needs of customers rather than the predilections of faculty. There is growing pressure on managers to fit more into their busy schedules. This is already making itself felt in terms of demand for shorter, sharper executive courses. As one American CEO observed: "If we can do without one of our people for two weeks, then we can probably do without him altogether."

"It's a growing issue in our internal programs," explains Yvette Elcock, management development controller at Britain's supermarket chain Tesco Stores. "The challenges of today's business mean managers want short, sharp, effective development interventions. The message for providers is, If you can do it in three days, that's better than doing it in five. We're constantly looking at delivery of our in-house training to see if it can be done better, using multimedia, for example. We review these issues all the time."

The other side of this particular coin is that companies are now more likely to respect the demands on managers during courses. Hans-Henrik Hansen, director of programs at the Copenhagen Business School, reports that program participants are much better prepared now than they used to be. In some cases, he says, managers will negotiate with their employers to attend a particular program

Women Students

School	*Percent*
Singapore	53
Norwegian School of Economics	50
Chinese University of Hong Kong	48
Stirling University (U.K.)	46
Birmingham (U.K.)	41
European Business School (U.K.)	40
Lancaster (U.K.)	40
NIMBAS (Netherlands)	40
Monash Mt. Eliza (Australia)	40
Sheffield (U.K.)	39
Southern California	38
Thunderbird	38
Weatherhead	38
City (U.K.)	37
Dublin (Ireland)	37
Hong Kong University of Science and Technology	37
Toronto	37
Ashridge (U.K.)	36
Asian Institute (Philippines)	36
Arthur D. Little	36
Durham (U.K.)	35
IE (Spain)	35

Source: George Bickerstaffe, *Which Executive Programme?* Economist Intelligence Unit, London, 1996.

before taking up a new post. Time away from work commitments is part of the deal.

PROGRAM CONTENT

Keep It Current

We attended a business school seminar recently and were privileged to see a case study that had been resurrected from the 1970s. This was a useful lesson in prehistory, but bore no relation to reality. Business school professors tend to be masters of hindsight. It will, we expect, take around four or five years for material concerning the Asian currency crisis of early 1998 to filter into mainstream business school programs.

One of the biggest problems facing business schools is how to ensure that what they teach remains current. Companies do not pay for lessons in business history—not knowingly, anyway. They want to be sure that what is taught in courses is both relevant to their industry and at the leading edge of management thinking. This creates a pressure on business schools to stay in touch with the cut and thrust of what is an increasingly fast-paced business environment.

This problem is especially acute when it comes to the latest thinking on information technology. IT and its use in information systems (IS) is an increasingly critical component of business education. No self-respecting business school graduate can walk out of a course without some understanding of the way IT is changing the business world. This is an area where the pace of change is so fast that simply staying up to speed is a full-time task—not just for managers but for members of faculty teaching the courses.

"Although universities create and acquire knowledge, they are seldom successful in applying that knowledge to their own activities," say academics Dorothy Leidner and Sirkka Jarvenpaa. "In fact, academic institutions typically lag businesses by roughly a decade in the adoption of new technologies. This is certainly true in terms of the application of information technology into the learning process: the blackboard and chalk remain the primary teaching technologies in many business schools even while the merits of information technology to improve communication, efficiency, and decision making in organizations are recognized and inculcated by IS researchers."[15]

"Information systems have an ever-increasing role in today's business environment," says Dr. Benita Cox, senior lecturer in Information Systems Management at Imperial College, part of London University. "However, the volatile and dynamic nature of IS presents educators in this area with a constant challenge. On the one hand, they must be aware of the theoretical advances in the field of IS. On the other hand they need to get close to business to ensure what is incorporated in their courses is relevant to business needs. Finally and most challenging, they must keep up with technological advances.

"Without this knowledge they are unable to deliver advice on how best to tailor emerging technology to meet business requirements. It is therefore essential that business needs, technological capacity, and theoretical wisdom are integrated. Failure to integrate any of these elements would lead to courses which would either be teaching about outdated technologies or about technology which is not relevant to business needs. In addition, without knowledge of the academic background to IS, teaching becomes no more than interesting rhetoric."

Develop Leadership

Virtually every survey of managerial skills identifies deficiencies in leadership. Though this subject is covered by most business schools it is often regarded as peripheral to the core functional programs. Other providers—such as the Center for Creative Leadership—have mined this potentially lucrative niche. If the next generation of business leaders is to succeed, business schools need to grant greater resources and commitment to the serious study of leadership. At present, there are too many theories and not enough leaders.

Move Beyond the Functional

Business schools "live and think in terms of organizational charts. But life is a spiderweb," says Ross Perot.[16] Business schools have traditionally presented a tidy version of reality with content neatly subdivided by function.

Clearly, the basic functional skills—finance, marketing, operations, human resources, and strategy—remain relevant. But it is no longer so easy to justify constructing entire programs around them. More imaginative—and realistic—programs increasingly construct entirely new foundations while still covering all the major elements of the functions. At present, European schools lead the way in this area.

But U.S. schools are beginning to get the message. At Stanford, Gale Bitter notes a trend among course participants is to come with their own agenda. "Often participants come onto the program with a particular problem or challenge in their mind. They then apply what they've learned to that issue when they get back into the workplace. Or it might be more formalized. So maybe the CEO or a senior manager in the organization will say, 'Here are some issues the company is facing in the next few years. How can what you learn on the program help us with them?'"

Learn from Outside Business

Peter Drucker has written extensively about the management of nonprofit organizations and the lessons they can teach their private sector brethren. Business schools have been slow to follow in Drucker's footsteps. Where they involve themselves in this area at all, it tends to be in the role of teaching nonprofit managers how the private sector does it.

There are many other walks of life that have lessons for management development. Attend an executive program at Milan's SDA Bocconi and you might encounter Franco Zeffirelli, the famous film maker, who contributes his own insights on such issues as project management and managing talented people. This is an area that is so far largely ignored by U.S. schools. (There is hope, however. We understand that Oprah Winfrey is to teach a course at Kellogg on the dynamics of leadership.) It is an area they should explore further. Imagine Steven Spielberg on the role of vision, for example, or Madonna on brand management.

TYPES OF PROGRAMS

Question Involvement in Public Programs

In some cases, it is debatable whether schools should continue to offer public programs. Their broad-brush, generic approach sits uncomfortably with any notions of specialist knowledge and expertise. It is not effective for highly talented and highly paid faculty to deliver programs on finance for nonfinancial managers, for example. Business schools should stick to areas where they can add real value to the customer's learning experience. In many cases, public programs are delivered more effectively, and certainly more cheaply, by small local or virtual providers.

Use Custom Programs to Cement Partnerships with Companies

Custom programs have been the great success story of the last decade. They offer business schools a chance to get involved with corporate transformation. They are a major opportunity to demonstrate value and to foster long-term partnerships.

Clearly, custom programs represent a major investment by the company in terms of both cost and commitment. As a result, the level of support for the program has to be much greater, and is likely to actively involve senior management. Narayan Pant, deputy chairman of executive programs at the National University of Singapore, says, "Companies no longer want to be told that program providers know what's good for them and they should quietly accept what they're given. Increasingly, they want to be involved in the process of program design and implementation, perhaps even using their own facilitators to put the program content into the company's own context."

The enormous growth in custom programs in recent years suggests that companies are now using this type of executive program for a different purpose. Whereas open programs have traditionally been seen as a development tool to transfer specific skills, custom programs are often part of a corporate transformation process. Providers are responding by encouraging companies to work more closely with them—concentrating on developing partnerships rather than products.

Stanford, for example, is best known in the executive education market for its prestigious public programs. But according to Gale Bitter, in recent years the school has begun offering more focused programs for some corporate clients, and is looking to work closely with a handful of truly innovative companies. A valuable way for companies to support managers in these programs, she says, is to set the strategic challenges in advance. "With the more focused programs what we like to do is have the CEO or senior management team think about the key strategic issues or challenges before the program starts. Then participants can really focus on those key issues as they move through the program. It's a very effective technique to ensure the program adds maximum value to the company. It also sets a clear agenda for everyone."

Cement Partnerships with Consulting Firms

The same point applies to the use of custom programs with consulting firms. Consultancies are often called in to bring about major change. But consultants are good at analysis, not at changing behaviors. Business schools are better geared to that activity. Consultancies need partners who can support them with implementation. If business schools don't create these relationships the consultants will go elsewhere—or more likely build capacity themselves. It is surely just a matter of time before major consultances start buying an independent business schools for the brand.

MBA PROGRAMS

Handle the Brand with Care

The stretching of the MBA brand was always a dangerous game. Now the ultimate general management program is at risk of becoming drowned by specialties. There is, for example, an MBA in Church Management. "We need to think of the worshipper in the pew as the person we serve," says one of the clerics involved. "It is about a useful harnessing of management skills and insights to our theological and missionary work." While the MBA in Church Management may well boost attendance—and fill the coffers—of churches, it hardly enhances the credibility of the MBA as a premier qualification. It would be better for the long-term survival of the qualification if churches sent their managers to be trained in conventional MBA programs.

Make Business Ethics a Part of Every MBA Program

Other professions recognize the importance of ethical guidelines and frameworks to support individuals. If management is to be taken seriously as a profession it must do the same.

Engage Young Managers

The new generation of managers have new perspectives on business schools and MBA programs. Their agenda is radically different from that of executives in the 1980s.

Bruce Tulgan has made a career out of studying the career aspirations of his generation. In his book *Work This Way*, Tulgan continues the themes he started in his influential book *Managing Generation X*. In a "memorandum to the workforce of the future," he offers a new career manifesto for the "post job era."

"It's all over," he says. "All of it. Not just job security. Jobs are all over. We have entered the post jobs era and there's no turning back."[17]

Generation Xers are realists. As far as they are concerned, traditional jobs are something their fathers and mothers had. They are from another era. "Conditioned to practicing self-reliance by our latchkey childhoods, Gen Xers expect to depend on our natural entrepreneurship to attain security in an uncertain future," Tulgan observes.

They pack parachutes when they fly with Corporate Airways. They've seen too many crew members escorted off the premises in midflight. As far as they're concerned, business schools are selling career parachutes.

Jay A. Conger, a former visiting professor at Harvard and INSEAD and now at the University of Southern California, has carried out extensive interviews with Generation X managers, and confirms a significant shift in attitudes. According to Conger, the Silent Generation—born between 1925 and 1942—was made up of people who were children during the Great Depression of the 1930s, or whose parents still remembered the experience vividly. They were influenced by their parents' hardships to value job security. The concept of the "company man" was invented for this generation; they were the managers of the 1950s through to the 1970s.

Then came the Baby Boomers. Born between 1942 and 1963, they grew into the Yuppies of the 1980s. Their rebellious attitude was influenced in America by Vietnam and Watergate, which taught them to distrust authority. Following the Baby Boomers are the Gen Xers. The product of dual-career families and record divorce rates, they are better educated than their predecessors and want to judge—and be judged—on merit rather than on status.

The Gen Xers share the Baby Boomers' distrust of hierarchy, preferring more informal arrangements. They are also far less loyal to their companies than previous generations. According to Conger, the contract of lifetime employment, which began to deteriorate for the Baby Boomers, feels practically nonexistent to the Gen Xers. They will demand changes.

Gen Xers are also much more likely to go to business school. Tulgan spells out the new career agenda. Gen Xers will not remain in the same job or with the same employer for anything like the same periods as previous generations.

They will use business schools like pit stops to update their skills. Tulgan reports: "Applications to MBA programs are increasing again (by 7.5 percent in 1995) and almost 200,000 people will apply to MBA programs this year (1998). The best among the 50,000 who complete the two-year MBA program will go right down the water slide into high pressure corporate jobs, working eighty hours a week or more, until they get rich or burn out. Many others will find that the degree is too general and not prestigious enough to get them the kind of job they were hoping for."[18]

FUNDING, STRUCTURE, AND ORGANIZATION

Clarify Funding

It's essential to clarify and communicate criteria for donors. Business schools are currently noticeably reticent in publishing any guidelines by which financial donations are screened. Would, for example, a donation from a tobacco company be welcome today at the Fuqua School at Duke? Would MIT's Sloan School accept an endowment from an arms manufacturer? Unless criteria are published, schools leave themselves wide open. Transparency and accountability are no longer just words on a business ethics course.

Adopt Freeflowing Structures

Business literature is full of celebrations of companies that have organized themselves flexibly. Free of burdensome hierarchies, they are fast moving, talent-based, geared to innovation. Some believe that business schools already fit the bill. "The kind of business a b-school seems to resemble the most is a capital-markets trading unit, or a Paris couturier, a repertory theater, or perhaps an Americas Cup boat. In short, any enterprise that lives or dies by the quality of its ideas, its ability to anticipate trends and its skill at crafting strategies against real needs and executing them brilliantly," says Glen Urban, dean of MIT's Sloan School of Management.[19] Urban is right: this is how schools should look—but few do.

Work in Partnerships

One consequence of the partnership idea is that business schools cannot limit their activity to the delivery of an educational program. More and more they need to take responsibility for the application of concepts in the partnering organizations. This does not imply that they have to go into the consulting business. But it does imply that business schools have to take more responsibility for what happens before and after the program. Participants who come well prepared to the management education program get a lot more out of the faculty and other participants. Understanding the specific goals of the program, or coming to the program prepared with a set of concrete problems that the participant wants solved during it, may help tremendously in increasing the return on the investment in training. It also makes it easier for a business school to react to the specific needs of the participant and to indicate what the potential tools for the implementation of certain ideas and concepts are.

Finally, as we know, no learning is more effective than learning by doing. Sitting on a school bench for several hours and listening to a dry lecture is a very artificial exercise for a modern manager. A real partnership requires that business schools should take a share of the responsibility for the diffusion and application of what the participant learned. Thus the implementation side must feature prominently in business school programs. Action learning through project work, structured debate, and exchange of experience between participants will have to gain importance in program portfolios. Again, to make this work business schools require the active support of their partner companies.

Eliminate Bureaucracy

For all their talk about business efficiency, business schools come laden with more than their fair share of forms to fill in and outdated, unwieldy hierarchies. Harvard had a committee overseeing the design of its Web site—this took full and awesome responsibility for the typeface used. Faculty were not allowed to order Post-it notes in any color other than yellow.

Dean Kim Clark has been at war with bureaucracy ever since taking over. He has moved power downward to the heads of the school's academic units. "In an era when forward thinking managers were flattening hierarchies and fostering teamwork, America's high church of management education remained a sclerotic bureaucracy that seemed to do everything in its power to promote rivalry rather than co-operation among its students," observed *Business Week*'s John Byrne.[20] Harvard's labyrinthine rules are not unusual. Schools with university links are particularly prone to bureaucratic overload. Says Kenan-Flagler's Robert Sullivan, "Universities look like fourteenth-century institutions."

Use Technology as a Tool, Not a Toy

Information technology is often regarded by business schools as a decorative extra rather than a powerful tool to deliver learning. Those who use it for the former will be overtaken by those who use it for the latter. Beware those lying in ambush.

"It's one thing to get computers around the place; it's another to use them in an innovative way," says David Blake, president of the American Assembly of Collegiate Schools of Business.[21] In too many business schools, technology is decorative. Don't be dazzled by it; turn it to your advantage.

Recognize That Knowledge Work Is Universal Now

"The knowledge worker sees himself just as another professional, no different from the lawyer, the teacher, the preacher, the doctor or the government servant of yesterday," wrote Peter Drucker in his 1969 classic, *The Age of Discontinuity*. "He has the same education. He has more income, he has probably greater opportunities as well. He may well realize that he depends on the organization for access to income and opportunity, and that without the investment the organization has made—and a high investment at that—there would be no job for him, but he also realizes, and rightly so, that the organization equally depends on him."[22]

Drucker was exploring the implications of knowledge being both power *and* ownership thirty years ago. If knowledge, rather than labor, was to be the new measure of economic society, then, Drucker argued, the fabric of capitalist society must change: "The knowledge worker is both the true *capitalist* in the knowledge society and dependent on his job. Collectively the knowledge workers, the employed educated middle-class of today's society, own the means of production through pension funds, investment trusts, and so on."

Drucker has developed his thinking on the role of knowledge—most notably in his 1992 book *Managing for the Future*, in which he observes: "From now on the key is knowledge. The world is becoming not labor intensive, not materials intensive, not energy intensive, but knowledge intensive."

This is now accepted as a fact of corporate life. It is notable that while Drucker was pontificating on the subject many years ago, business schools were strangely silent. Yet the entire notion of knowledge workers has ramifications for the ways in which business schools are organized and deliver their product. To survive and prosper in the knowledge society, business schools will have to become true communities of learning, with knowledge and information flowing freely both in and out.

And finally: Remember that management is pocket science, not rocket science.

Further Reading and Information

Books

George Bickerstaffe, *Which* MBA? 9th ed. (Menlo Park, Calif.: Addison-Wesley, 1997).

Phil Carpenter and Carol Carpenter, *Marketing Yourself to the Top Business Schools* (New York: Wiley, 1995).

Stuart Crainer, *Which Executive Program?* (London: Financial Times Management, 1998).

Robert French and Christopher Grey (eds.), *Rethinking Management Education* (Thousand Oaks, Calif.: Sage, 1996).

Godfrey Golzen, *The Association of* MBAs *Guide to Business Schools, 1997–98* (London: Pitman, 1998).

Robert Reid, *Year One* (New York: Avon Books, 1994).

Peter Robinson, *Snapshots from Hell* (London: Brealey, 1994).

Albert Vicere and Robert Fulmer, *Leadership by Design* (Boston: Harvard Business School Press, 1998).

Web Sites

http://www.aacsb.edu Home page of the American Association of Collegiate Schools of Business—includes lists of donors to business schools and details of deans, as well as latest information from the AACSB.

www.cranfield.ac.uk/som/cclt/links.html This site, at Cranfield's School of Management, provides a listing of business schools throughout the world and links to their Web sites.

www.dartmouth.edu/tuck/bschools/ The Tuck business school's home page offers the most comprehensive listing of business schools and links to their sites—and to associated business school sites.

http://www.mgeneral.com Home page of Management General—includes short "ezzays" by leading business thinkers as well as ratings of the best business books produced by commentator and consultant Tom Brown.

http://www.suntopmedia.com Home page of the authors with details about their other publications as well as suntop media reports and newsletters.

Appendix

Quick Guide to Methodology Used for Business School Composite Ratings

The following explanation is from John E. Wehrli, creator of the composite rankings featured in Chapter Eight.

Rankings: What You Will Find in the New Business School Rankings

- A composite ranking of the top 30 business schools and top 55 overall
- An average ranking of the top 55 schools according to the nine major published sources
- The most recent rankings and a historical average of each of all the major published rankings
- Student caliber rankings, including grades, GMAT scores, and selectivity
- Other measures including school size, starting salary, and placement

How the Composite Rankings Were Determined

1. Rankings for the nine sources shown below were collected for all business schools since each publication first initiated such rankings.

U.S. News & World Report, since 1987; *Business Week*, since 1988; The Gourman Report, since 1980; U.S. News Academic Reputation Survey, since 1987; U.S. News Recruiter Reputation Survey, since 1987; *Business Week* Corporate Ranking, since 1988; The Carter Report, 1977; The MBA Advantage, since 1994; The *Chronicle for Higher Education*, Faculty Rankings.

2. The average rankings for each publication were then determined for the composite of every year but the present. For example, the rankings for *U.S. News* were determined for the years 1987–1995.
3. Next, the current ranking for each publication was noted (i.e. 1996). This number was then averaged at a weight of 50 percent with the historical number from above for that publication. This results in an average number for each business school which is weighted at 50 percent for the most recent ranking and 50 percent for its historical ranking.
4. Next, for the publications that rank every law school in the nation, the schools were sorted according to their average ranking for all those publications. This means a sort of every publication except the MBA Advantage, *Chronicle for Higher Education*, and the Carter Report.
5. Next, for schools not ranked by the MBA Advantage, The Chronicle for Higher Education, or the Carter Report but falling within the top 50 (statistically the top 55) in the previous sort, rankings were assigned according to their rank in the previous sort. This way schools who are not ranked are not penalized since they retain their relative rank from the previous sort, while schools ranked by these publications benefit from the extra metric. This method is statistically rigorous and such numbers are shown in italics in the detail table.

6. The remaining 55 schools were then sorted according to their average ranking for all six published measures. The result is the top 55 schools as ranked by all reliable published measures available to the public over the past 20 years.
7. The top 30 schools from the previous sort were then selected for a composite ranking that incorporates student caliber and placement data.

   Based on a study of variances about the mean, according to published rankings, the top 30 form a definite separation from the next 20. Similarly the next 25 form a definite separation from the remainder, again according to variance from the mean. The second 25 represent a transition zone of sort to the top 30 with a handful of schools close enough to possibly penetrate the top 30. There is also a clear statistical division between schools ranked 1–6, those ranked 7–19, and those ranked 20–30. Also by isolating only 30 schools, factors used for student caliber and placement become more reliable for comparison.
8. Next, the median GMAT & GPA scores for the most recent class were obtained from either the schools, John Byrne of *Business Week*, or *U.S. News & World Report*.
9. Next, a student academic score was calculated. The highest median GMAT and highest median GPA were identified. A particular school's GMAT and GPA was then compared as a percentage of the highest value. Then a weight of 50 percent was assigned to the GMAT score and a weight of 20 percent was assigned to the GPA. The GMAT is a better normalizing variable for comparison of student sample groups, since grade inflation and difficulty of major is filtered out.
10. Next, the percentage of students admitted to each school was calculated from raw data of applications and admits provided by John Byrne of *Business Week* via America Online and compared to data available from each school. The calculation was

simply total number of admits divided by total number of applicants. In some cases the results differed to a statistically significant level from that published by *U.S. News*. The 30 schools were then sorted and ranked according to selectivity.

11. Next the above selectivity calculation was weighted at 30 percent of the student caliber calculation. Thus the student academic score utilized GPA (20 percent), GMAT (50 percent), and Selectivity (30 percent). Schools were then sorted and ranked according to academic score to arrive at student caliber rankings. This component of selectivity reflects the quality of the student body. Since at top schools, the applicant pools are highly qualified, averaging 630+ GMAT at some schools, selectivity further indicates the caliber of the student body.

12. Next, school caliber was determined by assigning a weight of 50 percent to the selectivity calculation and 50 percent to the student academic score. The second component of selectivity reflects relative demand for schools among the top 30. Thus selectivity really accounts for 65 percent of the student caliber calculation. The schools were then sorted according to caliber and ranked.

These weights are based on statistical analysis of correlations with the published rankings and on available data concerning the quality of applicant pools for each school. These analyses indicated that top business schools admit based primarily on professional work experience, writing ability, and interviewing ability after applicants pass a 'numbers screen'. Such indicators of admissibility are only reflected in selectivity statistics. Remember that at many schools that admit, say, 20 percent of an applicant pool, the applicant pool may average 630 GMAT and the admit pool 650. What separates an admitted student and a denied one is not GPA or GMAT, but rather other factors for the top business schools. This method would not necessarily apply for schools outside the top 30.

13. Next, the percent of students with jobs 3 months after graduation was obtained from *U.S. News & World Report*. A sample of schools were selected for verification. These schools were then sorted by placement and ranked.
14. The median starting salary for the most recent class was then determined for each school. A sample was selected for verification. Schools were sorted and ranked accordingly.
15. A placement rank was then determined by taking a sort of the average of salary rank and percent employed rank. The result reflects both quantity and quality of placement assuming quality can be reflected by salary. The correlation for such an assumption is between .41 and .54 based on available measures for business schools.
16. Finally, a composite ranking of the top 30 schools in the nation was determined by assigning a 20 percent weight to the caliber ranking, a 10 percent weight to the placement ranking, and 70 percent to the average published ranking. Weights were based on statistical analysis of groups of data obtained from sensitivity analysis correlated to the published rankings. The result is that only a few schools differ by more than 2 places in the average of published rankings from the composite rankings.

Based on statistical analysis, the resulting composite score represents the most accurate ranking of business schools currently available. I provide detail tables, the presort of the average published rankings, and each individual ranking used in my calculations to enable you to test the method yourself and to provide full disclosure of my data. Statistics were calculated using MiniTab Statistical Analysis Software. Sensitivity analysis was conducted using an add-in to Microsoft Excel called Solver. Additional sensitivity analysis with multiple regression probabilities as risk variables was run using Decisioneering Crystal Ball, Version 3.0.

John E. Wehrli
wehrli@ilrg.com

Endnotes

Introduction

1. Alice Thompson and Des Dearlove, "Weekend Lessons in Leadership for Shadow Cabinet," *London Times*, Oct. 26, 1995.

Chapter One

1. Personal correspondence.
2. *Inside INSEAD*, Feb. 1998.
3. "Pillars of the Economy: The Contribution of UK Business Schools to the Economy," Association of Business Schools, 1997.
4. Albert Vicere and Robert Fulmer, *Leadership by Design* (Boston: Harvard Business School Press, 1998); Warren Bennis, "It Ain't What You Know," *New York Times*, Oct. 25, 1998.
5. Jennifer Reingold, "Corporate America Goes to School," *Business Week*, Oct. 20, 1997.
6. *Harpers & Queen*, Oct. 1997.
7. Paula Hawkins and Charles Piggott, "INSEAD: Is Its MBA Any Good?" *European*, Oct. 2, 1997.
8. Stuart Crainer (ed.), *The Ultimate Book of Business Quotations* (New York: AMACOM, 1998), p. 71.
9. Robert Townsend, *Up the Organization* (London: Michael Joseph, 1970), p. 68.

10. Katherine Bruce, "How to Succeed in Business Without an MBA," *Forbes*, Jan. 26, 1998.
11. Henry Mintzberg, "The New Management Mind-Set," *Leader to Leader*, Spring 1997, p. 48.
12. Peter Drucker, *The Age of Discontinuity* (London: Heinemann, 1969).
13. The feeling is mutual. Academia has not embraced Drucker. "Only now in my very old age has academia been willing to accept me," he says.
14. Founded in 1946, the school took its nickname from the old World War II pilot training base outside Phoenix where it began.
15. Indeed, Henley (founded in 1946) and Cranfield (which started management training in the 1940s) had a substantial head start.

Chapter Two

1. Victoria Griffith, "The Art of Good Business," *Financial Times*, Sept. 1, 1997, p. 13.
2. Stuart Crainer (ed.), *Financial Times Handbook of Management* (London: Pitman, 1996), p. 463.
3. Arie de Geus, *The Living Company* (Boston: Harvard Business School Press, 1997), p. 2.
4. James O'Toole, *The A to Z of Leadership* (San Francisco: Jossey-Bass, 1999).
5. International Management Symposium, London Business School, Nov. 11, 1997.
6. The 1998 survey of Britain's Top 100 Entrepreneurs makes interesting reading. Qualification is based on three criteria—job creation over five years, sales growth over the same period, and personal wealth. Interestingly, the list of one hundred contains just three MBAs—and two of the three are from the same company (Computacentre).
7. Personal correspondence.

8. Frederick Hilmer and Lex Donaldson, *Management Redeemed* (New York: Free Press, 1996).
9. Stuart Crainer (ed.), *The Ultimate Book of Business Quotations* (New York: AMACOM, 1998), p. 71.
10. Henry Mintzberg, "The New Management Mind-Set," *Leader to Leader*, Spring 1997, p. 48.
11. International Management Symposium, London Business School, Nov. 11, 1997.
12. George Bickerstaffe, "New Ideas from the Old School," *FT Mastering*, Feb. 1998, p. 8.
13. George Siedel, Graham Mercer, Jim Sheegog, and Brandt Allen, "Management Education and New Technologies," ICEDR Working Paper, May 1996, p. 12.
14. Peter Robinson, *Snapshots from Hell* (London: Brealey, 1994).
15. Crainer, *Ultimate Book of Business Quotations*, p. 72.
16. Personal correspondence.
17. Chris Argyris, "Teaching Smart People How to Learn," *Harvard Business Review*, May–June 1991, p. 99.

Chapter Three

1. Personal correspondence.
2. Stuart Crainer (ed.), *Financial Times Handbook of Management* (London: Pitman, 1996), p. 463.
3. George Bickerstaffe, "New Ideas from the Old School," *FT Mastering*, Feb. 1998, p. 8.
4. Henry Mintzberg, "Musings on Management," *Harvard Business Review*, July–Aug. 1996, p. 65.
5. International Management Symposium, London Business School, 1997.
6. "McKinsey Recruiting Gay Students," *Harbus News*, Nov. 20, 1995.
7. INSEAD press release, Feb. 5, 1997.

Chapter Four

1. Godfrey Golzen, *AMBA Guide to Business Schools* (London: Pitman, 1996).
2. George Bickerstaffe, *Which MBA?* 9th ed. (Menlo Park, Calif.: Addison-Wesley, 1997).
3. Peter Robinson, *Snapshots from Hell* (London: Brealey, 1994), p. xx.
4. Robinson, *Snapshots from Hell*, p. 13.
5. Cornell survey, 1997.
6. Bickerstaffe, *Which MBA?*
7. Survey by Universum, Sweden.

Chapter Five

1. Maria Saporta, "Allegations of Vandalism Doomed Sonnenfeld at Tech," *Atlanta Constitution*, Dec. 12, 1997, p. 2.
2. International Management Symposium, London Business School, 1997.
3. "Professor Porter PhD," *Economist*, Oct. 8, 1994, p. 97.
4. International Management Symposium, London Business School, 1997.
5. John Byrne, "Harvard B-School's Professor Fix-It," *Business Week*, May 20, 1996.
6. *Fortune*, Aug. 1995.
7. Arie de Geus, *The Living Company* (Boston: Harvard Business School Press, 1997), p. xiv.

Chapter Six

1. Katherine Bruce, "How to Succeed in Business Without an MBA," *Forbes*, Jan. 26, 1998.
2. Wharton press release.
3. Internet site at http://www.alumni.hbs.edu/fund/waysofgiving.html
4. David Charter, Don's Vote Puts £20M Gift for Oxford in Jeopardy," *London Times*, Nov. 6, 1996.

5. David Leonhardt, "Goldrush in the Ivory Tower," *Business Week*, Oct. 21, 1996.

Chapter Seven

1. Judi Bevan, "Leader of the Brand," *Sunday Telegraph*, Dec. 7, 1997.
2. Joshua Jampol, "Get the Power of Global Networking," *London Times*, Jan. 26, 1998, p. 11.

Chapter Eight

1. George Bickerstaffe, "MBA Special Report," *London Times*, Jan. 30, 1995, p. 5. Byrne did much to establish the credibility of the rankings. He has now relinquished his power to Jennifer Reingold.
2. Nadav Enbar, *Business Week On-Line*, May 11, 1998.
3. George Bain, former principal of London Business School, has made the same points.

Chapter Nine

1. Roger Trapp, "Learning Crusade," *Human Resources*, May–June 1996, p. 17.
2. 1998 Survey of Corporate University Future Directions, Corporate University Xchange, 381 Park Avenue South (Suite 713), New York, NY 10016.
3. Albert Vicere and Robert Fulmer, *Crafting Competitiveness* (Boston: Harvard Business School Press, 1998), p. 246.

Chapter Ten

1. Albert Vicere and Robert Fulmer, *Crafting Competitiveness* (Boston: Harvard Business School Press, 1998).
2. Lisa Gubernick and Ashlea Ebeling, "I Got My Degree Through E-Mail," *Forbes*, June 16, 1997.
3. As we write, the Apollo Group has announced a deal with Hughes Network Systems, the private satellite network supplier, to form a worldwide distance learning company.

4. "Wicks to Lead Pearson's New Management Education Business," Pearson press release, Jan. 5, 1999.
5. Gubernick and Ebeling, "I Got My Degree."
6. Joshua Jampol and Des Dearlove, "New Visions for Executive Education," *Time*, Mar. 30, 1998, p. 41.
7. Jampol and Dearlove, "New Visions," p. 41.
8. George Bickerstaffe, "New Ideas from the Old School," *FT Mastering*, Feb. 1998, p. 9.

Chapter Eleven

1. George Bickerstaffe, "New Ideas from the Old School," *FT Mastering*, Feb. 1998, p. 9.
2. Gary Hamel, International Management Symposium, London Business School, Nov. 11, 1997.
3. Ted Levitt, "Marketing Myopia," *Harvard Business Review*, July–August 1960.
4. *Herts*, short for Hertfordshire, is pronounced "harts."
5. Quoted in K. Napuk, "Live and Learn," *Scottish Business Insider*, Jan. 1994.
6. Peter Senge, "A Growing Wave of Interest and Openness," Applewood Internet site, http://www.the-wire.com/applewood/senge.html, 1997.
7. Bickerstaffe, "New Ideas," p. 8.
8. Bickerstaffe, "New Ideas," p. 8.
9. Bickerstaffe, "New Ideas," p. 8.
10. Gerhard Mumme, "Learning to Manage," *New World*, Feb. 1997, p. 28.
11. Della Bradshaw, "Remuneration Remedy," *Financial Times*, Nov. 11, 1996, p. 15.
12. Della Bradshaw, "Boardroom to Classroom," *Financial Times*, Oct. 6, 1997.

13. John Kotter, *The New Rules* (New York: Simon & Schuster, 1997).

14. "Comeback of the MBA," *Business Dateline*, Feb. 8 1996.

15. Dorothy E. Leidner and Sirkka L. Jarvenpaa, "The Use of Information Technology to Enhance Management School Education: A Theoretical View," *MIS Quarterly* (University of Minnesota), Sept. 1995, p. 265.

16. Katherine Bruce, "How to Succeed in Business Without an MBA," *Forbes*, Jan. 26, 1998.

17. Bruce Tulgan, *Work This Way* (Oxford: Capstone, 1998), p. 5.

18. Tulgan, *Work This Way*.

19. Colin Price and William G. Dauphinais, *Straight from the CEO* (London: Brealey, 1998).

20. John Byrne, "Harvard B-School's Professor Fix-It," *Business Week*, May 20, 1996.

21. Byrne, "Harvard B-School's Professor Fix-It."

22. Peter Drucker, *The Age of Discontinuity* (London: Heinemann, 1969).

Name Index

Subject Index

D

G